NZ$ 10.00 3/75

A MEMOIR OF
CHINA IN REVOLUTION

❊ CHESTER RONNING ❊

A
MEMOIR OF
CHINA IN
REVOLUTION

*From the Boxer Rebellion
to the People's Republic*

PANTHEON BOOKS

A Division of Random House, New York

951.04
R
C. 1

Library of Congress Cataloging in Publication Data

Ronning, Chester, 1894–
A Memoir of China in Revolution: From the Boxer Rebellion to the People's Republic.

1. China—History—1949–   2. China—History—1900–   I. Title
DS777.55.R565   915.1'03'40924   73–18720
ISBN 0-394-47255-1

Manufactured in the United States of America

FIRST EDITION

To
Inga Marie Horte

CONTENTS

vii

ILLUSTRATIONS

1966. Ambassador Ronning on a special peace mission to Hanoi
with Prime Minister Pham Van Dong of the
Democratic Republic of Vietnam.

(between pages 212 and 213)

*(Following photographs courtesy
of Audrey Topping)*

1973. At the Summer Palace in Peking. The author, with
former Ambassador Li En-chou, Audrey Topping, her daughter
Susan, and Mrs. Li of the Friendship Association.

1973. In the Great Hall of the People, Peking. The author
chatting with Prime Minister Chou En-lai and Acting President
Tung Pi-wu.

A visit during the peanut harvest, near Peking.

Exchanging pleasantries with a neighbor from Szechuan at the
Liu Pei-chuke Liang Temple in Ch'engtu.

Sitting on an unterraced hillside, being briefed by a
leading member of the Shashiyü commune.

A terraced hillside.

Cutting barley with a scythe and net attachment on a commune
near Fancheng.

Entering the Yangtse gorges.

"East Is Red #33," sister ship of "East Is Red #32."

The Nanking Bridge, built after the Russian technicians left China.

1971. A cotton textile factory in the author's hometown of Fancheng.

1973. Grasslands of Inner Mongolia.

Harvesting in the North.

The author visiting nomads in their yurts.

1973. The historic city of Kuelin, founded by
Ch'in Shih Huang-ti *ca.* 200 B.C.

1971. The author's daughter Sylvia in the Hangchow Gardens.

1971. The Laughing Buddha of Hangchow.

PREFACE

The Chinese have undertaken what may be the greatest revolution attempted in the history of mankind. Never before have so many people been at the centre of such a vast and rapid transformation from decadence and misery to a society in which the people themselves are deeply involved, participate actively, and increasingly make basic decisions.

My opinions are, of course, deeply influenced by the many years I have lived in China. Altogether I spent a quarter of a century in China over four six-year periods, as a child, teen-ager, teacher, and finally as a Canadian diplomat. Each period happened to coincide with important crises feeding the developing revolution, yet there was so much poverty, disease, malnutrition, starvation, exploitation, and injustice that I had never expected to see the Chinese authorities attempt a frontal attack upon all these evils. My hope is that through this account I may make some contribution to a better understanding of the people of China today and of the profound revolutionary changes which are creating a new China.

This account was originally intended to be mimeographed primarily for my own family: brothers and sisters, children, grandchildren, and great-grandchildren. It is based on letters to the family, notes which I recorded when the occasion warranted, and a diary which I kept intermittently.

CHESTER RONNING

Camrose, Alberta
November 1973

A MEMOIR OF
CHINA IN REVOLUTION

1

HOW
IT ALL
STARTED

It was in 1891, in the days of the Imperial Empress Dowager, Tz'u Hsi, that my parents went, with the first small group of Lutheran missionaries to central, interior China. That was the year when a so-called anti-Christian movement spread throughout the Yangtse River valley, which has a denser population than any other great river valley in the world. The movement was, in fact, anti-foreign rather than anti-Christian. Foreigners, however, preferred to call it anti-Christian to divert attention from the forcible seizure of concessions by foreigners in all of the important port cities of China, including Hankow, the heart of China's greatest natural water transportation system.

Through the "unequal treaties," granting extraterritoriality, all foreigners, including missionaries, enjoyed complete exemption from Chinese law and enforcement. The treaties also enabled foreigners to obtain important privileges in Chinese trade, commerce and customs. Foreign gunboats, especially British but also American, controlled the Yangtse River valley from Shanghai to Chungking.

The most important tributary of the Yangtse is the Han. The

shifting sands of the Han made that river too treacherous for foreign gunboats to patrol, and law and order were maintained by the Chinese junk-type gunboats. As a young boy I knew nothing about foreign control of China until my father brought me down the Han River in a Chinese junk to Hankow, where I got my first lesson in the real meaning of extraterritoriality. That lesson was a shock from which I did not recover until the "unequal treaties" were abrogated.

Coming from a walled city in the interior, where the only foreigners were a few missionaries, I had never seen a foreign city. As my father led me down a paved street in one of the foreign concessions, I stopped to stare at a large foreign house where a Chinese was chained by his feet to a huge block of cement. The prisoner carried an enormous square frame around his neck made of heavy wooden planks. He could reach his mouth only with great difficulty, through a small hole in the frame. Father tried to lead me off, but I held back to stare at the man and, growing more and more angry, I began to cry. How could Christians behave as only heathens were supposed to, treating a Chinese like this, in his own country? (Having known only missionaries, I thought all foreigners were good Christians.) Father said: "You are too young to understand. This is not China, but a foreign concession in China. The man has perhaps done something wrong and is being punished. You see, all foreigners in China have extraterritoriality. But that is too big a word for you." I certainly did not understand, but I did learn to understand why the Chinese were anti-foreign.

My father, Halvor N. Ronning, was born on a farm called Buskeronning in Telemark, Norway. After completing his secular education, he migrated to the United States, graduated from Red Wing Theological Seminary in Minnesota, and became a naturalized American.

Before my mother, Hannah Rorem, was born (in Illinois), her parents had migrated from Norway with their first daughter and four sons. The family had left a beautiful farm on the island of Ombo known as Rörheim.

Nearly a century later, while I was Canadian Ambassador to Norway, I visited my mother's ancestral home. Ombo is the largest island in Bokenfjord on the west coast of Norway. The central portion of the island is mostly dark rock. On the Rörheim farm, however, the soil is fertile, and in the lower valleys there are masses of delicious, wild plums. As I bit into one and looked out to sea, past the other islands, I asked a descendant of my great-grandfather: "How could my grandparents leave this lovely place with such fine fruit and scenery?" He replied: "Your grandparents with a large family could not live on wild fruit and scenery."

My mother was only a few years old when her parents moved from Illinois to Iowa. There she was trained as a schoolteacher before she volunteered to go to China as a missionary. My father had also volunteered. They crossed the Pacific to Shanghai and from there took a river boat up the Yangtse to Hankow. There they were married and there they remained for two years to study Chinese in preparation for their future work.

After mastering enough Chinese to get along, they travelled by passenger junk, known as a *man-kan,* 600 miles up the Han River as it winds in innumerable S-bends to the twin cities Hsiangyang and Fancheng, known as Hsiangfan. There they established a new mission station in the interior, walled, commercial city of Fancheng directly across the Han from the official, walled city of Hsiangyang.

I was born in Fancheng on December 13, 1894, the first non-Chinese baby in the County of Hsiangyang.

Even after we children were born, my mother continued her missionary work, which left us to spend a great deal of time with the Chinese of our household. We played with Chinese children, and the doors of our house were constantly open to our parents' co-workers—Chinese pastors, bible-women, teachers, and students. We were daily in and out of the school dormitories and classrooms. We naturally identified with the Chinese pupils. They shared their problems with us, and we shared ours with them. Very seldom did they classify us as foreigners. We dressed like them and talked like them. I did not realise until years later that there were any differences between us except in colour of skin, hair, and eyes.

We were most fortunate in our cook and amah. They were literate, belonging to a family which for generations had worked for the Tao T'ai, the super-mandarin in Hsiangyang. Through them we were introduced to the rich world of old Chinese folk-lore. To this day I remember the fables and still recite rhymes, riddles, proverbs, and old sayings. They were so much a part of our daily life that even my sister Almah, two years younger than I, who never returned to China after she was eleven, still remembers them by the score.

I also learned from childhood days to understand the problems which young Chinese faced. For example, many of my student friends had been engaged to be married, since birth, to girls they had never seen and would not be permitted to see before their wedding day. Their resentment against the old patriarchal family tyranny increased when they learned that in Western societies young people choose their own life partners. Many of the boys in our boys' school were interested in the girls in our girls' school. As the time approached to marry the girl of their parents' choice, they became moody, unhappy, and rebellious. They yearned to change the old traditions which deprived them of freedom—by revolution if necessary. Most of them, however, knuckled under when the patriarchs and matriarchs used patriarchal family pressure to force obedience.

It was more difficult for our parents to understand resentment of old traditions, even though they too spent most of their time with Chinese, spoke Chinese, albeit with a foreign accent, and wore Chinese clothes. My father even wore a false queue firmly attached to his skullcap. All Chinese teachers wore their queues both outside and inside the house.

I remember once how uproariously some Chinese laughed at my father when they discovered that his queue was false. It happened during the initial stages of the disturbances which led to the Boxer Rebellion of 1900. One day a large crowd of people had followed Father when he was returning from a visit to the shopping centre of Fancheng. The crowd suddenly became a mob. Shouting *"yang jen,"* foreigner, or *"yang kuei,"* foreign devil, they chased him up the street leading to our mission compound. Our gatekeeper heard the unpleasant noise and quickly barred the gate, unaware that my father was involved. Seeing the gate closed, Father made a desperate leap at the compound wall. As he scrambled up, a ruffian grabbed his queue and yanked it off, together with his skullcap. The angry mob suddenly began to laugh at my father, who sat dishevelled, without a queue, straddling the wall. The crowd roared with laughter. The man who had snatched the queue now stared at the object in his hand, apparently suspecting some evil foreign magic, and quickly carried the dangling queue to the gate. The gatekeeper was too frightened to do anything. Father descended from the wall, opened the gate, and thanked the frightened man for returning his precious queue. He then expressed gratitude to the smiling crowd for their kindness, placed the cap and queue back on his head, and invited them to visit him some time when they were not in such a hurry.

In 1899 my parents left China on their first furlough, travelling first to Norway and then to the United States. In Norway my older brother Nelius, a younger sister, Almah, and I had to learn Norwegian. Too soon afterwards in Iowa, at my mother's home, we were forced to learn a third language—English. Back in China, a year later, we were required by our parents to keep up all three. During our three formal meals a day, Mother spoke to us in English. We were made to answer in English, and she saw to it that we read books in English. Father spoke to us in Norwegian, we replied in Norwegian, and he gave us our religious education in Norwegian. Chinese, however, remained our best language and, away from the table, we got into the habit of speaking to our parents in Chinese. Soon after our return to China—after we had learned English—my brother and I were in constant demand by the senior boys of our father's school who wanted to learn English. Many of them could read English. When they proudly read aloud to us, however, we understood almost nothing. It sounded more like a chant of Chinese nonsense syllables. They had learned to read and understand English from correspondence courses and by using an English-Chinese dictionary. They had received pamphlets on the American and French Revolutions from students in Hankow. Actually, they taught us the Declaration of Independence. In their translations of the Declaration of Independence, they had substituted, to their and our amusement, the "Empress Dowager" for "George III," listing her corresponding crimes. Their parents would not dare to defy the ruler who reigned over them by the Mandate of Heaven, but the students scoffed and made fun of the old girl. The cultural revolution in China flourished in Christian missionary schools.

Although the students laughed when they listed the crimes of the old Dowager, they were deadly serious. One day, Nelius and I were invited to the room of the most senior student, Tung Tse-p'ei. He came from a village where he had been memorizing Chinese classics to prepare for the old-style Government examinations. When his father could no longer afford to pay the teacher, my father invited Tse-p'ei to our school. He was a hardworking, brilliant young man and organized, through instructions by correspondence, a local branch of Dr. Sun Yat-sen's famous United League (T'ung Meng Hui). All the senior students were members. Out of the Christian missionary schools of China came most of the early and many of the later revolutionary leaders in China.

One day, in explaining their objective to us, Tung Tse-p'ei suddenly bent forward and whipped his queue over his head from behind. "Look at this disgrace to all patriotic Chinese," he shouted. "You call it a pig's tail, and that's exactly what it is. We were forced to wear these miserable things because we have become pigs to show our inferiority to the Manchus." He looked up and, using his fingers like a pair of shears, added: "We are going to cut them off like this. We want short hair like yours. We are joining students throughout China to overthrow the Manchu Dynasty."

Before the session finished, he asked us not to tell "Lao Hutzu"—"Old Whiskers" (our father). He said that he would tell him later. He thought Father would probably not like to hear that they were plotting revolution, but that he certainly would be pleased to hear that China was to become a republic like the United States of America.

That was my first, but not last, contact with Chinese revolutionaries.

I am sometimes asked how we became Canadians. It happened simply because we passed through Canada on our return to China in 1901. We were to sail on the old Canadian Pacific steamship *Empress of China* from Vancouver to Shanghai. In Calgary, the train stopped for coal and water at the old CPR station. As we walked up and down the wooden platform, we passed a group of men excitedly talking Norwegian. My father asked them where they were from. They had recently taken homesteads southeast of Edmonton at a place which they had named Bardo. They had come originally from Bardo, near what is now known as Bardu Foss in the far north of Norway. One of the group, John Anderson, turned out to be a brother of Peter Anderson, who had been a fellow student with my father at the Red Wing Seminary in Minnesota. John strongly recommended to my father that he should invest in a half section, 320 acres, of CPR land in the Bardo district—some day he would surely need a home in case of sickness or retirement. The land was available at $3 an acre, with twenty years to pay and at a very low interest rate.

My parents discussed the possibility almost every day on the old *Empress of China,* and we all grew more and more excited about visions of prairies, woodlands, cattle and horses, and a home for the future. From Yokohama, the first port after Victoria, Father sent a cable to Peter Anderson to buy a place for us in Bardo.

After my mother's death in 1907, it was decided that my elder brother, Nelius, and I would go to her sister's farm home near Radcliffe, Iowa. We were to begin formal schooling for the first time, starting in grade seven. Before leaving China, we had worn only Chinese clothes. "Foreign" clothes, however, now arrived from America—generous gifts from relatives for our trip, and Father escorted us to Shanghai to be fitted out with "foreign" overcoats and hats.

When Father left us on the deck of the Pacific Mail SS *Mongolia* and was on his way back to the Bund in Shanghai, we stood sadly waving to him on the tender. A gust of wind suddenly blew my brand new hat into the yellow waters of the Yangtse. To this day, whenever I am hatless I still see that beautiful hat tossed like an egg-shell floating downstream headed for the Yellow Sea.

In the Radcliffe Public School, we were lost—utter strangers and completely ignorant of the ways of Americans. (We soon noted, however, that the boys wore caps, not hats, which helped me to get over the pain of losing my only hat.) We were daily subjected to the questionable honour of a great deal of attention, and during the first recess were treated to a chant of greeting in which all the natives joined:

> *Ching chong Chinaman eat dead rats*
> *Chew them up like ginger snaps*

We said nothing to our aunt about the reception. That night my pillow was wet with an uncontrollable stream of silent tears, and I longed to go home to China where the people were friendly and did not regard me as a foreigner.

It was not until my brother and I learned how to drive a team of horses to cultivate corn on Uncle Albert's farm that we were finally accepted by Radcliffe's school community. We continued, however, to clam up completely whenever the teacher asked questions about China.

After a year in Iowa, my brother and I went to our new home in Canada. A month later we were joined by our father and five younger brothers and sisters direct from China. We became Canadians when my father was naturalized with the help of the Honourable Frank Oliver, who hoped he would receive father's vote during an election campaign. He did.

Especially for Nelius and me, going from the United States to Canada and to a Canadian school meant another adjustment to a new community which was only somewhat less painful than our experience in Iowa. The difference was that now we were regarded as Americans as well as Chinese.

As Americans we had learned that we had won all the battles of the Revolutionary War as well as those of 1812. We had thrown off the yoke of British monarchy. We had rejected taxation without representation. In Canada, we were informed that Canada and Britain had won all the battles of the War of 1812. In the United States, pro-British Americans were classed as "rebels" and had been driven out of the United States. In Canada they were respected as "United Empire Loyalists." Our adjustment to those opposite views was painful but thorough. Eventually we were completely subverted, and I have never for a moment regretted my father's acceptance of the Honourable Frank Oliver's invitation to become a Canadian citizen. Canada became our family's permanent home. Years later I became Canada's Ambassador to Norway. That would have pleased my father, but he died when I was still in China as Chargé d'Affaires of the

Canadian Embassy. The posting to Norway and Iceland was followed by seven years as Canada's High Commissioner to India.

In 1913, our family moved from Bardo to an undeveloped part of the Peace River country. My brother and I finished our school term before going north over the famous Edson Trail to the area where my father had filed on three homesteads for himself, Nelius, and me. He had named the place Valhalla. On our trip over the Edson Trail, we were joined by Harry Horte, who later became a brother-in-law. We had a team of horses with a democrat, a saddle horse, and a pack horse for the trip of some 350 miles from the railroad at Edson. We were as green as grass about that sort of experience when we started and the laughing stock of some seasoned pioneers in Edson. We didn't even know how to tie the diamond hitch to pack a horse. At the end of that trip we were, at least in our own opinion, toughened pioneers.

I became so enamoured of the challenge of pioneer life in Grande Prairie that I soon developed ambitions to become a rancher. We raised a fine bunch of horses, and I spent a great deal of time in the saddle riding the range.

To "prove up" my homestead, I broke fifty acres of land with four oxen and the help of a young brother, Talbert. He sat on a great old ox named Charlie. His job was to keep the oxen plodding along. He used sweet, gentle persuasion and kind, loving words, punctuated by the use of a willow switch, and his method and language were very unlike those of other homesteaders. (Talbert is now the pastor of a Lutheran congregation in Chicago.)

My hopes of becoming a rancher, however, were suddenly dashed. The local school board called on my father, who had been instrumental in organizing the local school district, to say that they had lost their teacher and that no one would come over 300 miles from the nearest railroad town to teach school.

Father told them: "Please do not worry. Chester will teach our children. He is a born teacher." Those were the days when everyone and anyone could teach school. They were all born teachers. All the equipment necessary was textbooks and a strap. The school board provided the strap, and the children were required to supply themselves with books.

I loved the outdoors. I wanted to ride the range, but what could I do? I had been brought up in the "Honour Thy Father" tradition and bowed to the inevitable. The Department of Education in Edmonton willingly connived in the plot to trap me. The necessary "permit" was issued. That started me off on a career in education.

The first-graders flabbergasted me. What to do to keep them busy—that was the problem which haunted me. Fortunately, I found a pamphlet with instructions how to fold coloured pieces of square paper into caps, boats, and so on. The youngsters crowded around my desk to learn the creative art of folding coloured paper. I folded very slowly, sneaking peeks at the open instructions. I repeated each step out loud, as much for my own edification as for their guidance. Their eyes were glued to my fingers and the paper. They did not wonder why it took me so long my wonders to perform. Since that experience, I have always been of the opinion that kindergarten and first-grade teachers have the most difficult jobs. They require much more than I had with my "born-a-teacher" qualification and should receive the highest salaries of all teachers, including university professors.

After one term I decided that, if teaching was to be my destiny, I should go to Camrose Normal to get a teacher's certificate. I had received almost no salary for teaching. That no doubt was exactly what the school board thought it was worth. In any case, had I not obtained valuable experience practising on their children, including four of my own younger brothers and sisters? My problem was to finance my way through Normal School.

Dr. Lavik, President of the Camrose Lutheran College, rose to the occasion by offering me board and room if I would take charge of the men's dormitory and teach high school mathematics and agriculture. I accepted, even though I had never taken a course in agriculture. By the middle of the term, I was suddenly informed by the Department of Education that I lacked one prerequisite subject for the Normal School course I was taking —namely agriculture. I confessed my predicament to the class and eventually sat down with them at the end of the term, wondering if any of us would make the grade. We passed. My experience as a pioneer in the Peace River country did make the course in agriculture more interesting and intelligible than it would have been without any practical knowledge.

My experience there was not confined to agriculture, however. In Valhalla, I fell in love with Inga Marie Horte. She loved horses and owned a fine palamino mare named Flory. I sometimes wondered if she would have accepted me for "better or for worse" if I had not won a bet we made about Flory's first colt, Pet, a five-year-old gelding. Inga bet me that I could not break Pet to ride. Foolishly, I accepted. No money was involved, but the challenge was important. Without Inga's knowledge, I rounded up the horses and isolated the spirited buckskin in Chris Horte's corral, roped him, put a half-hitch over his nose to prevent him from bucking, and rode him bareback around the corral. I repeated the performance a few days later, and decided that since I could ride him bareback, it would be a "cinch" to ride him with a saddle. I invited Inga to watch me ride her favourite horse, but it was no "cinch." He resented the curb bit, which I held too tightly, and finally reared up so high that he fell over backwards. I managed to scramble out from under him, but not without some doubts for a moment that the magnificent beast was about to fall backwards on top of me. Fortunately, I got to my feet before he did and slipped into the saddle as he was getting up. This time I let him have his head and spurred as he burst into a dead run. I let him go until he was all a-lather before I reached down to pat him and talk to him. When he calmed down, I rode back to claim my "win."

After a stint at Fort Osborne, Winnipeg, as a sapper in the Royal Canadian Engineers, I returned to Valhalla on leave before transferring to the Royal Flying Corps as a cadet-for-pilot. During that leave Inga and I decided to get married.

We hitched up a team to Father's buggy and drove forty-five miles to Grande Prairie City to get a marriage licence. My father performed the wedding ceremony, and the young people of Valhalla gave us a good old-fashioned shivaree.

I had never given up the idea of some day returning to China. My brother Nelius and I had an understanding that we would join forces in China some time. After his death, during a geological survey in Great Slave Lake, I enquired about possibilities of work in China. In 1921, the opportunity came to organise and teach a course in education for teachers in the middle school of my home town in China.

I completed a course in education offered by the University of Minnesota (since at that time such courses were not available at the University of Alberta). Upon graduation, I was offered a more lucrative and comfortable position in Minnesota, but I was not tempted. Apart from the fact that I was anxious to return to China, Inga and I had chosen Canada as our permanent home and we refused to let anything change that. Teaching in China would be for a limited period.

With our three-year-old daughter Sylvia, we therefore sailed in the *Empress of Canada* to Shanghai and up the Yangtse by a Jardine Matheson river steamer to Hankow. We had intended to go by rail to Peking, but trains to and from Peking passing through Honan had been attacked by soldier-brigands of feuding war lords, killing innocent passengers. Instead we sailed back to Nanking to take the Blue Express via Tientsin to Peking.

We spent a most rewarding year in Peking, one of the most fascinating cities of the world. For me, however, it was most interesting to come again into contact with Chinese students in universities and middle schools. They were even more active than they were earlier in the century and had a deeper political and social consciousness. They suffered from China's humiliating defeats by foreign countries. There was a new dejection and indignation caused by the failure of the United States to oppose the sell-out of China to Japan at the Paris Peace Conference, coupled with a bitter disappointment in traitorous politicians of China's own corrupt, inefficient Government—a tool of war lords competing in the scramble for the Mandate of Heaven.

Installed as principal of the Hung Wen Middle School in my home city, I was delighted to find that the Associate Chinese Principal was my esteemed friend Tung Tse-p'ei, as brilliant and devoted as any person I have known. As a teen-ager in China, I had regarded him as a mentor. Since then he had gone to Cheeloo University in Tsinan, Shantung, and had returned with Western-style university degree in addition to his Chinese *hsiu-ts'ai*, B.A. He had continued his deep interest in revolution and had actively participated in the May Fourth movement, China's first modern mass movement, spurred by humiliation at Versailles and the breakdown of her traditional culture.

In the Hung Wen Middle School all of the members of the staff (with one exception, an old scholar who taught ancient Chinese classics, which was fast becoming unpopular with the students) and all of the students were members of the revolutionary Kuomintang, Sun Yat-sen's Nationalist Party. Staff and students were enthusiastic supporters of the new Government in Canton organised by Sun Yat-sen with the aim of wiping out the war lords, uniting China, and carrying out a programme based on San Min Chu-i, Three Principles of the People. The first Principle of Nationalism declared China must regain her

lost sovereignty and unity. The second declared the Chinese
Government must serve the people and be responsible to them,
and the third Principle of the People's Livelihood declared that
China's basic industries would be socialized and that the peasants
who tilled the soil should own it.

The teachers and students of our school and of the Government schools in the twin cities, the educational centre of northern Hupeh, divided into teams to visit all of the villages in the
area. Tung Tse-p'ei explained that the first phase was to organise
illiterate, ignorant peasants, most of whom were concerned
only with the problems of food, clothing, and shelter. Only after
they were organised could the next phase begin—the struggle
against the vicious landlord organisations. Millions upon millions
of China's people, he said, would die in the struggle before the
people reached the promised land envisioned by the revolutionaries. He doubted that very many really realised how great a
revolution was needed to free the people of China from the
ancient traditions which had such a firm grip upon Chinese
society. Sometimes he referred to Mao Tse-tung's policy of or-
ganising peasants as the soundest way of getting the revolution
started, a revolution which must come to save China. First, he
said, the peasants must be given the opportunity to become literate. That was why the staff and students of Hung Wen were
spending every week-end teaching peasants the basic ideographs
necessary to read newspapers and pamphlets written in "p'u-
t'ung hua," the common, spoken language. He hoped the missionaries would understand this.

I did, but I was certainly surprised by what happened one day
while I was in the midst of conducting a class of forty young
men. A student opened the door, walked quietly in, and whispered something to the boy next to the door. He in turn passed
something on to the chap sitting next to him. Some message was
passed from ear to ear until the whole class knew something
which I did not. A few minutes later the whole class rose and
walked silently out into the hall. I followed them, wondering if
this was some expression of anti-foreign feeling being directed

against me, since I was the only foreigner. But the halls were filled with all of the several hundred students, and they walked silently out of the school. I joined the other teachers. If they knew what was going on they said nothing. We followed the students down the street to the city gate facing the Han River. From the gate we saw hundreds of students coming out of the gates of Hsiangyang across the river. They boarded junks going upstream and forcibly seized all foreign kerosene and tobacco, stacked it in piles, drove holes into the kerosene tins, and set fire to the tobacco and kerosene. It was all part of the boycott campaign throughout China against Japan and Great Britain.

Foreigners who thought the Red Guard aspect of the Great Cultural Revolution of 1966 was something new in China failed to remember that, in the Twenties, young patriots seized and destroyed private property when Chinese leaders failed to take action to boycott goods from China's enemies.

In 1927, my wife and I with our three children—Sylvia, eight years old, Alton, two, and Meme, six months—were ordered by the British Consul in Hankow (Canada was represented at that time by Great Britain) to return to Canada. When we were still in Hankow, I received a request by mail from the Camrose Lutheran College to become head of the institution which I had attended during its first two years and where I had done some teaching while attending the Camrose Normal School. The offer was accepted after we returned to Canada, and Camrose became our permanent home.

In 1932, the United Farmers of Alberta (UFA) asked me to be their candidate to contest a by-election for the Legislative Assembly of Alberta. That summer, the UFA had joined the Cooperative Commonwealth Federation (CCF), headed by James Woodsworth. I happened to be the first person in Canada to run on the provisional CCF platform.

Not long after my campaign started, a supporter told me that a very damaging whispering campaign was spreading rapidly through the constituency about me. In his opinion, if I did not stop it, I would stand no chance of winning against my opponents. I asked my new friend what part of my dark past had been discovered. He said: "They say you were born in China. They also say," he went on, "that your mother was unable to supply you with milk and that cow's milk was not available in China. Is that really so?"

From the way he asked the question I got the impression that he could not vote for me if my reply was in the affirmative. So I had to explain that I had no intention of refusing to give credit to a kind Chinese woman who had saved my life so that I could contest this election as a farmers' candidate.

My friend finished by saying: "The worst of it is that they say since you were brought up on Chinese milk, you are partly Chinese."

I interjected that, according to that logic, I might have absorbed some of the traditional wisdom of the great Chinese philosophers, which should make me the best possible member of the Alberta Legislature to represent the farmers of the Camrose Constituency.

I tried to end our conversation by asking my friend to start a whispering campaign about my opponents.

"What do you know about them?" he asked.

"I have it on fairly good authority," I said, "that they were brought up on cow's milk."

I told this story at every public meeting I addressed after that, and the audiences seemed to appreciate its logic.

I won that campaign but I was thrown out on my ear in the next round. The electorate must have decided that I had not acquired the sagacity of the Chinese sages after all.

After returning from China in 1927, I remained in charge of Camrose Lutheran College for fifteen years. When Canada was involved in the war against Japan I was induced to join the Royal Canadian Air Force, to become head of the Discrimination Unit of RCAF Intelligence. In close cooperation with corresponding Canadian Navy and Army units, we intercepted Japanese communications throughout their expanded empire to obtain intelligence through traffic and cryptanalysis.

In the summer of 1945, shortly before the Japanese capitulation, the Canadian Department of External Affairs advertised for a Canadian who could speak Chinese to assist Canada's Ambassador in Chungking. The Under-Secretary of State for External Affairs, Mr. Hume Wrong, requested me to examine the applicants in their ability to speak Chinese.

Prior to VJ-Day, three candidates successively failed the oral examination. After VJ-Day, when my work in the service was finished, I was asked if I was willing to go to China for External Affairs. My daughters, Meme and Audrey, were so enthused about the idea that before breakfast the next day, it had been decided that the whole family was to be on its way to China, *pronto*.

I therefore replied to Hume Wrong that I would go to China on two conditions—first and most important, the whole family was to be included, and second, that we would try it for only one year. The Under-Secretary of State for External Affairs agreed and to make it legal he authorised me to administer the necessary language examination.

Because our Ambassador, General Victor W. Odlum, urgently required the services of an officer in Chungking, I found myself very soon on the way to China. With no preparations other than perhaps being a "born diplomat" as well as a "born teacher," I was classified as a First Secretary. It was assumed that my age exempted me from starting at the bottom as a probationary Third Secretary. I did not expect my appointment to last for more than a year and thought I would most likely be back to my real profession of teaching before too long. The new job continued, however, for more than two decades.

2

❀

ANCIENT
CHINA'S
COLLAPSE

❀

In 1922, after an absence from China of fifteen years I returned with my wife and a daughter to teach at the Hung Wen Middle School in Fancheng, the city of my birth. To welcome us, the staff and students invited us to a *"ch'a-hua hui,"* a tea-talk party, with songs, speeches, roasted watermelon seeds, and great quantities of hot green tea. The speech which interested me most was one by a young student who proudly tossed his head as he said: "My country has a recorded history of four thousand years. My country has a population of four hundred million people."

He probably underestimated the total population by at least one hundred million people, but the length of China's recorded history was not too far off the mark—only some 300 years. The first dynasty, Hsia, had begun before writing was invented. Writing on "oracle bones" established that writing had been invented during the second dynasty, the Shang Dynasty, which did not begin until 1766 B.C. After that invention some amount of time must have passed before history was actually recorded.

Some aspects of several ancient civilizations have survived —the Hebrew, for example. China's ancient civilization, however, is the only one which survived to modern times in all its various aspects; it has been the most continuous and stable of all ancient civilizations; it has also been in control of a vast area of Asia continuously for millennia.

China had perhaps the most perfect system of government ever devised for an ancient feudal, agricultural society in which the great majority of the people were illiterate peasants and workers. That social, political, and cultural system was eventually described, codified, and perhaps perfected by Confucius, who, as a result of his work, has often been credited with inventing the system. The system was by no means as foolproof as it has been said to be, nor was it pulled out of the blue sky by one of the greatest pragmatic philosophers of all time. Confucius was actually an idealistic, political adviser in an ancient feudal and decadent society which was fast disintegrating. Only centuries later was the Confucian system of government adopted by the Han Dynasty. As a result, the Hans became the greatest empire builders of all the ancient dynasties. The Mongol Yuan Dynasty, which re-established the rigid examination system and the bureaucratic imperial organization, thus coupling the Confucian system with the driving energy of mounted desert warriors, succeeded in expanding the empire to cover nearly half of continental Asia.

China's ancient system had probably been worked out through millennia of a continuous trial-and-error struggle beginning with the invention of agriculture, which necessitated the gradual introduction of more sophisticated organizational changes in the earlier, relatively simple, pastoral, hunting, and fishing social structure. The form of China's civilization which emerged was firmly based on, and adapted to, China's primitive agriculture. The two essential elements in the primitive agricultural society were a body of willing young peasants and village industry workers and a small group of experienced village elders and leaders.

The greatest threat to the life and prosperity of village agricultural society was rebellion by young peasants and workers. The tendency, therefore, was for the village authorities to govern in a manner satisfactory to the working peasants and technicians to encourage loyalty and prevent rebellion. The elders were under great pressure to prevent dissatisfaction in the labour force. The wiser men in the community were therefore most frequently elevated to positions of local authority by the choice or consensus of the villagers. On the other hand, the tendency for individuals or groups of young workers in an agricultural civilization to rebel was effectively curbed by their inability, if expelled from the village, to find land to till for a living. Arable land was already cultivated by other villages. The economy and security of a village gradually became completely dependent upon the wisdom of the elders and the filial piety of the able-bodied workers and young peasants.

While Mao's interpretation of Marxism-Leninism inspired his pragmatic development of China's modern urban factory and rural commune society, it is also true that the new social system in China bears some relationship to China's ancient agricultural system. Involvement, participation, and consensus are modern expressions of certain aspects of the old social system. This may explain why the necessary modern innovations are acceptable, particularly to the young.

In the decadent depths to which Chinese agricultural society had fallen during the periods of the latter Manchus, the war lords, the civil war, the Japanese occupation, and the Nationalist corruption, China's peasants lost nearly all of the desirable aspects of China's old system. They had become the tortured victims of exorbitant tax collectors, unscrupulous money-lenders, cruel landlords, corrupt officials, and foreign competition. Mao Tse-tung restored modern versions of the good aspects of the ancient system.

In ancient China, internal pressures developed from amalgamations of primitive agricultural communities expanding into larger political organizations, nations, and kingdoms. Confucius was concerned with the growing pains which the Chou Dynasty experienced when the Warring States were gradually being amalgamated into the Ch'in Empire. Mammoth undertakings became necessary—for example, the Great Wall was constructed for the security of a growing empire against Northern nomads.

Complex situations demanded new and sophisticated solutions to prevent chaos and decadence. This became the burden of men like Confucius, who deplored the discord of his own time. He proposed the philosophical foundation for a political, social, and economic structure to perpetuate peace, prosperity, security, and harmony. His system of government, perhaps more than any other single factor, enabled the ancient civilization of China to endure.

A common explanation of the phenomenal endurance of Chinese civilization has been that China was isolated by natural barriers of deserts, mountains, and seas. She had escaped the foreign invasions which brought about the collapse of other ancient civilizations. Also it was assumed that China had almost no contact with any other great empire as strong as herself and that she had, therefore, been able eventually to absorb and overcome invaders. There is some truth in those explanations.

The historic fact, however, is that China did for centuries have very extensive contacts, by sea and land, with countries bordering the Mediterranean, with the Middle East, with Indo-China, Japan, and India. The contacts were instigated chiefly by China. During the Yuan Dynasty (1279–1368), which was imposed upon China by Mongol power, especially during the reign of the great Kublai Khan, there was a significant influx into China of foreigners. They were used by the Mongols for administration and included Persians, Turks, and other peoples from Central Asia. Marco Polo was one of these and to this day he is enshrined as a "Lohan," Bodhisattva. As a student in Peking, I was surprised during my first visit to the "Wo Fu Ssu," Temple of the Sleeping Buddha, in the Western hills to suddenly see a foreigner among the huge statues of distinguished Chinese "Lohans." Underneath his statue I read the transliteration, "Ma K'o Po Lo," Marco Polo. The people of my home city still talk about the visit of Marco Polo to Hsiangyang when it was stormed by the Mongols.

While the Confucian system prevented a collapse of China for more than 2,000 years, Confucius' ideals of peace and harmony did not always characterize Chinese civilization. China has perhaps had more than her share of war and bloodshed.

Confucius may not have foreseen that all the feudal aspects of the Chou Dynasty would be perpetuated by his teaching. While he taught that it was the duty of a sovereign to satisfy the needs of his people, whatever democratic aspects his teachings had were cancelled out by the sacredness of his traditionalism. The Chou Dynasty system was his ideal. Traditionalism, not democracy, became basic in Confucianism. His commitment was to stability, not to change. Youth was to be submerged by age; there could be no deviation.

More than 2,000 years passed before the Confucian system, which was conceived to be eternal, finally collapsed. The corruption and stagnation inherent in the old system were sufficiently offset by other characteristics of the system to enable China to survive until the whole structure finally collapsed when she came into confrontation with the dynamic, ruthless, industrialized empires of the West. They were in search of new sources of raw materials for the modern factories of Europe and North America and new markets for the products of the new labour-saving machines powered by steam and electricity. And they were backed by superior military power, which easily crushed China's resistance.

When China was brought to her knees by the *yang-jen,* Ocean people or foreigners, the Emperor, despite his Mandate of Heaven, the ministers, the mandarins, and the intellectual elite were forced to accept unequal treaties, grant concessions, and yield national sovereignty. These demands caused deeper hatred and more humiliating kowtows to the *yang kuei-tzu,* foreign devils, than any obeisance the Chinese may have tried to exact from foreign diplomats before they were subdued by military power.

I have always felt that historians, who stress the "degrading humiliation" expected by Chinese rulers from foreigners, forget the infinitely more degrading humiliation foreigners demanded from the Chinese after crushing China by superior Western military weapons in the Opium and subsequent wars.

More important by far, however, the people of China suffered the disastrous effect which Western exploitation had upon the village economy of China.

China had been able to deal effectively with all previous invasions, chiefly because China was actually governed by an aristocracy of the intelligentsia which had been continuously revitalized by new blood. The examination system, despite petty corruption, did bring to the top of government administration a constant stream of the most able young men. The sons of butchers, bakers, and candlestick makers could become Prime Minister if they had the brains to pass the examination which provided recruits for the imperial bureaucratic elite. No aristocracy of wealth or of blood could have pulled China through more than 2,000 years of turbulence.

When emperors toppled, it mattered little to whom the Mandate of Heaven fell—the Chinese bureaucratic society continued to function. More important, no new dynasty, not even a foreign one, had ever crippled the village economy upon which the agricultural civilization of China was based.

China could, and perhaps always did, tolerate a high degree of corruption and inefficiency. The peasants and village industry workers did sustain not only the wealthy merchants, the landlords, the scholarly aristocrats, the armed forces, and the luxury of mandarin and imperial families and their armies of retainers. They also bore the brunt of supporting a vast number of professional, parasitic organizations, such as tea-house gangs, yellow ox gangs, beggar gangs, and armed brigands. The corruption and stagnation of the old system could be, and was, endured by the patient, long-suffering peasants as long as the rot was sufficiently curbed to prevent a breakdown of the village and its ability to raise grain, produce goods, and render the services of labour.

When the merchants of the West came with their flood of foreign goods—better, cheaper textiles, kerosene and lamps, cigarettes and opium—the old Chinese system collapsed. The Government could do nothing to stem the tide. It had given up essential sovereignty in the face of superior military power.

The proud imperial bureaucracy and the mandarin elite could do nothing. They were entirely ignorant of the new forces to which China was subjected. Their training had been in the old Chinese classics, and their experience had not prepared them to meet the new challenge. The scholarly elite were no more capable of dealing with the situation than the eunuchs who served the wives and concubines of the Imperial families in the Forbidden City.

Extraterritoriality had sterilized China's courts. Foreign merchants, diplomats, and missionaries were not subject to Chinese law. Even Chinese Christians were protected by the treaties which had been exacted from weak and useless governments in Peking. The treaties provided that Chinese Christians were not to be "persecuted." Persecution was sometimes interpreted as prosecution, and mandarins did not dare to prosecute a Chinese Christian in court regardless of his guilt. During the anti-Christian demonstrations of the Twenties, the criticism was not of Christian teachings but of the practice of Christian organizations taking advantage of extraterritoriality.

When I was a teacher in China, I saw a beautiful cathedral built chiefly by money contributed by grateful winners of law suits in the local court. The magistrate feared to make any decision against a member of a Christian congregation. If he did, he ran the risk of being reported to a foreign legation in Peking. The Foreign Minister would report the case to the Foreign Office, which in turn would notify the Provincial Viceroy, who would then discipline the local magistrate who had violated the sacred unequal treaty granting foreigners extraterritoriality.

Sincere Chinese Christians deplored this situation. Most of the missionaries did everything they could to prevent such practices, but there were sufficient violations to arouse antagonism, especially among the youth of China.

The commercial invasion of China by the West was certainly

not the only, or perhaps even not the chief, cause for the break-down of a civilization in the 19th and 20th centuries which had endured for millennia. It was, however, much more than the proverbial straw, which in addition to the accustomed overload broke the back of China's agricultural society—the village economy.

By 1850, conditions throughout China, especially in the South, had deteriorated to perhaps one of the lowest levels in China's history up to that time. Peasants and unemployed workers organized secret societies in protest against the authorities at an alarming rate. They lacked leadership to take action, but rumours gave rise to deep rumblings of a pending revolt. Then a strange and most unexpected development took place.

Robert Morrison, the first Protestant missionary to China, had come to Canton at the beginning of the century in a British ship carrying a cargo of opium from India, which the British had compelled the Chinese to accept. Morrison had studied the Chinese classical language for years. With the assistance of Chinese scholars, he had prepared and distributed some Christian tracts. Some of the tracts, which dealt with the promise of a kingdom of heavenly peace on earth, came by chance into the hands of one, Hung Hsiu-ch'uan. Hung had been suffering from deep, melancholic depression. He had failed to pass the examination which he hoped would qualify him for a position in the imperial bureaucracy. He studied Morrison's tracts and was suddenly seized by an idea which had astonishingly explosive power. Why not transform China into a "Taiping T'ien Kuo," a Kingdom of Heavenly Peace? The only way in China to persuade heaven to remove the mantle of the Mandate of Heaven from the ruling emperor was to use military power.

Hung visited the secret societies and spread the spores of rebellion which mushroomed throughout South China into an army before which all Manchu armed forces capitulated. The army was trained, indoctrinated, and well equipped. Cities fell and, to make a long story short, a Government of the Kingdom of Heavenly Peace was established in Nanking. Except for an army of Chinese and foreign mercenaries, led by "Chinese

Gordon," a foreign mercenary, Peking would have fallen, and the Manchu Dynasty would have been terminated half a century before it was. The mercenaries crushed the Taiping Rebellion, and Manchu troops slaughtered millions of Chinese who had actively or passively supported the Taipings. A few escaped to Southeast Asia to become Overseas Chinese known as *hua-ch'iao*. The cities that had welcomed the Taipings were razed; every man, woman, and child was brutally murdered.

More than half a century later, I visited the site of one of those cities not far from the present city of Shasi on the Yangtse River. The city walls had been torn down, and every building in the city had been reduced to a heap of shapeless rubble. As I looked at the devastation, I imagined the horrors of the inhuman butchery and wanton destruction of that terrible day. No one had since returned to the cursed city. There were too many ghosts there.

The Taiping Rebellion had been crushed. The first phase of China's modern revolution had been nipped in blossom. China seethed with hatred against the Manchus and the foreign mercenaries who had intervened in a civil war and which had made possible one of the greatest massacres of all time.

Nearly a century passed before the Chinese people rose again successfully to establish a kingdom of genuine peace—the People's Republic of China—which ended another fratricidal civil war.

After the Taiping Rebellion, revolutionary reform raised its head again in the "Palace Revolution" before the end of the century. A new class of modern intellectuals had gained the confidence of the young Emperor in Peking. They persuaded him to issue edicts which heralded an ambitious programme of reforms that would have begun the modernization of China. The notorious Empress Dowager, however, aided and abetted by her wily minister Yuan Shih-k'ai, nipped that effort in the bud.

Very soon after the failure of the "Palace" reform effort of 1898, extremely bad crops and floods in parts of North and Central China caused the widespread uprising of peasants, directed by a secret organization known as the Boxers. The Empress Dowager, Tz'u Hsi, very cleverly diverted the movement, which was originally directed at the Manchus, against foreigners. Missionaries were killed. Although official instructions were issued to protect foreigners, the Empress issued secret instructions to the contrary.

The Boxers were invited into Peking. In a wild orgy of rapine and pillage, the German Minister was murdered. The Manchus declared war on the foreign powers, and the "siege of the legations" began. An international force was organized by nine foreign powers, which saved the foreigners from a general massacre, ordered by the bigoted Empress Dowager, with the encouragement of her vicious favourite eunuch.

As my parents were preparing to leave for their first furlough in 1899 after a decade in China, they learned that a number of missionaries had been killed in areas more disturbed by Boxer disorders than ours. We were on our way down the Han River by junk to Hankow when we had our first scare. After being anchored for a night not far from a small city on the banks of the Han River, we were suddenly awakened by the terrifying, continuously repeated raucous cry of the Boxers, "*Sha yang-jen,*" kill foreigners. As the sound drew nearer and nearer, my father urged the captain to set sail. Our boatmen, terrified because they were helping foreigners, hurriedly got the junk loose and out into the stream. It was the first and last time we heard that Boxer slogan by a large mob, but for years I carried the memory of that terrifying sound.

We were back in China by 1901. The classical examination system was abolished in 1905, and my father's school, the only modern one in the area, suddenly became popular. The only requirement to qualify for public service was a certificate from one of the new schools. Until the founding of new government schools, which eventually appeared in nearly all county seats, the alternative was to go abroad. Students went to Britain and to the United States. Everyone wanted to learn English. France attracted many. Japan was nearer home and cost much less. Students flocked there by the thousands. A stint in a Japanese military academy was the way to become a general. Schools throughout China became centres where the youth of China were exposed to revolutionary ideas. A new, modern, revolutionary class of intellectuals was rapidly replacing the old elite Confucian scholars. Cells of Dr. Sun Yat-sen's revolutionary organization, the T'ung Meng Hui, mushroomed in almost every educational institution. New publishing houses, newspapers, and magazines were circulating and being avidly read by students and teachers, who were eager to participate in reforming and modernizing China.

After the "Palace Revolution" and the Boxer Rebellion, there was universal agreement in the new intellectual circles that the first step must be to crush the Manchu Ch'ing Dynasty and establish a republic. Without military power, however, there was no way of depriving the Manchus of the Mandate of Heaven. It was essential to win the support of powerful military men.

The decaying dynasty was itself disintegrating and incapable of hanging on to the Mandate much longer. The disastrous rule of the vindictive Empress Dowager and her diabolical Grand Eunuch was rapidly weakening the power of imperial structure.

The Emperor Kuang Hsü died on November 14, 1908. It was suspected that Tz'u Hsi had herself poisoned him the day before she died. The Emperor had no heir, so his nephew, P'u Yi, became his successor as Emperor Hsuan T'ung. Kuang Hsü's last order had been that Yuan Shih-k'ai be executed for his betrayal of the Emperor and the "Palace Revolution" advisers in 1898. The order was not carried out by Prince Ch'un, the new Regent, brother of Kuang Hsü and father of P'u Yi.

With an infant on the Dragon Throne and a weakling Regent, the time was ripe for action by Sun Yat-sen's T'ung Meng Hui to act. A bomb exploded in Hankow a week before a planned uprising was scheduled. A commanding officer was killed by a soldier. The Revolution was off to an unpropitious beginning. It ended when Yuan Shih-k'ai outwitted Sun Yat-sen, the Provisional President of the new Republic. Yuan became the First President and stopped at nothing to become the founder of a new dynasty. He ordered the assassination of T'ung Meng Hui leaders. Yuan's National Congress of Representatives unanimously invited Yuan to ascend the throne. On December 12, 1915, Yuan accepted. The idea of a Republic had been cherished for so long by so many that opposition was overwhelming. Yuan's China broke up. On March 12, 1916, three months after his ascent to the long-coveted Imperial Throne, Yuan Shih-k'ai formally decreed the end of the Hung Hsien Dynasty.

Yuan died on June 6, 1916. Rumour had it that he was helped to join his non-imperial ancestors prematurely by poison in his swallow-nest soup. He had betrayed his Empress, the Manchu Dynasty, and the Republic. Sun Yat-sen had hoped that Yuan would live long enough to be suitably punished for his crimes against China.

It has often been said that Yuan was the only man in China strong enough to hold the country together after the Manchus were eliminated and that China fell to the war lords after he died. The truth is that many of the provinces had declared their independence of Peking when he declared himself the founder of a new dynasty. It was perhaps more likely that China could have been held together if Yuan had not held on for four long years.

Vice-President Li Yuan-hung assumed the Presidency when Yuan Shih-k'ai died. In 1911, Colonel Li Yuan-hung had been a potential revolutionary, but had no intention of participating in an open rebellion. In fact, he had to be dragged out of hiding in Wuhan to lead the military rebellion which eventually resulted in the establishment of the Republic.

President Li resurrected the provisional constitution of 1912 and restored Parliament. He was unaware that the powerful Peiyang leader, Tuan Ch'i-jui, who controlled the best armies, had no intention of letting Li or anyone else control the Peking Government, which was gradually reduced to a ridiculous sham. Under "Tu-chün," super-war-lord rule, Parliament became a political football in a game for power played by the most adroit Tu-chüns, each hoping to inherit the Mandate of Heaven and the Dragon Throne.

Chang Tso-lin, reputedly a descendant of the traditional red-bearded bandits of Manchuria, became the most powerful Tu-chün of the North. When Sun Yat-sen organized a new revolutionary government in Canton in 1923 to challenge the sham government of Peking, Chang Tso-lin saw an opportunity to use it as he had used the weak Peking Government to further his ambitions. With this same end in view, he offered Sun Yat-sen his support before Sun's death in Peking in 1925. Chang also feared the rivalry and rapidly increasing power of Central China war lord Wu P'ei-fu, whom Sun had sworn to defeat. Sun wanted Hankow as the seat for his Government and the new capital of China.

War lords became great by swallowing small war lords. If the lesser ones were subsequently regurgitated, they resorted to banditry. There were always defeated troops finding themselves far from home and eager to share in the loot of periodic raids.

Two notorious and powerful bandit leaders—"Lao Yang-jen," old foreigner, and "Pei-lang," white wolf—conducted extensive periodic raids in Honan and parts of Hupeh, where I lived with my wife and two children. Late one night I was awakened by the gatekeeper with news from Tsaoyang, a city near bandit headquarters, that one of these bandit groups had occupied the city. Two missionaries had been severely wounded by gun shots. Reverend John Gronli set off immediately on a rescue mission with sedan chairs for wounded foreigners.

Early next morning, a second messenger brought news that a doctor was urgently required. Gronli had apparently been unable to get through an area where villages were burning after pillage and looting. I went immediately to an embryo war lord who was temporarily in control of the twin cities, Hsiangfan. He agreed to assist provided I would accompany one of his lieutenants. It took more time than I had thought necessary, but we started off that afternoon in an old Model-T Ford one-ton truck on which a rickety wooden body had been built. Two planks, one on each side, provided seats for passengers. I was surprised to find a squad of twenty fully armed soldiers packed into the truck. We started off on the forty-mile drive to Tsaoyang, the driver having little experience but lots of nerve. He pulled the accelerator down as far as it would go and kept his hand on it while he guided the vehicle over the rough, winding narrow road with the other. The truck rattled, bumped, and twisted. Each soldier sat holding his rifle between his knees with fixed bayonet. I sat with my back to the cab. By turning sideways I could see the road through the windshield.

The soldiers quickly fell asleep, and the bayonets klinked. We came to a tributary of the Han and crossed on a barge. After crossing the river, the lieutenant wakened the troops and invited me to change places with him as we would soon be coming to the area held by the brigands. He thought we would have less difficulty getting through if a foreigner was seen in the front seat, distracting attention from the armed troops, who would not be seen unless we were stopped and inspected. He had orders not to shoot any bandits unless it became absolutely necessary to get through.

It became pitch dark. The headlights penetrated the darkness with two long cones of light which lit up the countryside. We passed through a few small villages. Not a human being, not a flicker of light came out of any of the mud-walled, straw-roofed huts. On the eastern horizon a reddish glow appeared, and gradually the whole sky reflected the fire of burning villages. Still not a sign of life. We thundered past burning houses on both sides of the road, black smoke curling above leaping tongues of fire as we passed through the centre of larger villages. If there were bandits, they remained discreetly silent and motionless. The headlights of our vehicle had warned them. It was uncomfortably hot as we dashed through narrow streets past livid flames. Not a word was uttered. The driver had nerves of steel. He turned and twisted the old Model-T through crooked streets dodging fire on both sides. Sometimes it appeared as if we were about to crash into a wall of fire. The driver never for a moment lifted his heavy hand from the little lever, and we finally came out in an open area between the burning villages and the city of Tsaoyang.

We arrived at the city gate and learned that the wounded missionaries had been rescued. The rescue party had taken a road north of the regular road and were probably not far from Hsiangfan on the way back. Without a word, the lieutenant ordered the driver to return the same way we had come. He had learned that the bandits were camped in villages north of the city and might return and he did not wish to annoy them. In any case, this was not an area for which his General was responsible for law and order. We drove back through still-smouldering villages.

When I got home, the missionary and his wife were in the Hsiangyang Hospital, both of them seriously wounded. She survived, but he died. I had known her when she was a small girl. Her parents, the Reverend and Mrs. Kilen, had been very good friends of my parents.

During the chaos of the war-lord days, thousands of Chinese had been killed and wounded, thousands had lost their homes and all their possessions. Millions of young Chinese were determined to end this senseless chaos which China had gone through so many times to determine who would inherit the Mandate of Heaven to rule China.

3

THE
"GREAT REVOLUTION"
AND THE
1927 DISASTER

The Northern Expedition, conceived by Dr. Sun Yat-sen and commanded by Chiang Kai-shek, marched triumphantly into Hankow in 1927. When I arrived in Hankow from Fancheng with my wife and three children, the British and other foreign concessions had been seized by the Chinese. Most of the foreigners in Hankow spent their nights in foreign gunboats anchored along the bund, while they waited for stragglers like us from the interior. All foreigners in Central China had been ordered by their respective consulates in Hankow to leave.

Until law and order was fully established in the city by the new regime, there was considerable chaos. Coolies were charging five silver dollars to carry suitcases from ship to shore—the usual charge had been a few coppers. If the cost of a rickshaw ride was not agreed upon beforehand, which was not the custom of most foreigners, the demand for money upon arrival was sky-high. Payment was quickly made, however, when passengers were subjected to physical violence and loud cursing. Foreigners' extraterritorial privileges had vanished. Port-city foreigners were terrified. Missionaries from the interior who did not insist upon their extraterritorial advantages and habitually dealt with the Chinese fairly had almost no difficulties.

The new intellectuals of China had initially pinned their hopes on the Republic of 1911 to begin a reform of the old Confucian system and the modernization of China. Their dreams were rudely upset by the personal ambitions of numerous military contenders striving desperately to inherit control of the old Empire.

Chinese intellectuals eventually lost their faith in Parliamentarian democracy as far as China was concerned and began to examine other Western solutions for their political and social problems. Such reforms could be dealt with only if political power could be attained. Even Dr. Sun Yat-sen became disillusioned in the hope of getting help from the United States or Great Britain. He was finally urged by Moscow's agents in China to collaborate with the USSR. By inviting Chinese Communists to join the Nationalists, Dr. Sun Yat-sen expected to unite all Chinese revolutionaries.

Many young Chinese went to Moscow to study. Revolutionary Marxist cells had already been organized in China by Comintern representatives. On July 1, 1921, the Chinese Communist Party was launched, with Ch'en Tu-hsiu as Secretary-General. Mao Tse-tung from Hunan, Tung Pi-wu from Hupeh, and ten others were charter members.

To prepare for a military expedition against the Peking Government, Sun Yat-sen sent Chiang Kai-shek to lead a politico-military mission to Moscow. The Russians sent Michael Borodin to be a personal adviser to Dr. Sun and official political adviser to the Kuomintang, the Nationalist Party. The KMT was remodeled on the pattern of the Communist Party of the Soviet Union.

The stage was being set for what the Nationalists called "The Great Revolution." The Government in Peking had neither power nor will to cope with the chaos throughout China caused by numerous contending war lords. They collected taxes for a steadily increasing number of years in advance to keep vast armies of soldiers to fight other war lords instead of protecting the peasants from roving bandits and disbanded soldiers. The Chinese peasantry had not been as disturbed since the Taiping Rebellion.

Borodin had brought some forty advisers to China. The Soviet Union promised arms. A new military academy was established at Whampao near Canton, and Chiang Kai-shek was appointed its head. A Soviet general, Vassili K. Bluecher, alias Galen, became Chiang's Chief of Staff and Chou En-lai his Deputy Political Commissar in charge of indoctrinating the army and Whampao cadets for the anticipated Northern Expedition.

Sun's Northern Expedition to drive out war lords and move his Revolutionary Military Government north, however, was still awaiting the extension of greater control in the South.

Sun Yat-sen died in Peking in 1925 while negotiating with Chang Tso-lin, the most powerful Tu-chün of the North. Sun's so-called allies, Chang Tso-lin and Tuan Ch'i-jui, controlled the nation's capital. The time seemed propitious to launch the Northern Expedition, which had been Sun Yat-sen's dream for many years. Chiang Kai-shek made that decision on July 9, 1926, and Pai Ch'ung-hsi became his Deputy Chief of Staff.

The drive against the most powerful war lords of Central China, Wu P'ei-fu, succeeded with little difficulty, and Changsha, Hunan's capital, fell. The Expedition drove on to capture Wuchang, the capital of Hupeh, hitherto considered impregnable. (Chinese labour battalions which had returned from France after World War I had been drafted to dig trenches around the walled city. Wu P'ei-fu had been assured that no army could penetrate these modern defences. Some of my students from Fancheng had joined the Northern Expedition as troops. One of them related to me how well the troops had been indoctrinated by Chou En-lai and his assistants at the Whampao Military Academy. Wuchang was captured despite the French trenches on October 10, the fifteenth anniversary of the 1911 Revolution.)

The Expedition secured control of the whole of the important upper Yangtse valley, including Hunan, where peasant uprisings had been inspired by Mao Tse-tung, and Szechuan, whose generals joined in the fight against Wu P'ei-fu.

These victories released reinforcements for the fighting in Kiangsi. The Nationalists captured the important city of Nanchang, and Nationalist forces pressed on to take over the provinces of Fukien and Chekiang. Shanghai was captured. Chou En-lai had organized an uprising of Communist-organized workers inside the city, which made possible the entry into Shanghai by the Eastern Route Army of the Expedition.

After Shanghai, the Nationalists entered Nanking. They attacked resident foreigners. Missionaries and a British consul were killed. Foreigners in the northern part of the city were saved by two foreign gunboats, one American and one British, anchored in the Yangtse River.

My wife and I witnessed the escape of the foreigners over the northern city wall of Nanking. They were being let down outside the wall in baskets on long ropes. From there they joined us aboard the Jardine Matheson steamer on which we were travelling from Hankow to Shanghai. With us were our three children, the youngest of whom was Meme, five months old. The American gunboat, commanded by Lieutenant Olds, together with the British gunboat lobbed shells into Nanking to prevent the Nationalist troops in the southern part of the city from attacking the foreigners in the northern part of the city who were being helped to escape. Twenty-one years later, Meme was married to an American naval officer, David Westlein, by the last American Ambassador in China, Dr. Leighton Stuart. One of our guests was Admiral Olds, the gunboat lieutenant of 1927.

The Revolutionary Government had been moved from Canton to Hankow in January and was controlled by left-wing Nationalists, including Sun Fo, Sun Yat-sen's son by his first marriage, Foreign Minister Eugene Ch'en, and Soong Ch'ing-ling, Sun Yat-sen's second wife. Comintern representative Michael Borodin was still an adviser of the Government.

Mao Tse-tung's influence and activities in his home province of Hunan had blossomed into an organization of some two million peasants. Mao Tse-tung had good reason to predict that the peasants of China were capable of "rising like a tornado to liberate peasants from money-lenders and landlords."

The right-wing Nationalists of the Kuomintang, however, many of whom had landlord connections, were opposed to any "liberation" movement by peasants. Chiang Kai-shek had his own reasons for encouraging the Nationalist military officers from landlord families to oppose the turbulent peasant movement. Chiang had never understood, or agreed, that a revolution was necessary in China. It was frequently said that he had ambitions to succeed where Yuan Shih-k'ai had failed in the attempt to restore a Confucian-type empire.

Chiang Kai-shek completely lost his influence and control of the Hankow Government. He had, however, close connections with the moneyed interests in Shanghai. He decided to force the issue by requesting the Hankow Government to move to Nanchang. He had obtained substantial loans from powerful financiers in Shanghai and was thereby freed from the former reliance on the Soviet Union for aid.

To satisfy his Shanghai friends, Chiang then attacked the labour unions in Shanghai, who had helped the Nationalists to enter the city. The blood bath of Shanghai followed. For months not only every Communist but also all Nationalists who were suspected of supporting the Government in Hankow were hunted down and executed. The few who escaped fled to more remote rural areas or went underground. Chiang Kai-shek's hatchet-men cut down five-sixths of the total Communist Party membership. The Party organization, however, some of the key leaders, and a hard core of fighting men survived. Chou En-lai made his escape to Hankow by the skin of his teeth and found himself surrounded by old friends and former subordinates, including Ch'en Yi, when the Hankow Government did not go along with Chiang Kai-shek's purge.

The Kuomintang Central Executive Committee passed a resolution condemning Chiang and recommended that he be dismissed from all his offices and sent to the Central Government for punishment. Chiang's reaction was to organize his own Nationalist Government in Nanking.

The Hankow Nationalists subsequently swung to the right and expelled their Communist allies from the Kuomintang, and another phase of the purge began. The revolutionaries were put to the sword, and a wave of executions which began in Shanghai was extended to Wuhan and into northern Hupeh, where many of my friends who had organized peasant associations were hunted down and destroyed as revolutionaries and radicals. The peasant movement was crushed.

It mattered little to Chiang Kai-shek that the Hankow Government removed him from office or that his own Chief of Staff and generals refused to carry out his orders. He would retire for a period and return more powerful than before.

In 1927, after his temporary fall from grace, Chiang had retired to Japan. He emerged from retirement when the Nationalist Party was in a shambles, and the need again arose for a strong man. His rivals out of the picture, Chiang was restored as the Commander-in-Chief of the Nationalist Army and Chairman of the Kuomintang Executive Committee by the financial moguls of Shanghai. A Nationalist Government functioned again in Nanking.

Chiang would dominate the Nationalist Government in Nanking until driven out by the Japanese, then for a period in Chungking, and finally back in Nanking until the People's Republic of China came to power. Chiang was not a political philosopher. He was never by any stretch of the imagination a revolutionary or even a reformer. Because Sun Yat-sen was the acknowledged father and founder of the new order, his Three People's Principles were considered sacred, and all loyal citizens were expected to revere them as essential for necessary and safe reforms. However, the great founder had provided, at least for the time being, for a system of one-party "tutelage" by the Kuomintang. The controlling Kuomintang faction was the right-wing group, most of the left-wing faction having been massacred. The right-wingers were such conservatives as the brothers Ch'en Li-fu and Ch'en Kuo-fu, Chiang Kai-shek's military generals, and powerful Shanghai financial and commercial figures. The Nanking Government, by its composition, was bound to be identified with the maintenance of the social, political, and economic *status quo*. It was, in fact, merely a continuation of the strong-man tradition of Yuan Shih-k'ai, Tuan Ch'i'jui, and Chang Tso-lin.

Chiang Kai-shek was so steeped in this tradition that even twenty years later, when under pressure from General George Marshall, he flatly rejected any reform even to save his own regime. He could never make any change that would conflict with his "destiny." He fully expected to be called upon to accept the Mandate of Heaven and cannot accept that in 1949 it fell to the genuine revolutionaries of China.

4

THE
LONG MARCH
AND THE
SIAN INCIDENT

China's foundation was her agricultural economy. She had almost no proletariat, only millions of peasants. In the villages of China lived the people who were rapidly becoming ripe for revolution. All they needed was organization. Many of China's revolutionaries did not fully realize this situation. It was Mao Tse-tung, who had worked in the more remote villages and mountainous areas such as Chingkangshan, who finally drew their attention to this fundamental truth about the country.

Conditions in agricultural China had been rapidly deteriorating for decades owing to the demands of a rapidly increasing population, limited arable land, high rentals, usurious interests charged by money-lenders, war lords, collection of future taxes, and conscription of manpower by irresponsible generals for military adventures. For a century, foreign goods had been destroying villages industries; drought and famine occurred in China's northern provinces; the soaring prices of rice and wheat impoverished a high percentage of the population, already ravaged by banditry; ownership of land was passing from impoverished peasants to landlords and money-lenders. The peasants of China, driven to desperation, were ripe for revolution.

After the 1927 purge, driven away from urban centres to China's villages, the Chinese Communists eventually realized where the real problems lay. Mao Tse-tung and a small band of followers had retired to the hills and mountains of the Kiangsi-Hunan border area in Chingkangshan. There they were joined by General Chu Teh and his ragged troops. Chu Teh, who had fought against the Manchus as well as against Yuan Shih-k'ai, became the Commander in Chief of the new army and Mao the Political Commissar.

The Central Committee of the Chinese Communist Party had gone underground with headquarters in Shanghai. It continued to keep in touch with the Comintern, but its ties were gradually cut off when Chou En-lai finally joined Mao. Later, Moscow's advice was defied by Mao's unorthodox revolutionary approach. Mao denounced Li Li-san, who had transmitted Moscow's directives. The break with Moscow was complete. Mao Tse-tung became the real leader.

On November 7, 1931, the first Soviet Congress was convened at Juichin in Southern Kiangsi. A Provisional Soviet Government was set up, and a Provisional Constitution adopted. The first international decision of the Juichin regime was to declare war on Japan, which won enthusiastic support throughout China in a wave of spontaneous nationalist resentment against the Japanese invaders. Chiang Kai-shek, who could have won similar support with such a gesture, preferred to use his military forces to destroy the Communists and seemed to be toying with the idea of eventual compromise with the Japanese.

Economic conditions continued steadily to deteriorate. The Chinese Communists no longer constituted an immediate threat to the Nanking Government, but they were steadily gaining public support by pressing for mobilization against the "devils from the base of the sun," and Japan had launched an attack on Manchuria which deprived China of some of her sovereignty. Despite everything, Chiang continued to be in favour of appeasing the Japanese. Why did he devote all his military power against the Communists instead of the Japanese? Why was the cream of a whole generation of China's new intellectuals destroyed to save China from change? Because these were the people Chiang feared as the greatest threat to the restoration of a Confucian-type system.

The Japanese would undoubtedly accept a restoration of the old Empire provided certain concessions were made to satisfy the increasing Japanese demand for China's raw products. Such a deal could be mutually beneficial to two Empires and be the easiest way to finance the increasing needs of China's growing population. Wang Ching-wei later proved that the Japanese would choose to rule through a Chinese Government. If it could be a government that was not only Chinese but had the Imperial Mandate, the Japanese would certainly co-operate and would perhaps even prefer it to be an equal rather than a mere puppet. Chiang would drive a hard bargain. The people of China would accept such a solution only if revolutionary Communist influence was completely eradicated. Hence Chiang's choice was first to unify the country to save China from Communism and then to deal with the Japanese threat to China's sovereignty.

The Sian incident suddenly changed Chiang Kai-shek's well laid plans, but in the meantime Chiang was unswervingly consistent in his determination to destroy Communism in China.

In 1930, to eliminate the Communist pockets of rebellion, Chiang appointed General Ho Ying-ch'in as Commander-in-Chief for Bandit Suppression, the name given to a final effort to wipe out the Communists. The "bandits" were to be suppressed "within three to six months at most." The campaign, however, failed miserably. General Ho lost two divisions. A Nationalist report gave six reasons for the failure. The sixth reason was a very frank admission of the real situation: "The bankrupt condition of the peasantry, unemployment among the artisans and workers, and the general economic distress among the people which supplied inexhaustible fuel for the growth of Communism."

A second bandit-suppression campaign was launched in 1931 against the "ragged, poorly-armed Communist rebels." It ground to a halt in five months, with the Communist forces again enriched by captured arms and defected Nationalist troops.

Chiang then assumed personal command of the third offensive to wipe out the Red rebellion. Rewards were posted: "50,000 yuan each for Mao, Chu Teh, and P'eng Teh-huai, alive, or 20,000 for each, dead." Chiang reported that the campaign had been successfully completed. The Government sent a message of congratulations to the "victorious Commander-in-Chief."

The victory, however, was less than total, and Chiang ordered complete eradication of Red banditry by the end of the month. A week later, Chiang rushed to the front to take personal command. The Communists, however, caused a critical situation. They avoided decisive actions and counter-attacked the Nationalist flank and rear and cut up two Nationalist divisions. After another battle, Chiang again announced: "The Red bandits, having suffered a bitter blow, certainly cannot rise up again." The Reds, however, were still to be "wiped out."

The fourth bandit-suppression campaign was commanded by General Ch'en Ch'eng with 250,000 troops. Like its predecessors, it failed ingloriously. It was out-manoeuvred by the mobile enemy in mountainous terrain and three divisions were lost. The Communists had actually grown in strength with each "suppression" campaign.

A fifth bandit-suppression campaign began in October 1933 and bore the influence of Chiang's new German military advisers. This time, the Communists were blocked off by a new strategy of encirclement—concrete blockhouses connected by barbed wire. All lines of communication were heavily guarded; all trading was stopped. The Communists began to feel the pinch in such essential supplies as salt, fats, and medicines. The iron ring was drawing tighter, continually advancing the line of fortifications. The odds were against the Communists; they were outnumbered by 700,000 Nationalist troops against 150,000 commanded by the embryo Juichin regime.

After a preliminary failure due to a rejection of Mao's strategy, the Communists led by Mao and Chou En-lai decided to save themselves by an early escape. It was, however, not done in panic. It was carefully planned, and the peasants who had joined the Red Army were given ample warning so they would not remain behind to be wiped out. In October 1934, one year after the fifth campaign started, the Red Army, divided into five corps, broke out of the Kiangsi-Fukien base area where they had been trapped. Marching by different routes and accompanied by a mass of peasants carrying supplies, they started out in search of a refuge. The fifth Nationalist campaign had cost the Communists 60,000 men, but there were still some 80,000 under arms ready to leave. Mechanics, technicians, bank clerks, factory workers, and the whole technical staff were needed for the march. To begin with, there was an attempt to keep the move secret, but that proved impossible.

Battle-tested local guerrilla units replaced regular Red Army units for the anticipated breakthrough of the Nationalist encirclement. General Chu Teh led the First Army Corps flanked by the Third and Ninth Army Corps and spearheaded the attempt to crash through the iron ring of fortifications. The elite Thirteenth Division was assigned to fight a rearguard action. Mao Tse-tung, Chou En-lai, and other leaders moved in the very centre of the column, together with the women's political propaganda corps led by Teng Ying-ch'ao—Mme. Chou En-lai.

The Reds threw their concentrated military weight against the unsuspecting Nationalist unit under cover of darkness, broke open a gap in the siege, and pushed on through three more layers of Nationalist fortifications before they got out of Kiangsi and Hunan and into Kweichow.

The units flanking the main army struck out in two separate directions to distract the enemy, while the main retreat column detoured again and again, often retracing their steps and making loops to elude pursuers and dodge local resistance.

It became the duty of Chou En-lai to plot these daily changes. He spent long hours each night planning each movement, based on information from radio reports and from scouts and supporters along the route.

It was not a march to victory; it was rather a serious retreat from overwhelming Nationalist military superiority directed by expert German strategists. Nationalist troops continued in relentless pursuit.

It took three months to reach Kweichow, where the marchers rested eleven days, the longest rest during the entire one-year trip. At each stop, the women's propaganda corps and the political workers immediately spread out to drum up support among the residents. Money and supplies were handed out free to the city poor. Peasants along the route proclaimed that the Red Army was carrying out the Mandate of Heaven.

The radio man brought in the news every evening. Chou En-lai would move his stool close to the candle to read it. When the radio man stood up to leave, Chou would always call to him to remind all the comrades to return everything they had borrowed for the night—boards, beds, scissors, and needles borrowed from the women—to their owners.

Chou En-lai held all his comrades, including the ranking generals, answerable to the Chinese Communist Party through the troubled days of the Long March, as he had in the Kiangsi Soviet. He used gentle persuasion and iron discipline.

When the marchers reached northern Szechuan, they ran out of food. The nearest cereal field often lay as far as ten miles from their camp. Everyone had to join in gathering half-ripe cereal, including Commander-in-Chief Chu Teh, who, at forty-nine, carried a load of 100 pounds and marched at the head of the labour column. Chou's associate in his Paris days, Hsü T'e-li, over sixty years old, also joined the carrier squad. Only Chou En-lai, because he had to stay up nearly every night to chart the next day's retreat route, often was forced to spend the day taking catnaps on a stretcher.

The marchers pushed on through Yunnan and Western Szechuan, where they frequently had to cross deep gorges between sheer rock walls thousands of feet high. Each crossing was a test of their ingenuity and courage. The local troops had been alerted by the Nationalists to haul away all grain in storage and burn what could not be hidden, to cut the bridges wherever there were any, and sink the ferry boats where there were no bridges. With each crossing, the Reds escaped one more Nationalist trap, and at each moment of critical decision Chou En-lai and Mao Tse-tung were there, studying the map together with the vanguard commander.

After crossing the Tatu River, a swift stream near the Tibetan border, under enemy fire behind a dozen dare-to-die volunteer comrades who crawled along iron chains (since the cross-tie boards on the bridge had been burned by Nationalist troops), there was suddenly no road. The marchers picked their way in single file through the jungle. Adding to their misery was the presence of Lolo tribesmen, who were traditionally suspicious of the Chinese and unable to understand their language. Fortunately, one of the vanguard commanders was familiar with the Lolos. Before he obtained permission for the safe passage for his comrades, he had to drink a bowl of rooster's blood with the Lolo chief and swear brotherhood forever.

The 6,000-mile trek from Kiangsi to Shensi, through some of the most rugged and uninhabited lands of the world with enemy troops lying in wait all along the route, certainly wrote a remarkable page of military history with the unbelievable survival of the core of the Chinese Red Army. The Long March started as a retreat, but wound up a memorable triumph. Less than half of the marchers reached their destination, but not all were lost. Some were purposely assigned to remain behind along the route to form Communist nuclei.

At the end of the Long March, in December 1935, the Communists settled down in the Province of Shensi and established their headquarters in the caves of Yenan.

Despite the failure of five successive "bandit-suppression" campaigns, Chiang Kai-shek, still determined to wipe out the Red Army, stationed his best troops in areas not far from Yenan almost simultaneously with the Chinese Communist proposal, on February 21, 1936, that all parties and factions in China should unite to resist the Japanese invasion of China. A few months later, as the Japanese continued their advance encountering no Chinese resistance, Mao Tse-tung, Chou En-lai, and Chu-teh proposed a formal truce with Chiang Kai-shek. Ch'en Li-fu, the Nationalists' political security chief, was appointed to meet Chou En-lai. China's neutral groups and third parties, including independent intellectuals, heartily supported the proposal and organized the all-China National Salvation League to end the civil war and unite all Chinese against Japan.

Chiang Kai-shek's highest priority was nevertheless given to winning the civil war. The key of the plan was to use Chang Hsueh-liang, a dashing young marshal, former playboy and son of the super war lord Chang Tso-lin. The young marshal was forthwith transferred to Sian, capital of the Province of Shensi, as the Deputy Commander-in-Chief for "bandit-suppression" in Central and North China.

Chiang Kai-shek's strategy backfired, however. Chang Hsueh-liang used his new headquarters to play a key role in forcing the Generalissimo into military action to save China from Japanese occupation regardless of Chiang's plans.

Political opposition to Chiang existed even in the Generalissimo's own family. His son, Ching-kuo, who had been sent to Moscow to study in the Sun Yat-sen University and the Red Army Academy, refused to return to China. When ordered by his father to do so, young Chiang defied him and wrote to his mother to condemn his father for conniving with the Japanese to destroy the Communists.

At the time of the Mukden incident of 1931, Chang Hsueh-liang had committed 100,000 of his best troops south of the Great Wall to bolster up Chiang's forces in the civil war. Chiang had warned the young marshal to avoid any provocation of the Japanese in retaliation for the Mukden incident. Anti-Japanese sentiment in China resulted, however, in widespread opposition to Chiang's failure to abandon the civil war to resist the Japanese. Chiang was either ignorant of, or completely ignored, the fact that anti-Japanese resentment was already deep in the hearts of the young marshal's Manchurian troops. Most of them would have preferred to protect their own homes rather than fight in a civil war south of the Great Wall.

The Communists were firmly established in the province to which the Generalissimo had sent the young marshal and his Manchurian armies. The Communists lost no time in establishing secret contacts with Chang Hsueh-liang. The liaison developed rapidly to the point where the Communist representatives actually took up residence in Sian, the headquarters of the young marshal's army.

Chiang Kai-shek had expected that Chang Hsueh-liang would win for him a victory in his sixth "bandit suppression" campaign and undoubtedly also hoped that the young marshal's armies would be so damaged in the fight that they would no longer be a major factor in Chiang's balance-of-power scheme. Chiang's strategy was to use one war lord against another to eliminate both. That had been the practice that had enabled Chiang to rise to the status of a Generalissimo.

The Communists were in the meantime completing their concentration of forces in the Northwest and had become nearly as strong again as they had been before the Long March. When Chiang Kai-shek made a trip to Sian to confer with Chang Hsueh-liang about the sixth campaign to wipe out the Communists, he was confronted with proposals to stop the civil war and establish a united front to resist the Japanese.

Two months after his first call, the Generalissimo returned and ordered the young marshal to start the sixth "bandit-suppression" campaign. But Chiang Kai-shek was suddenly arrested, and a circular telegram was sent to Nanking demanding reorganization of the Government on a coalition basis and the immediate cessation of the civil war in favour of armed resistance to Japan.

Nanking was shocked. General Ho Ying-ch'in, who had long cherished ambitions of his own, proposed a punitive expedition against Sian employing bombers that had been concentrated for the "bandit-suppression" campaign. General Ho was not too concerned about what might happen to the Generalissimo during the aerial bombardment of Sian, where the Generalissimo was a prisoner.

The arrest of Chiang Kai-shek had been precipitated by General Yang Hu-ch'eng of the Northwestern armies, who was aware of the secret truce agreement which had been reached between Chou En-lai and the young marshal. Yang was violently anti-Chiang. When Chiang arrived in Sian, the young marshal feared someone might assassinate the Generalissimo, and General Yang was therefore kept out of top-command conferences. Yang could wait no longer and ordered the immediate seizure of Chiang Kai-shek, who was then placed under house arrest. Chiang attempted an escape. Pursued over rocky ground at night, he stumbled, and was reported to have broken some of his teeth in the fall.

Chou En-lai rushed to Sian from Shanghai. He did not want Chiang Kai-shek harmed or killed. In fact, he wanted the Generalissimo to order all Nationalist armies to resist Japan.

Chou played a key role in working for a united front to drive Japan out of China. He visited his former boss of the Whampao Military Academy. Whatever understanding was reached between Chiang and Chou has never been reported by anyone. It was perhaps a gentleman's agreement of some sort to the effect that Chou would get the young marshal and General Yang to release Chiang and let him return with dignity to Nanking if he would join forces with the Communists and all other factions in China to take united military action against the Japanese.

There was no written agreement. In any case, the young marshal was satisfied that all would be well and offered, despite a warning from his top advisers, to accompany the Generalissimo to Nanking. Chang Hsueh-liang was jubilant at the prospect of participating in military action to recapture Manchuria for the people of his home district. Also he wanted to avenge the death of his father, who had been killed by Japanese bombs which wrecked the train in which the famous super war lord was returning to his headquarters in Manchuria.

Before Chiang's release, Mme. Chiang Kai-shek and her brother, T. V. Soong, had arrived by plane from Nanking to participate in the discussions. Chiang was released on Christmas Day 1936, two weeks after his arrest.

Chang Hsueh-liang accompanied the Generalissimo to Nanking and was promptly sentenced to ten years' imprisonment. Subsequently, he was placed in the personal custody of Chiang Kai-shek. In 1949, when the Generalissimo escaped to Taiwan, the young marshal continued to be held under the Generalissimo's surveillance. Chang Hsueh-liang's partner, Yang Hu-ch'eng, who actually precipitated the Sian kidnapping, was murdered in a prison camp in Chungking when Chiang Kai-shek fled from the mainland.

It has sometimes been assumed that the settlement in Sian with the Generalissimo was the result of pressure on the Chinese Communists by the Comintern in Moscow.

In 1946, our Ambassador, General Victor Odlum, and I were guests of the Generalissimo and Mme. Chiang Kai-shek on Kuling, the summer resort near Kiukiang. One afternoon, Ch'en Li-fu, Chiang's Minister of Education, called on us and talked about the Sian incident for over an hour. He claimed that he persuaded Moscow through a Comintern representative in China to direct Chou En-lai to negotiate the release of Chiang Kai-shek and that he had himself negotiated on behalf of the Central Government with Chou En-lai.

Ch'en Li-fu further claimed that he had himself induced Chou En-lai to visit Sian to talk to the Generalissimo, when he was under house arrest, and persuaded the representative of the Third International in China to wire to Moscow to suggest that a telegram be sent by Moscow to Chou En-lai directing him "not to pour oil on fire." The Comintern representative had agreed to Ch'en Li-fu's proposal. The reply from Moscow was terse and characteristic, giving the necessary instructions to Chou En-lai in Sian. To me this was preposterous—Moscow had stopped giving orders to the Chinese Communists a decade earlier. Ch'en nevertheless claimed that this was the explanation of Chiang Kai-shek's release.

It was true that Ch'en Li-fu had negotiated with Chou in Shanghai prior to the Sian incident. The facts were, however, that it was Chou En-lai who had taken the initiative to negotiate with Chang Hsueh-liang. Ch'en Li-fu was anxious to create the impression in General Odlum's mind that the Chinese Communists were dangerous to world peace because they were controlled by Moscow. The fact that Chang Hsueh-liang's proposals may have fitted in perfectly with the Comintern's directive as reported by Ch'en Li-fu was not a determining factor with the Chinese Communists. They had accepted no advice from Moscow after the Juichin Soviet Government had been formed. Mao Tse-tung had defied Moscow ever since he had been convinced that revolution in China was possible only on the basis of peasant organization. As soon as they had established headquarters in Yenan, the Chinese Communists had themselves urged a coalition with the Nationalists to defy Japan's threat to China's sovereignty. Chou En-lai had maintained some contact with the Comintern before his final escape from Shanghai, but never after the establishment of the Juichin Government.

Chang Hsueh-liang had been eager to fight Japan long before the Sian incident, and it was Chou En-lai not Ch'en Li-fu who persuaded Chang Hsueh-liang to release the Generalissimo if he would agree to join in hostilities against Japan. Yang wanted to execute the Generalissimo and then unite for the war against Japan.

Negotiations between the Nationalists and Communists dragged on in Sian for over a year. When the Japanese openly attacked the outskirt of Peking at the famous Marco Polo Bridge on July 7, 1937, all China rose in protest against the Government's failure to take action. Chou En-lai hurried to meet Chiang Kai-shek on Kuling. A compromise was reached. The Military Chief and Political Commissar of the Whampao Academy were allies again, despite a relentless and savage ten-year man-hunt to exterminate Chou. The Generalissimo had apparently responded at long last to the demand of the people of China to stop Japan's aggression.

5

CHUNGKING

To secure transportation for the journey from Ottawa to Chungking in 1945 was no easy task. It could be provided only by the armed services, and I spent seventy hours in the air and fifteen days to travel a 15,000-mile route. From Montreal to Cairo I was flown by the Royal Canadian Air Force aboard a Liberator bomber. It took five days with stops in the Azores, Rabat, and Malta. After a week's delay in Egypt, I obtained passage in an Empire Flying Boat to Karachi. The trip took four days, with stops at the Dead Sea, Lake Habbaniyah, Basra, Bahrein, and Fort Sharjah.

In Karachi, I was the guest of the Prime Minister of Sind before being flown in another Empire Flying Boat to Calcutta, with stops at Rajamund and Allahabad. In Calcutta, I had the good fortune to meet one of the charter members of the Communist Party of China, Mr. Tung Pi-wu. Before leaving China in 1927, I had come to know his reputation as an important theoretician of the embryo Party, highly respected by China's revolutionaries. Tung had just returned from San Francisco, where he represented the Chinese Communist Party on the

Chinese delegation to the founding Conference of the United Nations. He was accompanied by Chang Han-fu, the well-known editor of a Communist journal in Chungking. We flew over the "hump" in the same aircraft from Calcutta to Kunming, the base of the Flying Tigers.

During the trip, Tung, who, like myself, is from the Province of Hupeh, told me that the Soviet Union had given the Chinese Communists no assistance whatever in the war against Japan. Soviet arms and ammunition had gone to the Nationalists only, and they had not co-operated too well with General Stilwell to fight the Japanese, despite massive American military supplies. The Communist forces, without foreign aid, had liberated extensive areas in North China from the Japanese. When I asked Mr. Tung what the Chinese Communist attitude was to Moscow, adding that I knew something about the differences which began in 1927, he replied that he would let me draw my own conclusions. He then added that the Chinese Communists would never approve of the recent agreements between the Chinese Nationalists and Moscow granting important concessions to the Soviet Union in Manchuria. The Chinese Communists considered these concessions to be as unacceptable as the unequal treaties.

It was evident to me that the gulf between Chinese and Russian Communists, between Mao Tse-tung and Stalin, had widened during my eighteen years in Canada.

The Canadian Embassy

I was driven to the embassy, on Shen Hsien Tung Kai (Street of the Fairy Grotto) by our chauffeur, Lao Chu, who had been a driver on the dangerous Burma Road.

I liked him on sight.

Our Ambassador, Victor W. Odlum, stood at the door of the embassy to welcome me with his firm military handshake. He stood erect as a ramrod in a neat, carefully pressed civilian suit which did not conceal his military bearing. General Odlum was always every inch a soldier.

After introducing me to Liao, the major-domo of the whole establishment, and to the locally-engaged secretaries and clerical staff, the General took me inside.

Liao conducted me to my second-storey room, which had an old-fashioned bay window almost overhanging the Street of the Fairy Grotto. I could look down on the street traffic and see the activity in the tea-shop and eating place across the street. It was all very lively and something like the main street of my home city, Fancheng. The accent and tones of Szechuanese were similar to the language of my province, yet different.

Liao said he had prepared a hot bath for me, and I had better get ready very soon as hot water was severely rationed and we had to take turns for baths. I followed him to the bathroom and got into about four inches of hot water which Number Two servant had brought in two buckets. Liao apologized and said that was it. I had had no baths since Calcutta and wallowed in the luxury of hot water. I had come to the spartan life of Chungking. There was no heat in any of the rooms, regardless of chilly weather.

Dressed and back in my room, I was surprised to hear the sound of a small gong tapped by a soft mallet. I stepped out into the hall to see if the servants had admitted the monkey trainer into our residence-cum-chancery. I knew that sound from childhood days when the master of performing monkeys would summon a crowd into the street by tapping what the children called a "monkey gong." When I saw it was only Liao, I asked what the idea was. He explained that he had orders to summon everyone to dinner twenty minutes before seven and that there would be another one five minutes before and suggested that I might wish to be on time. "But," I said, "that is a monkey gong." "Yes," said Liao, "we know that, but the Ambassador doesn't, and he wouldn't believe it if I told him." Liao added that there would be similar "monkey" warnings before break-fast at seven and lunch at one.

In the dining room I found that our four young lady secre-taries were already standing at their places—two on each side. Liao showed me to my place at one end of the table and went promptly to the other to stand behind the Ambassador's still vacant chair. There followed the sound of quick steps on the cement floor—there were no carpets—and the Ambassador walked smartly to his place at the head of the table. We all sat down simultaneously with a precision which I had not practised since I learned from a British army sergeant how to form fours in the Canadian Engineers.

During the soup, I suddenly caught sight of Liao standing behind the glass door to the kitchen making signs to me. There was no mistaking his sign language. He kept rapidly pumping his cupped hand up to his open mouth and down again. I got the idea and hurriedly finished my soup. Numbers One and Two promptly cleared everything away from the table and served the main course. The food was good. The General regaled us with some stories of his experiences in World War I in France and then announced that breakfast would be served at seven. I hied me to my unheated room to watch the night life of Fairy Grotto.

It was not long before I learned that the mud walls of the embassy had been penetrated by a complex system of tunnels with openings into every room of the building. Chungking rats occupied the building and were in open competition with the human inhabitants for anything edible.

The first night I slept so soundly that I was not even aware of the invaders. In the morning, however, I saw that nearly all of my soap had been eaten. The next night I was awakened by the noise of the soap dish falling on the floor. When I turned on the light, a brigade of the bandits, crowded on the top of the clothes cupboard, stood their ground and defied me to throw my shoes at them. I did. They scattered and left through several openings chewed through the floor boards. As soon as I turned the lights out, they returned, and I saw a row of eyes reflecting the dim light from the street lamps all along the top of the big cupboard. This time, I hurled both shoes without turning on the lights. The disadvantage of this tactic was that my shoes landed on top of the cupboard and stayed there. I left them to be retrieved in the morning. I left the light on and was not disturbed any more that night. In the nights that followed I never succeeded in hitting a single rat, nor were they scared away for long. One night several rats learned that by leaping onto my bed while I slept, they could reach the soap which I had suspended from a string to outwit them.

I had no idea that so much of a foreign service officer's time was taken up with activities necessary just to exist. I firmly decided to find a rat-proof brick or stone house for the embassy when the Government prepared to move from Chungking, the wartime capital, to Nanking.

Beginning in Chungking in November 1945, I tried to write a circular letter each week to my family in Camrose, Alberta, to my father in Valhalla, Alberta, and to my brothers and sisters, all of whom were in the United States. Following are extracts from some of these letters and from my diary over the years.

November 28. . . . I am at long last in damp, chilly Chungking. Conditions here are pretty grim, yet not fully as bad as I had expected. But oh how it drizzles and fogs up! The air never seems to move. I have not caught even a glimpse of the sun so far.

It is extremely interesting meeting people, some of whom are close friends from Fancheng. The people of China are changing their attitude and thinking. One senses an undercurrent which surfaces in the most unpredictable ways. The Chinese are desperately attempting to modernize against the tremendous momentum of the oldest tradition, which continues to swallow even the most ardent revolutionaries.

December 7. . . . Chinese language periodicals published here reflect the opinions of Chinese intellectuals, including non-partisans and partisans of some of the minor parties to which a number of independent thinkers still cling in the hopes that greater freedom of the press will result from the presence here of General George Marshall. These periodicals have a wide circulation through sale in bookstores, as many intellectuals are not brave enough to become regular subscribers.

There is an astonishing degree of unanimity of opinion in regard to China's most urgent problems, such as:

Opposition to Civil War. The editors desperately desire immediate cessation of hostilities. They denounce all who advocate force or instigate war. They have no confidence in the use of military power to settle China's problems. They regard present hostilities as a national disgrace.

Reorganization of Chinese Government. Until more democratic methods of choosing a government become practical, the editors are more or less united in the demand for an immediate dissolution of the present government and the formation of a *coalition government* of representatives from the two major and all the minor parties.

Nationalization of the Army. With a coalition government established, the editors consider it essential that the present Party Armies be reduced and reorganized into a National Army controlled only by the National Government.

Early Return of American Forces. Considerable animosity is expressed to what is termed American interference in China's internal affairs. It is feared that the goodwill engendered during the war is rapidly being replaced by suspicion and hatred. American economic imperialism is frequently discussed.

High Hopes Placed on Marshall. The editors are optimistic regarding the hopes that Marshall's appointment indicates that the

President, the Senate, and the people of the United States will promote peaceful settlement of dispute between the Communists and the Kuomintang.

Fear China To Be Used as Asiatic Base. Many editors express the fear that unless internal dispute is rapidly settled China may become the battleground for the next world war between the US and the USSR.

China's Political Problem Most Urgent. The editors agree there is little profit to be derived from discussions of China's economic or social problems or plans for China's rehabilitation and industrialization until the basic political problem is settled. China must have a government which can establish peace and unity as a foundation for the solution of China's other great problems.

The articles from which the above conclusions are drawn were written solely for Chinese consumption. While some of them are mere academic discussions, they do reveal a deep concern by serious people regarding China's problems. Perhaps the most encouraging aspect is that the editorials are unanimous in expressing the hope that, in spite of the many failures, democracy may still become a reality in China. The frequent references in Chinese periodicals to the recent British elections indicate that the democratic miracle of replacing a national war hero without bloodshed has made a profound impression upon the Chinese.

January 2, 1946. . . . I must tell you about my visit to the famous, or notorious, Dr. H. H. Kung, depending upon your point of view. He is the husband of one of Mme. Chiang Kai-shek's sisters. He lives in a palatial house located on top of one of Chungking's miniature mountains. Lao Chu parked our car outside the gate, and I handed my calling card to the gate-keeper. He returned with a young secretary who spoke to me in Chinese. He accompanied me to a commodious house of foreign style. The halls were decorated with huge porcelain vases and carpeted with heavy, beautiful Tientsin rugs. I was seated in the famous financier's office which had a large portrait of Dr. Sun Yat-sen and a marble bust of the Generalissimo.

Very soon, excellent Lung-Ching tea was served in the old-style cups fitted into saucers with covers to keep the tea warm. The tea was followed by the entrance of the English-trained secretary, Mr. Ch'iao, who entertained me until a third secretary finally arrived and announced that the Doctor would receive me in another residence as he was not feeling well, having just arrived from his country home.

Two of the secretaries accompanied me through the garden, where the dwarfed and twisted spring plum blossoms were in full bloom, filling the air with sweet fragrance. In the second residence, which was even more luxuriously furnished than the first, I was seated in the drawing room, where I was served scented tea in the most comfortable furniture I had sat in since coming to Chungking. Before I had finished the hot tea, a fourth secretary came to say that the Doctor would receive me in an upstairs drawing room.

The room was done in blue with a cozy charcoal fireplace. A servant brought in a third brand of tea, which must have been "his tea." Dr. Kung came in dressed in a long satin fur-lined robe over which he wore a black satin *ma kua,* the old fashioned wide-sleeved short jacket originally designed for equestrians.

One could not help being impressed by this apparently old-style Chinese gentleman. I could not dislike him immediately, despite all the stories about his financial wheeling and dealing. He had an amiable personality. Most of his conversation was an explanation of why he was no longer in the thick of things. He has been superseded by his able and ambitious brother-in-law Dr. T. V. Soong.

The venerable, aging Doctor told me about crossing Canada in 1892, two years before I was born. He was in no hurry, and we spent a long time just chatting after our business had been satisfactorily concluded. Then he accompanied me downstairs, in spite of my repeated "*pu sung*," do not escort, and "*liu pu*," save steps, and escorted me all the way to the outer door with old-fashioned courtesy. People in Chungking say that is not usual.

Judging by some of his reminiscencing, I felt that he would have wished that Chiang Kai-shek had not driven out of Dr. Sun Yat-sen's Kuomintang nearly all Chinese progressives and liberals to establish a one-man government, excusing his failure to accept the democratic principles and ruled by the pretext of "tutelage of the Party" until the people were ready for democracy.

On the way back to the gate, I paused to admire a particularly dainty dwarf tree planted in an oblong flower pot. It formed a leafy canopy for a tiny ridge of rocky mountains in the crevices of which were minute plants and mosses. I had not seen anything quite as attractive since I last visited Chu-ke Miao, the temple dedicated to the great hero, Chu-ke Liang, up the Han River from Hsiangyang.

Old H. H. was truly a Chinese gentleman of the old, old order. Can China afford them today? I must agree with the Communists—No! China must be modernized to end the misery, poverty, corruption, and skullduggery suffered by the masses who sustained this luxury and culture for the wealthy, privileged few. China can no longer afford old H. H. Kungs!

January 15. . . . A "Committee of Three," consisting of three Generals, George Marshall as mediator on behalf of the United States, Chang Chih-chung for the Nationalists, and Chou En-lai for the Communists, have reached an agreement on a cease-fire ending all hostilities. The Marshall Mission, working quietly and without the fanfare of Hurley's efforts, appears to have been successful.

Nationalist troops have entered the Mukden area, but the Russians have apparently not yet taken their departure. There seems to be some uncertainty as to whether or not the truce agreement specifies Manchuria. At any rate it does not say that Manchuria is "not involved."

The Soviet Union, which was to have withdrawn from Manchuria in December, has now announced the departure will be delayed until February 1.

. . . On a recent Sunday evening, I attended a Chungking Symphony Orchestra concert. I didn't even know there was such an organization here. The power was off. There were no lights. A feeble candle was shared by each pair of players. There was no resonance at all in the brick building with a cement floor. Everything was against the brave musicians. They were under the leadership of a very talented German-trained leader and played astonishingly well. There was a large, appreciative audience, nearly all Chinese. I was surprised to see that so many Chinese have learned to appreciate Western symphony music. On the way out, I heard many comments, and all of them were laudatory.

. . . I have now met several of the Chinese Communist leaders who are here for negotiations conducted by General George Marshall to reach an agreement to stop the civil war.

A few days ago I acted as interpreter in a spirited conversation between the famous Communist General Yeh Chien-ying and General Odlum. General Yeh was the man who assisted Chou En-lai at the time of the Sian incident.

Our Ambassador was trying to persuade the Communists to lay down their arms, stop fighting for power, and submit to the will of the people, as we do in Canada. He strongly urged that in the interests of the people of China the two Armies, which were now doing with bullets what we in Canada did with ballots, should be merged into a National Army under the sole control of an elected Government. General Yeh replied with as much conviction and volume that if the Communists gave up the one weapon which Chiang Kai-shek respected they would suffer the same fate as the other opposition political parties—physical extinction. He shouted at our Ambassador and asked if he knew that distinguished members of the Democratic League were taken out of their universities and executed as examples to their students and colleagues not to engage in political activity in criticism of the Government.

I would say that the argument ended in a draw, but each General was cock-sure he had won hands down.

I have also just had a half-hour with Chou En-lai. He has invited General Odlum and me to dinner. His wife, Teng Ying-ch'ao, will be there.

January 22. I have been working all evening on a report to External Affairs on the activities of the Political Consultation Conference, at present in session. They consult and advise. Chiang couldn't care less.

This afternoon, I acted as interpreter for Mr. Wang Ping-nan, a representative of the Communists, who visits us regularly. He marshals his arguments in masterly fashion and makes a good impression, occasionally sprinkling his explanations with interesting anecdotes. He has a degree from Germany and has a German wife—Anna Wang, a close friend of Mme. Sun Yat-sen, Soong Ch'ing-ling, one of the three famous Soong sisters.

Tomorrow I am to dine with Mr. Ho Pai-hen. He is in charge of hydroelectric development in this province. Canada may become interested in assisting one of his hydro projects. Canadian projects are more modest than American plans and are perhaps more in keeping with the needs of Szechuan. Ho is a fine, tall, dignified Chinese gentleman with an almost one-track mind devoted to hydroelectric power. His redeeming feature is a fine sense of humour.

Last Sunday afternoon, I made a trip by car into the mountains as a guest of a well-to-do silk merchant. Mr. Fan has a beautiful little place in a beautiful garden. His yellow, waxy winter plum blossoms were still in full bloom. Mr. Fan also had the pink and the red double-blossoming spring plum trees. Then there were a number of the white variety of blossoming plums, which are very rare. The Chinese call them "green," and they do have a delicate greenish shade. Grandfather Halvor Ronning would have said that garden was as close as you could get to paradise on this earth.

January 31. . . . Moscow has informed the Chinese that enterprises in Manchuria which had been used by the Japanese Army were properly regarded by the Soviet Union as "war booty" and have proposed joint Chinese-Russian control of such enterprises.

. . . Tomorrow I fly to Nanking. That is, the jeep and I fly. I am to find a building for the Canadian Embassy. We are to move to Nanking. I'm prepared to accept almost anything with one basic qualification. It must be built of bricks or cement which rats cannot chew. Last night I used a cane to drive dozens of them out of my room.

Last night I attended a big dinner at the Soviet Embassy. All the Soviet officers speak Chinese with a Manchurian accent which they have learned in the Chinese Language School in Moscow. The First Secretary, my opposite number, is a Mr. Federenko. He speaks Chinese not only well, but he is a scholar who has done research on classical writers which is highly regarded in China. Another distinguished member of the Soviet Embassy is General Roshchin, the Military Attaché, who also speaks Chinese well and is considered to be the best informed foreigner in China on Chinese military development. For me it was a most interesting evening. I wish Canadians would attach more importance to the necessity of training at least a few foreign service officers in Chinese.

Odlum's Essay on "Squeeze"

Our Ambassador, General Odlum, was a remarkable person. He was hard-working, conscientious, and a prolific writer. He occasionally handed me copies of his old reports, and I kept some of them with my notes and diary. In the following report, he expresses his opinion about "squeeze" and other unsavoury aspects of management in China at the time.

Worst of all, there is a general lack of public honesty, even in high places. The "squeeze" is typical of China; and foreigners and Chinese alike laugh, as though the "squeeze" was rather a funny little Chinese way rather than rank dishonesty. One might smile if the squeeze stayed on the lower levels amongst the poor. But it does not. It goes a long way up. And it is "recognized." Army officers are paid on such a low level that there is nothing for them to do if they are to live but to rob their own men and defraud the Government. And they do rob and defraud. Everyone in the Government, including those right at the top, knows it and accepts it. It seems to be counted to a man for righteousness if he looks after his family, even though it be by robbing someone else, or better still by robbing the whole people. And they are not punished. The highest Government officials, denying the value of the income tax, say frankly that it is simply impossible to get an honest return. Businessmen keep two complete sets of books.

Along with dishonesty go sheer inefficiency and actual indolence. An official is not ashamed if he has nothing to do but still continues to draw his pay. The whole "philosophy" teaches that scholars do not work. They grow long finger nails. Only coolies work, and coolies do not have long finger nails. It is the educated group which seems most disinclined to work. It is willing to write and talk, but it will not use its hands. That is where the Chinese Air Force came a cropper. Young officers, trained to a point, felt that they knew all. Above all, they would not tinker with their planes, using their hands. They did not personally supervise the servicing of their planes. They did not even take the trouble to know if they were serviced or not. They found out only when they were up—and then crashed. The wastage was terrific. The Chinese Air Force, as an organization, has ceased to exist.

The interest rate alone indicates Chinese level of efficiency. Farmers pay up to 10 per cent per month for money. This does not mean that their profits are great enough to warrant these rates. They are not. The interest is actually taken out of the meals they eat. They live on less. They almost starve. But the money owners have no other profitable use to which to put their money. They do not work, and their money must support them. They go to the market which provides the highest rates. Businessmen of the top ranks pay the banks 7 to 8 per cent per month for money. The bank will allow almost as much for time deposits. An economic structure based on such interest rates must either crash or sustain itself on the misery of the poor. It does the latter.

The coolies live as close to the margin of starvation as do the peasants. The coolie and peasant class get no sympathy or protection. They work. They make soldiers.

There is an authentic report that a coolie who had interfered with the progress of an empty sedan chair belonging to a rich man was mercilessly beaten by the police. His arms were shattered. A huge crowd looked on without sentiment, because the poor fellow was only a coolie. There was no trial. One was not necessary. It was only a coolie.

The coolies and peasants bear the loads, carry the sorrows, and do the suffering for China. They are China.

The peasant will grow more and pay more to his landlord, to his banker, and to his Government. He will go on having children because he needs them. The huge population of China will continue to hug close to the edge, living by slow starvation. That is, it will unless the leaders arise with vision, understanding, and a great unselfish love for the Chinese masses.

Are those leaders in the group now directing Chinese Destiny?

In this essay, General Odlum put his finger on one of the real problems of China. When he wrote this report, he was still hoping that Chiang Kai-shek would provide leadership with "vision, understanding, and a great unselfish love for the Chinese masses." He ended his report by referring to Chiang's ghost-written book. The more often General Odlum talked to the Generalissimo, the more was he certain that Chiang was the leader who would direct "China's Destiny" and that China would be in safe hands as soon as the Communists accepted democracy and gave up the use of armed force to achieve the reforms about which they talked so frequently.

When the Government of the People's Republic of China had been in power for a few years, General Odlum reversed his appraisal of Chiang Kai-shek and approved of the reforms which the new regime had begun.

General Patrick Hurley

In Chungking, one of the main topics of conversation in diplomatic circles was General Patrick Hurley, who frequently boasted how he had persuaded President Roosevelt to fire General Joseph Stilwell. Stilwell was influenced by the "Dixie Mission" in Yenan and had accepted the recommendation that the United States should supply arms to the People's Liberation Army to fight the Japanese.

The names of the "Dixie Mission" most frequently mentioned were John S. Service and Colonel David Barrett, although John Paton Davies was considered to have initiated the idea of keeping a political-military group of American observers in direct contact with the Communists in Yenan.

Hurley was the American Ambassador. Since our Ambassador was also a general and also Irish, it was natural that the two ambassador-generals would hit it off on a "Pat" and "Vic" basis. They kept a well-beaten path between their two embassies and exchanged views constantly on the destiny of China. Both pinned their hopes on a Nationalist-Communist coalition under the control of the "great Generalissimo." In their opinion, there was no other way to keep China safely in the "democratic, free world." Neither of them held the Generalissimo personally responsible for the corruption of the Nationalist regime. They accepted corruption as unavoidable in the "Chinese way of life" and put their faith in Chiang's determination and capacity to introduce acceptable Western reforms as soon as the Communists agreed to amalgamate their armies with the Nationalist armies under Chiang Kai-shek's control.

Hurley frankly admitted to Odlum that he had attempted in 1944 to get a working coalition of Nationalists and Communists to fight the Japanese. In fact, he had gone to the Communist headquarters in Yenan, where the "Dixie Mission" had been in direct negotiations with Mao Tse-tung and Chou En-lai. Hurley had signed a proposal by Mao and Chou of terms for a coalition which he celebrated by giving his best rendition of the wild and terrifying Choctaw Indian war-whoop.

When General Hurley returned to Chungking, the Generalissimo refused to consider the proposal Hurley brought from Yenan and was displeased with Hurley's visit to Yenan. Hurley responded by claiming that he had been "tricked." That may have been the final reason for Hurley's decision to send Davies out of Chungking and for his quarrel with the "Dixie Mission."

"Hurley," said Odlum, "usually spoke with a low but impressive voice—except when he gave that terrible war-whoop, which he did at the drop of a hat. Then he really startled people."

Once, General Odlum said, he had heard "the sound of heavy guns reverberating along the American Embassy front." He was referring to an occasion when Hurley had sounded off about what he was going to do with members of the American Embassy staff who were undermining Chiang Kai-shek.

Odlum thought Hurley was very much like General Douglas MacArthur, especially in one respect: "He has a high degree of histrionic ability and, like MacArthur, he is tall and good-looking. Either man would be an impressive figure on the stage. In fact, he would be impressive anywhere and is an excellent companion, unless one has a burning desire to talk."

Hurley also told Odlum that he had recommended that the former Ambassador, Mr. C. E. Gauss, should be recalled. Ambassador Gauss's animosity, Hurley had said, was not important.

Gauss had been ready to retire in any event. He was tired of China. His influence was negligible.

Hurley told Odlum that John Paton Davies had to be sent home because of irregularities in his correspondence with Washington. He was a junior who thought he knew much more than did his senior and undertook to set the State Department straight. It appeared, alleged Hurley, that the American junior service abroad had developed a regular technique of writing to opposite friendly, junior members in the State Department, expressing private opinions in conflict with the official opinion of the mission, and unsparingly criticizing and exposing their chiefs. The result, he claimed, was that the State Department itself had broken up into warring cliques and groups whose differences of opinion were revealed occasionally in unseemly public disputes and acts. When Davies was fired from his post in Chungking and sent home, the State Department, Hurley said, was inclined to let him out of the service altogether, but he intervened on his behalf. Hurley added, however, that he regretted having done so.

It was a sad day for China and the United States when Hurley succeeded in "ridding" the American Embassy of the officers who warned that if Chiang Kai-shek started a civil war he would lose it to the tough leaders in Yenan whom Chiang Kai-shek had been unable to exterminate in nearly two decades of continuous, intermittent warfare.

It was said in Chungking that General Hurley had recommended to Washington not to accept an offer made to President Roosevelt by Mao Tse-tung and Chou En-lai through the "Dixie Mission" to go to Washington for direct talks on military co-operation in the war against Japan.

Tung Pi-wu told me that Mao Tse-tung was favourably impressed by United States participation in the war against German fascism and Japanese imperialism. American participation had strengthened progressive elements throughout the world. In April 1945, Mao had predicted victory against Japan due to President Roosevelt's leadership. The Communists, therefore, hoped that the US would demand KMT reform before continuing to supply war material to Chiang, which Chiang was hoarding to fight Chinese Communists. Stilwell was aware of the corruption of the KMT. That was why the Generalissimo wanted Stilwell recalled. After Stilwell's departure, coalition with the Nationalists would be difficult if not impossible. Both of the great powers, the US and the USSR, had given assistance only to Chiang Kai-shek, who had sat idly by waiting for the United States to win the war against Japan. The Communists, Tung Pi-wu said, had, on the other hand, advanced into vast rural areas in North China and Manchuria, where the Japanese were able to hold only the larger cities with isolated garrisons.

Hurley feared that a coalition with the Communists would spread Communist influence throughout China and become a threat to the new world order and the safety of Western political supremacy and economic hegemony in Asia. He saw no alternative therefore to bolstering up the corrupt regime of Chiang Kai-shek.

Despite Washington's apparent acceptance of some of General Hurley's recommendations, continued frustrations resulted in his resignation.

Upon my arrival in Chungking, it was rumoured that General Hurley's replacement would probably be General George Marshall, who was as quiet as Hurley was loud and perhaps as wise as Hurley was not.

Chou En-lai

Chou En-lai was a name with which I had been familiar for twenty-two years when I returned to China in 1945. As a student in Peking in 1922, I met Chinese students, especially those who had been in Europe, who spoke of a brilliant, energetic, devoted, and revolutionary young man named Chou En-lai.

The following year at the Hung Wen Middle School, I listened almost daily to informal discussions among members of the staff and senior students about important political developments in China. Their hopes had been raised, and they were excited about the organization by Dr. Sun Yat-sen of the new Kuomintang Revolutionary Government in Canton. Sun declared war on the Northern Government in Peking, which had come under the control of powerful war lords. Chiang Kai-shek had been assigned to take charge of the Whampoa Military Academy near Canton to develop an elite army for the Northern Expedition. China was to be liberated from the chaos of rival war lords who were ravaging nearly all of China. China was to be united under the new Government, which would be moved to a new capital in Central China if and when the march north from Canton eliminated the great war lord Wu P'ei-fu.

In 1924, Chou En-lai, already famous for his activities and experience in revolutionary organizations in France and Germany, was appointed Deputy Director of the Political Department in charge of political training in the new army.

When I came to Chungking in 1945, I learned that Chou En-lai was negotiating with the Nationalists on behalf of the Communists under United States auspices to patch up the disintegrated united front against the Japanese. Ambassador Patrick Hurley had failed miserably, and civil war between Nationalists and Communists was breaking out. General Marshall finally succeeded, on January 10, 1946, in getting an agreement signed ordering a cease-fire. President Chiang's Secretary-General, Governor Chang Ch'un, signed for the Nationalists and Chou En-lai for the Communists.

The right-wing factions of the Nationalists, however, were aware of the Generalissimo's determination not to co-operate with the Communists but eventually to wipe them off the face of China. They soon found the desired flaw in the wording of the agreement to justify the resumption of military action against the Communists in Manchuria, claiming that the cease-fire agreement had not specified that area. Negotiations for a coalition nevertheless continued, and the representatives of Yenan, headquarters of the Communists, were active in Chungking.

Marshall had the impossible job of coalescing oil and water, but if anyone could accomplish the task of uniting the Nationalists and the Communists, that person was General George Marshall. He had gained the confidence of the Communists, and Chiang Kai-shek had become completely dependent upon American aid. Chinese of all political shades, including many who were close to Chiang Kai-shek, wanted a peaceful settlement of the civil war after the horrors of Japanese occupation, even if it meant making important concessions to Mao Tse-tung. Civil war had continued with few interruptions for nearly two decades, and all patriotic Chinese wanted to build a new nation along the lines visualized by Sun Yat-sen and they thought that could be accomplished only by a coalition.

When Chiang's representative signed the cease-fire in Chungking, the reactionary C.C. (Ch'en brothers) clique knew Chiang Kai-shek had no intention of actually ordering his troops to stop fighting the Communists. Plans were underway to drive the Communists out of Manchuria, to be followed by similar military action throughout China.

I had been in Chungking only a few days when I had the opportunity to meet Chou En-lai. General Odlum and I were invited to dinner at his headquarters. I was not disappointed. He was a confident, modest man. His bearing was almost that of a Chinese gentleman-scholar. His language, however, was direct and forceful, with none of the flavour of the pretentious, polite old Chinese clichés. He carried not the slightest sign of the tough experiences of the long march nor of life in underground Shanghai, when he escaped the man hunts organized by Chiang Kai-shek's hatchet man, Ch'en Li-fu. At the dinner table one would never have guessed that Chou had recently come from the spartan life of Yenan.

There were only four of us at that dinner in Chungking. General Odlum sat opposite General Chou En-lai, and I sat opposite the interpreter, Chang Wen-chin. At one point, I thought the interpreter softened considerably both the intent and the language of both Chou and Odlum when the discussion became more than a little controversial. I was immediately asked by Chou to repeat exactly what Odlum had said. Our general was on his favourite subject—urging the Communists to amalgamate the Red Armies with the Nationalist Armies and trust the people of China to decide the issue as to which party should govern China. Odlum in turn asked me to repeat Chou's reply and the conversation became more spirited as well as more controversial. I could not help understanding Chou's point of view that no political party in China had the ghost of a chance against Chiang's totalitarian government without an army.

Soon after the cease-fire signing ceremony, we entertained Chou En-lai and his brilliant wife, Teng Ying-ch'ao, who, together with her husband, had played a key role in the Long March, and Chang Wen-chin. Seeing the famous Teng Ying-ch'ao and listening to her, one would never suspect that this cultivated, modest person could have endured the gruelling hardships of the 1927 massacre and the terrible march which lasted a whole year.

There are three men who are perhaps most responsible for the phenomenal rise to power of the People's Republic of China since the Communist Party's beginning in 1921, when a few inexperienced idealists met in a small room of a girls' school in Shanghai. They are Mao Tse-tung, Chou En-lai, and Chu Teh.

Mao Tse-tung, after years of serious differences with his Communist comrades, emerged as the leader who first realized that revolution in China could be based only on the peasantry. This was contrary to European Communist theory, which insisted that only the proletariat could be a sound basis for revolution. Mao insisted that China had mostly peasants. Mao was, therefore, considered *persona non grata* by the Comintern. Mao pulled out and began working methodically with peasants in the villages of the Kiangsi-Hunan border area.

After the *débâcle* in 1927, it was Chou who began assembling and reorganizing scattered remnants of the armies of the Northern Expedition, who continued to support Sun Yat-sen's Canton Government after it was established in Hankow.

Chou converted many of the officers of Chiang's crack divisions into eventually becoming Communist cadres. His experience for that work began when he was a student organizer in the Nankai

Middle School and University. In France he continued his activities and recruited many young Chinese, who later became Communist leaders in the early days of the Party. Ch'en Yi and Li Li-san were his comrades in Paris. He gathered a sufficient number of the members of the Central Committee of the Communist Party after 1927 to form a nucleus which carried on clandestine activities when Chiang Kai-shek forced them underground for survival. Chou En-lai was the enthusiast who never gave up. He participated in the armed insurrection in Shanghai. He helped to organize the revolt in Nanchang which was accepted as a beginning of a completely independent revolutionary military movement, and therefore August 1 is celebrated as People's Liberation Army Day.

Chou achieved a position of leadership in the Central Committee of the Communist Party and often disagreed with Mao on their politico-military strategy. There were times when Chou, clad with the authority of the Central Committee, differed seriously with Mao in efforts to hold the Party together.

The most serious dispute between the two, whose friendship and co-operation became perhaps the most important single factor which enabled the Party time and again to escape utter extinction, came after the Central Committee was driven out of Shanghai. Chou En-lai, disguised as a foreigner with a long, black moustache and a clerical gown, escaped to Mao's headquarters in Juichin after Mao's move from Chingkangshan.

Mao's strategy had been to lure Chiang Kai-shek's troops into the mountainous heartland of Kiangsi, cut them off from their base of supplies, and destroy them one group at a time. After the arrival of the Central Committee in Juichin, Chou En-lai, as Chief Commissar of the Red Army, overruled Mao and planned a head-on attack on Chiang's troops. The result was that Chiang Kai-shek's armies succeeded in taking one of the Communists' most important outposts. Ch'en Yi was severely wounded. Chou En-lai finally accepted Mao Tse-tung's guerrilla strategy. Chou, Mao, and Chu Teh agreed that a frontal attack on Chiang's armies, which always outnumbered the Red Army units, was suicidal. Chou En-lai found himself in complete agreement with Mao for the first time. This was the beginning of a combination of representatives of the two most important elements in Chinese society—peasant power and intellectual leadership—which, when working together, could move mountains. Mao had in Hunan and Kiangsi organized the peasant backbone of Chinese society, and Chou had enlisted the new intellectuals.

Chou recognized in Mao a leader inspired by revolutionary Western ideas and a creator of a new pragmatic Chinese philosophy based on his experience as a peasant's son. Chou was not obsessed by personal ambition. He saw in Mao qualities of leadership which were unique. Here was a man with deep roots in China's peasantry dedicated to modern revolutionary changes which could modernize and save China.

Mao saw in Chou a wise, tolerant, superb organizer and administrator completely dedicated to a cause for which he was prepared to make any sacrifice. He recognized Chou's unique qualities of being able to inspire others to devote themselves to the revolution which could save China from external oppression and internal stagnation.

In the middle of the 19th century, Japan had been intrigued by the West's industrialization and militarization as the way to build a great nation. China, however, was intrigued by Western ideas which could rejuvenate an ancient society that would otherwise perish. The Chinese intellectuals had traditionally been concerned with philosophical concepts which had desirable political and social implications. When China collapsed from internal corruption and stagnation, coupled with external exploitation and domination, Chinese thinkers suffered from a deep sense of humiliation and a desire to reform the philosophic foundation of Chinese society along Western lines. The new revolutionaries were attracted by Western liberal, political, and social ideas studied in Christian missionary schools—the first modern educational institutions in China.

Chou En-lai was one of the thousands who attended missionary schools. He would have preferred to go to the United States to continue his education, but had to settle for France. He had already been very active among students who were conscious of the deplorable situation in China and eagerly participated in revolutionary movements.

Chou En-lai had a talented and very kind mother. She was literate and had studied Chinese classics; she was considered very good in calligraphy and painting, which are closely related in China. But she died when her son was still very young, and Chou En-lai was adopted by an uncle who lived in Shanghai. His foster mother was illiterate, but an extremely capable person, who ran an organized and well-disciplined family. Her own son was much younger than Chou. She named him En-chu, which indicated he was a brother sharing one character in his given name. Against the wishes of many, she invited some Western missionaries into the home to teach her children "the new knowledge," including English. Chou En-lai's ability to deal with people who had conflicting personalities, inducing them to work together for a common cause, may have at least been partly due to the training he had in the home of his foster mother. He was always attentive to her and even after he had become an active revolutionary, he would sometimes, on the appropriate dates, carry out old Confucian family ceremonies.

Chou En-lai was taken by another uncle to attend a missionary-operated school in Mukden, the Sheng-ching Elementary School. There he was exposed to Western ideas by Chinese teachers who kept in touch with new developments in China. Through these men, he was introduced to thinkers like Rousseau and learned something about constitutionally guaranteed human rights.

Although his uncle did not approve, Chou En-lai later insisted on attending the famous Nankai School in Tientsin, which had acquired a nonconformist reputation and was said to be one of those modern schools which were breeding grounds for rebels.

Many missionary schools in China were run by Chinese teachers who were revolutionaries. The Yenching University in Peking, Harvard in China, whose President for many years was Dr. Leighton Stuart, the last United States Ambassador in Peking, was turning out graduating classes annually, many of whom went over to the Communists the moment they graduated. Why? Because that was the only way a young man who opposed Chiang Kai-shek's Government could stay alive. Those who joined the Democratic League, for example, were likely to be executed if they engaged in political activity not approved by the authorities. The Communist Party was the only political party other than the KMT with an army.

6

NANKING
AND CHUNGKING
1946

February 2. . . . When the jeep and I arrived by air in Nanking today, I heaved a sigh of relief. During the flight, the old jeep broke loose from its moorings and charged back and forth as the aircraft soared and dived in the mountainous gorges between high ranges above which the Dakota could not rise. The crew and I finally got the reluctant jeep tied down again before it could wreck the Dakota and leave us stranded in some of the wildest and most terrifying terrain on earth. Looking down, I wondered how in the world the Long March marchers ever made it through those seemingly impassable, deep, dark, narrow gorges.

My friend Brigadier Bill Bostock, our military attaché, met me at the Nanking airport, took charge of the jeep, and drove us to the old British Embassy building.

Bill had spent three weeks trying to locate suitable buildings for the Canadian Embassy and had drawn a complete blank. The situation was infinitely worse than when Brigadier Kay, our former attaché, had been promised three houses in December. Two of the houses were occupied by Chinese officials. One was available, but the Japanese had wrecked the house, tearing out all the plumbing and heating equipment. We would have to start from scratch.

February 9. . . . I have been here for a week. Coming here was like coming into a heaven of sunlight from a Hades of everlasting shadow. What a grand and glorious feeling it was to step out of the aircraft into brilliant dazzling sunlight, to realize again that there really was a sun and that it would shine and that it was warm and bright!

This week, Bill and I must find a house or two. All last week we chased around to no avail. All the houses we saw had been badly destroyed and looted by the Japanese.

February 10. . . . You should see the Japanese troops here. They walk around the streets by the thousands as if they were guests instead of prisoners. Occasionally some of them sweep the streets. They carefully mask themselves in white gauze for protection against the clouds of dust they raise.

February 16. . . . It is two weeks since I arrived in Nanking. Nearly every day Bostock and I have been driving around looking for houses. I cannot begin to tell you all the experiences we have had, so let me select one.

A Chinese general informed us of a large house for rent at a certain address. We drove to the place as soon as possible and knocked gently on the compound gate. The gate-keeper opened the iron gate just a little.

"We are from the Canadian Embassy," I said in Chinese. He looked blank, so I added, "We are looking for a house to rent and have been told by General Pao that this place is for rent." "No," he said. "This house is not for rent." "But does this house not belong to Mr. Tso?" "Yes, but he is living in it himself, and it is not for rent." "May we come in the compound and look at the house from the outside?" "Yes, come in, but the owner is not in just now so you cannot come in the house."

We went in and decided that the house was suitable for our purposes. I thanked the man, and we left. We drove back to General Pao. He was not in his office, so we spent the rest of the day looking over houses that had been stripped by the Japanese.

The following day we again interviewed General Pao and were assured that the house was for rent. We promptly drove back. This time, the gate-keeper did not open the big gate but peeped through a little slot. He looked cross when he saw me.

"Well," I said, "here we are again."

"Again? Have you been here before?"

"My friend, do not tell me that your 'remembering heart' is not well."

"What do you want?"

"We would like to see the house proprietor in order to rent the house."

"It's no use. The house is not for rent, and we have never heard of this General Pao you talk about."

The argument continued and, although I tried to inject a little humour into the situation by saying that we would be warmer inside and that it was tea time for foreign diplomats, the gate-keeper was not amused. He steadfastly refused to open the gate. Suddenly, someone pushed him aside and looked out. I saw the face of a lady with brown hair and brown eyes. Just as I had decided that some other foreigner had already rented the place, the big gate was opened, and the lady stepped out into the street and said: "I am very sorry that our gate-keeper has been so rude. I thought some Chinese gentleman was trying to get in with a view to taking the house for himself. We had no idea that it was a foreigner. Come in, come in and speak to my brother-in-law, who owns the house."

We went into a luxuriously furnished reception room and were soon drinking scented tea and eating delicious cakes and candies. When I said that our military attaché could not speak Chinese, the lady spoke to him in perfect English. She also spoke French and German, and I decided that one of her parents or grand-parents must have been European.

Her sister, a very elderly lady, came in. There could be no doubt that she was full-blooded Chinese, so I guessed that they were only half-sisters. I went through a complete review of all our requirements for a house in great detail thinking that the sister was the "house proprietor," but she was more interested in my Chinese accent than in houses and ferreted out of me all about my early days in Hupeh.

"Well, well! Isn't that interesting! We are really neighbours. I am the daughter of Marquis Tseng of Hunan." The Eurasian lady repeated this in English for the benefit of Bostock. Everybody in China, of course, knew about Marquis Tseng. She added: "We may have lost our position and our wealth after the war, but no one can take from us our royal blood."

More tea and delicacies were served while we were regaled with exploits of the famous father and were shown the scrolls upon which their ninety-three-year-old grandmother had written before she died. The old lady must have been a powerful old dowager. The characters were at least three feet in height and seemed to be excellent calligraphy.

At last, the lord and master came in. He was a rather old-fashioned Chinese, so we had to have fresh tea and more cakes. He said immediately that his house was not for rent but that our presence illuminated his humble dwelling and he desired to obtain from us morsels of our great knowledge. I replied that we were very sorry to disturb him in his palatial mansion but that we were glad of the opportunity to share his learning. The conversation drifted to the "good old days" of the Manchu Dynasty when "Tao T'ais" were "Tao T'ais," super mandarins, and were respected and had great power. When he became too classical I asked him to use the common people's language, giving as an excuse that our military attaché was not too familiar with Chinese expressions and that it was difficult for me to convey to him the noble ideas expressed in the relatively barbaric language of our humble country.

*The church that the Reverend Halvor Ronning built
in Fancheng in 1901 (photo 1971).*

*1898. The Reverend Halvor Ronning and
Hannah Rorem Ronning in Fancheng with Chester,
Almah, and Nelius (left to right).*

1901. The family returning to China after the Boxer Rebellion. The children, left to right: Almah, Chester, Talbert, and Nelius.

The house in Fancheng that the Reverend Halvor Ronning built in 1895 (photo 1923, Chester Ronning with daughter Sylvia).

Valhalla, Alberta, 1917. Chester Ronning mowing wild hay on his homestead.

ABOVE LEFT: *Valhalla, 1918. Wedding of Inga Marie Horte and Chester Ronning (on home leave from the Canadian Engineers).*

ABOVE RIGHT: *1922. The author's family in front of their house in Peking.*

RIGHT: *The Ronnings (Inga on far right, Chester on far left) with friends on the Great Wall.*

Returning to Canada in 1927 with Sylvia,
Meme, and Alton (left to right).

Squadron leader Ronning (center) as Director of the Royal Canadian Air Force Intelligence Discrimination Unit (1942–5).

Chungking, 1945. General Odlum and staff, Canadian Embassy.

Nanking, 1947. Judge T. C. Davis (front row, second from left) presents his credentials to President Chiang Kai-shek (front center) as second Canadian Ambassador to China. The author stands in the third row, to the right of center.

1945. The Canadian Embassy in Chungking.

April 1954. Opening of the Geneva Conference.
Front row: Acting head of delegation Chester Ronning with
Canadian Secretary of State for External Affairs Lester B. Pearson;
third row: Prime Minister and Minister of Foreign Affairs Chou En-lai,
representing the People's Republic of China.

1966. Ambassador Ronning on
a special peace mission to
Hanoi with Prime Minister
Pham Van Dong of the Demo-
cratic Republic of Vietnam
and the Canadian representa-
tive to the International
Control Commission.

I could see that he wanted to rent his house, but could not say so directly, since that would have been beneath his dignity—merchants, not scholars, discuss business. So he took us around the house to see some of his scrolls and treasures, hoping that we would form an opinion of the desirability of the house.

Finally, he said that, although his house was not for rent, he had a friend who had a big house with six bathrooms. Were we interested? When I said that we were, he said that the rent was at least $1,000 per month. Would that be a serious impediment? I said that I did not think it would present too many difficulties. So he said that if his friend's house with six bathrooms was worth $1,000, how much would his house, with three bathrooms, be worth? I replied that that would be a matter for him to decide. But he fell back on the fact that his house was, of course, not for rent. This kept up intermittently during the inspection.

The brown-haired lady insisted we accept goodies from her tins of American peanuts and cookies. (We later understood where they came from when we found an American officer waiting for her outside in a big car.)

After we had inspected the garden with its winter plum trees in full bloom filling the garden with sweet fragrance, the whole family and all the servants escorted us out to the street with much bowing, and we made arrangements to call again.

In addition to the search for a suitable house for the Canadian Embassy, there is the work of negotiating for it on behalf of the Department of External Affairs with the Chinese Foreign Ministry, the City of Nanking, and the Chinese Army Headquarters—quite a daily merry-go-round!

February 22. . . . There are student demonstrations in Chungking today to insist that the Soviet Union withdraw from Manchuria. The Chinese people demand recognition of their sovereignty in North East China.

Reconciliation between the Communists and Nationalists, especially in Manchuria, seems to be falling apart.

February 26. . . . The night before last, I was a guest of the famous General Ho Ying-ch'in, who is the head of the Chinese Nationalist Army. He is feared more than anyone in China except the Generalissimo.

Last night I dined with the Mayor of Nanking. The food was superb, the mayor being Cantonese. In China, everyone knows that "for food, there is no place under Heaven like Kuangchou," Canton.

During the past month I have done more negotiating than I would have thought necessary to get an international treaty ready to sign—with the result that we now have a house, owned by "Kidding" Wang, the popular chef de protocol of the Foreign Ministry. It will probably become the Ambassador's Residence, and in a few days we hope to secure a house for our Chancery at Number 3 Heavenly Bamboo Road. Bill and I have moved in.

March 8. . . . The Canadian flag flies in Nanking. It was raised for the first time yesterday, March 7, 1946, an eventful day for me in more ways than one. In childhood days, I used to admire the paintings in the history books of the great explorers and conquerors who threw their heads back and their chests out while they raised the flag and made great claims, especially if they had been sent out by a queen. Well, we had our ceremony too and we raised our flag in the hope that it would always stand for friendly relations between China and Canada.

Immediately after breakfast, the barber arrived. Bill and I were duly "barbered," sheared and most vigorously shampooed in preparation for the ceremony, which we had planned the night before.

Even our servants entered enthusiastically into the spirit of the day. The house-boy, who would have been a college graduate if the Japanese had not cut his educational career short by depriving his father of his means of livelihood, was obviously very impatient about something. He finally explained that he could not wait any longer for the arrival of the flag pole climber. This important figure in our plans for the day had promised faithfully to arrive at nine o'clock sharp to thread the rope through the pulley at the top of the flag pole. Members of the flag pole climbing profession are apparently somewhat dilatory about arriving at the scene of their activities—like men about to be hanged, realizing that nothing important will take place before their arrival.

Shortly after nine, the pole man arrived together with a silent assistant. I did not know until later that his wife had no intention of allowing his assistant to be the substitute collector if her expendable husband should become incapable of collecting the fee.

With great agility, our pole performer put on an exhibition worthy of the circumstances and really gave us our money's worth. Pausing halfway up, he hung by his feet and one hand while he tapped his chest with the other and gasped for breath. His subsequent groans would have done credit to a professional wrestler. Finally, he reached the pulley, where a painful series of staccato grunts punctuated the threading operation. With the rope between his teeth, preventing further oral entertainment, he treated us to the thrill of an astonishingly rapid descent. It was a fitting climax to his part of the proceedings. As he was about to collect his fee, who should appear on the scene but the sad pole expert's wife. With the index finger of her right hand she indicated on the palm of her left the correct strokes of the characters to be inscribed on the receipt in representation of her husband's name. She then pocketed the fee and departed.

Before the ascent, which the ascender described as a most dangerous feat, it was necessary to negotiate and finally fix a suitable fee. The man asked the sum of 6,000 yuan. Having been previously informed by our loyal house-boy that the Dutch Embassy pole had been ascended for 5,000, I offered four as a starter. The sad-faced poler replied that even the Embassy of Holland had paid more than that and surely this honourable Embassy could not lose face over the paltry sum of 4,000 yuan. He was prepared, on this occasion, to come down to a rock-bottom fee of 5,000 yuan, but that was the lowest possible figure for which he could risk life and limb. His offer was accepted. In Canadian money it amounted to about $2.50, and perhaps there was some truth in the claims about the risk.

Raising the flag was only the beginning of the excitement of this memorable day. Soon after settling down to our regular duties, I thought I heard the sound of running water. This seemed very strange, since the water pressure in Nanking had been insufficient to boost the water above the level of the ground floor, and this sound certainly came from upstairs. I went to investigate. As I opened the door of the room which is to be the Ambassador's when he arrives from Chungking, I found to my horror that water was pouring down from the ceiling in a young cloud-burst. I yelled most undiplomatically, and Bill Bostock came bounding up the stairs. Brigadier Bostock had experience with the Canadian Army in Holland and knew exactly what to do in the case of floods. He was soon emulating the young Dutch hero who sat all night with his finger in the dike. Water had been spouting furiously from the open end of a pipe in the attic, and Bill was trying desperately to stem the tide.

I should explain that we have resorted to every possible device to get our water system to function during the week we have been living in our newly acquired building. We even invited the stoker of the British Embassy furnace to help us find the trouble. He came to the profound conclusion that our trouble was due to the plugging of a pipe, which, he said, admitted air into the circulation of the system. This sounded so logical to us that we merely gazed in gratitude as he removed the plug. Whereupon, he took his fee, his departure, and the plug.

In the meantime, the Nanking Municipal Government had managed to replace certain machinery which had been removed from the waterworks by the Japanese, and the water pressure was suddenly restored. A wooden plug was eventually substituted for the Brigadier's finger, and our private downpour ceased.

March 9. . . . Bill and I feel we have to get out for long walks occasionally. One afternoon, we went with some American pilots to the top of Purple Mountain, east of the city, to see the remains of an American aircraft which had crashed. The mountain is just a little over 1,600 feet high. The plane, a Douglas Dakota, crashed into a rock ridge at the very top, less than twenty feet below the peak. The crew of four, who were to have been sent home to the United States in a few days, were killed instantly. The plane exploded and was scattered all over the top of the mountain. Only the tail remained in the spot where the accident occurred as a mute marker of the tragedy.

Not far from the site of the plane accident was a small blockhouse. One of the American pilots climbed on top just to get a better view of the surrounding country. He noticed a small hole in the roof. Looking down, he saw the face of a man looking up at him. The pilot knelt down and looked more closely. To his great astonishment, he saw four Chinese, their hands tied behind their backs with barbed wire. The men stood in complete silence. Their wrists were swollen; the barbed wire had sunk deep into the flesh. I immediately found some Chinese guards not far away and asked the meaning of this cruel treatment.

One guard informed me that two Red Army spies had been trying to destroy the wireless installations on the mountain top. "But you have four people tied up in there," I said. He replied, "Yes. You see, one of the two got away, and we took his relatives from that village in the valley." I asked if they had destroyed very much equipment. The answer was, "No, we caught one before they did any damage." I asked if they had had a trial. The guard said, "No, not before we get the one who ran away." China is a police state.

March 24. . . . Nanking is perhaps the only place in the world where you can walk in the country inside a city. When the city walls of Nanking were built, a vast area outside of the city was enclosed. In the southern part of the city, there is more than ample room for an airfield; in the northwestern part, there are farms, vegetable gardens, and small villages. The city is surrounded by twenty-seven miles of walls built with monster bricks in the style of a medieval fortress and in the magnitude of Bunyan's Holy City. Nanking sportsmen frequently hunt wild pheasant, found in abundance in the shrubbery of the hills.

The fields and gardens start just across the street on the west side of the Canadian Embassy building, so Bill and I haven't far to go to start our walks. Yesterday we took a narrow path between a winter wheat field on one side and a bean field on the other. Just as we began elaborating on how fine it was to walk in the country and breathe its invigorating air, I was suddenly slapped squarely in both nostrils by a most powerful and revolting stench. I could tell by Bill's twisting nose that he also had been hit. We had not far to seek the cause—a pit plumb full of fresh night filth in the middle of the path right in front of us. Chinese farmers have replenished the soil from time immemorial with this most potent of all fertilizers, and in the vicinity of all villages, small or great, are pits and pits, ranging in size from an earthenware crock buried in the ground to great vats and huge cisterns, all filled with human or animal manure in various stages of putrefaction, held in reserve for use at the appropriate time. And how it makes things grow!

Some distance further on, a healthy farm woman sat at the side of a pond washing the family clothes, while other women were weeding a garden. They looked up at us. One said: "Only two foreigners out playing."

The path took us past the family graves. In fact, the whole hill was covered with the graves of many families. China needs a law providing for the cremation of the dead. They occupy too much space and deprive the living of vast areas of fertile land.

We came upon two small, earth-god temples in a bad state of disrepair. Some local worshipper had, however, plastered the usual red paper scrolls on either side of the opening to the inner sanctum, probably at Chinese New Year's. One of these announced to those who could read the sacred characters but who might be inclined to scoff at such lowly spirits as mere earth-gods, that "Out of the Earth Comes Yellow Gold." And sure enough! We had gone only a short distance beyond the homes of the little dirt-gods, when I saw Bill bend over and pick up two green ten-yuan bills lying in the field close to the path. He felt so generous at being so richly rewarded after his first acquaintance with earth-gods that he immediately gave the greenbacks to a young man who was wielding a hoe in the field. The young yokel took a quick glance at the money and scornfully threw it away, exclaiming: "Bah, puppet money!" The Brigadier walked off, but I picked up the bills. I had not seen puppet money and besides I liked the colour and picture of Dr. Sun Yat-sen's tomb.

Beyond the village, we walked through the quiet of a bamboo grove. Here I saw a blue jay with the longest tail I have ever seen adorning a flying bird. It seemed to unbalance its proud possessor as he perched impertinently on a far too fragile branch. Past the grove, the valley became gradually smaller and finally terminated in a narrow gorge. I climbed a little way, but soon decided to rest on a stone while Bill explored the summits of the hills above. Not far off was a wrinkled old woman gathering twigs for firewood. I called to her, and she approached, perhaps glad of an opportunity to rest and chat.

"Today, the heaven is clear."

"Yes, it is so hard to gather firewood when it rains."

"How great an age are you?"

"I am sixty. And how great an age are you, teacher?"

"Oh, I am a young man compared to you."

"You are also much better off than I am. In spite of my age, I still have to do bitter labour. You see, my people were all killed by the Japanese in my own province of Anhui. I came here as a refugee and ate the bitterness of the people of the Land of the Rising Sun for eight long years. Even now, after they are no longer our masters, I must work for my food."

"Were the Japanese fierce?"

"Fierce? If the war had lasted another month, they would have killed us all at the rate they killed off my people."

"But they fed and clothed you, did they not?"

"Look, teacher, my clothes—all patches. I have not had a foot of new cloth for eight years. And when I came here to gather firewood, they caught me and took my clothes away from me."

"Do you know that man cutting down the sapling?"

"Oh yes. He was captured by the Japanese in Honan and forced to work for them. They took him away from his father, mother, wife, and four small children. He has not seen the youngest yet. He cries every night. I can hear him through the wall."

"Why does he not return to his home now?"

"Go home? He has not got a cent for travelling. By the way, teacher, are you also from Honan? Your 'mouth sound' is a little like that of this poor man."

"No, my old friend. But you have a very good ear. I come from Hupeh—not very far from the border of Honan."

Bill returned, and I had to bid the old woman farewell. She asked me to come again and "play" in the hills.

March 27. . . . The Committee of Three have agreed to dispatch truce teams to Manchuria. There are rumours that the extreme right-wing group of the Nationalists headed by the notorious Ch'en brothers is deliberately sabotaging the truce teams, claiming that the truce agreement was not intended to be applicable to Manchuria.

The Nationalists have finally occupied the city of Mukden,

and the Communists have occupied the strategic city of Ssuping between Mukden and Changchun.

March 30. . . . On first arriving in Nanking two months ago, I had a feeling of being suddenly cut off from a great nerve centre of political activity. In Chungking nearly everyone, especially the people who came to the Canadian Embassy, discussed Chinese politics when they were fresh and in the making. One could feel the political pulse beats of a great nation.

To the Canadian Embassy came men of all shades of political opinion. In the atmosphere which prevailed, these men and women seemed to drop their habitual defensive shells. They discussed in the frankest and friendliest manner policies about which many of them had deep convictions.

In Nanking, however, one gets a feeling of political isolation which extends beyond the foreign community to Government offices. The only topic which arouses universal interest is the eternal question of housing, rents, landlords, broken contracts, and success or failure in the occupation of rented buildings. As far as Chungking's authority is concerned, it decreases rapidly with the distance from that seat of power.

This attitude changed over night on the day before the Generalissimo arrived upon the scene. Nanking suddenly became a hive of activity. Flags appeared everywhere; streets were swept; trees were trimmed. National and Municipal Government employees were alert and unusually solicitous regarding foreigners' housing difficulties, Chinese soldiers saluted smartly, and thousands of lazy, well-fed Japanese soldiers were brought into the very centre of the city to repair streets.

But when the artificial respiration ceased, the city's heart beat dropped quickly back to its former rate. Nanking breathed a great sigh of relief upon the departure of the great man.

The tempo of activity in Nanking is nevertheless rising rapidly. As the time approaches when it is anticipated that the Government will arrive with all its departments and foreign embassies, the city will undoubtedly get into full swing. Preparations are being made for the reception of everyone from Chungking, and the return of the capital after long years in exile is eagerly awaited.

When I arrived here two months ago, this old city seemed to be just coming to life. Few rickshaws, fewer automobiles, and even fewer pedestrians were to be seen on the streets. I had never seen a Chinese city so thinly populated. The people had fled before the Japanese advance. Now, however, the streets are full of people, and all kinds of vehicles from tricycle-pedicabs to mule carts frequently jam the traffic.

On the river front, junks and steamers are loading and unloading. The Bund is alive. Public buildings are being renovated. The population is growing at an astonishing rate. Commercial enterprises seem to be increasing at the rate of geometric progression.

The rapid development taking place in Nanking is also reflected in the number of dailies and periodicals being published here. Twelve daily newspapers and ten weeklies have commenced publication. Three of the weeklies are published by the Communist Party. Otherwise all Nanking's papers and periodicals either support the Government or claim to be independent. Editors, even of the publications which are supported by the Kuomintang, are frequently critical of the Government's policies. This may be an indication of new independence which is gradually being generated by the hope of the removal of the severe censorship that has prevailed during the past years.

April 5. . . . I arrived here in Chungking on a China National Airways Corporation plane yesterday afternoon and have been chasing around the city in a hot car making preparations for the departure of the Ambassador to Nanking on April 23 by RAF plane.

The plan is that I am to remain here to wind things up and

go down to Nanking by ship—a trip I am looking forward to. Ever since I was a youngster, I have heard and read about the famous Yangtse gorges between here and Ichang. I will probably leave here soon after May 1.

April 10. . . . The cease-fire which General Marshall arranged in January is crumbling. The civil war continues to gain momentum, especially in Manchuria.

The United States continues to aid the Nationalists. It is reported here that $500 million have been appropriated to sustain the Chiang Government.

The notorious "Four Families" continue to reap the benefit. The Chiangs, the Ch'ens, H. H. Kung, and T. V. Soong jointly operate the Government economic monopolies and through this "bureaucratic capitalism" they amass wealth in very profitable commmercial, banking, and industrial organizations. US aid is funnelled through these organizations, leaving only a trickle for Nationalist troops holding isolated strategic cities in a vast countryside controlled by the People's Liberation Army.

Last night the Ambassador and I were dinner guests of Chou En-lai and Mrs. Chou (Teng Ying-ch'ao). A number of other prominent Communists were also guests. We had a *hai-shen,* sea slug, feast with *t'ien-chi,* paddy chicken (frogs' legs).

Chou En-lai is a handsome man with a sculpturesque head and bushy black eyebrows. His pitch black hair has a wave, which is very unusual in China. His argument is forceful and logical, his earnestness convincing, his enthusiasm contagious. He is completely unpretentious. In his conversation, he is direct and almost blunt. He said to the Ambassador two or three times: "You do not understand the actual conditions here because you have a totally different background."

One of the dinner guests who greatly impressed me turned out to be Liao Ch'eng-chih, son of the famous Liao Chung-k'ai. The father, born in San Francisco, had been a close friend and co-worker of Sun Yat-sen in Sun's revolutionary organization, the T'ung Meng Hui. Old Liao was assassinated in Canton in 1925—the year of Sun's death.

Young Liao became an ardent revolutionary at a very early age and openly announced that he represented the Communist Eighth Route Army in Hong Kong. In 1942, he was arrested on the orders of Chiang Kai-shek, who had collaborated with his father when Chiang had been selected by Dr. Sun to lead the Northern Expedition.

Young Liao told me that for two years and eight months he was kept in solitary confinement and did not see daylight. He was then brought before the Generalissimo and urged to join the Nationalists to be given a high position or return to prison. He chose prison and was not released until 1946, after another two years and a few months of solitary confinement. He had just arrived from prison and was pale and sickly, but confident that China would be liberated from the corrupt regime of the dictator. Young Liao had regained his freedom during the peace negotiations and was anxious to get to Yenan to continue the work to which he had dedicated his life. His prison term had made him even more determined to play his part in liberating China. These people are prepared to make great sacrifices for their convictions.

His father, he said, had been only one of a host of overseas Chinese who had supported and financed Sun Yat-sen.

April 18. . . . General George Marshall has returned to China after a visit to Washington. The situation, especially in Manchuria, has deteriorated very seriously during his absence. The truce agreement seems no longer to be in effect.

April 19. . . . This morning I attended a meeting with representatives from every country represented in China to discuss arrangements for tomorrow's exodus to Nanking. Yesterday

I sent off a lot of our luggage by transport plane. All the foreign embassies were at the airport with their baggage, and there was a mad, "unprotocolish," international scramble for first place in having the stuff weighed in.

April 30. . . . I sit alone in the Canadian Embassy. The Ambassador and the whole staff have gone. I have been responsible for the arrangements of all the details of three shipments by air of personnel and baggage, and it has been a hectic week. Now I have the furniture to crate for the river trip.

A few nights ago I had a most interesting experience. I was the only foreigner invited to a farewell dinner given in honour of the famous "Christian General," Feng Yü-hsiang. He is about to leave for the United States to study water conservancy and hydroelectric projects such as the TVA and return to China to start similar projects on the Yellow River. Cynics say that the Christian General has more experience with water than anyone else in China, having baptized thousands upon thousands of his troops using great fire-hoses to ensure total immersion.

When Feng talks, everyone listens. He speaks simply and directly in the common language, without ostentation. I remember him as a most colourful character since the day I first met him in 1923 at the Nan Yuan parade grounds just south of Peking. There, the Christian General addressed tens of thousands of his troops and catechized them in true military, staccato monosyllables through a megaphone. He remembered me and said that when he learned I was in Chungking he had asked our host to invite me.

It did not take me long to realize that the host and hostess and all the guests were anti-Chiang Kai-shek. They were unanimous in their opinion that Chiang Kai-shek feared that General George Marshall would insist upon a Presidential election if a coalition was established and that Chiang was getting Feng out of China because he knew perfectly well that Feng would be a candidate and was so popular that he would win hands down. Hence the pretext of sending him to study water in the United States.

May 3. . . . Moscow has announced that 300,000 Soviet troops have been evacuated from Manchuria. The Nationalists have failed to reap the fruits of the Soviet withdrawal. The Communists are apparently in control of all the northern area of Manchuria, and the Nationalists remain in control only of the greater cities in southern Manchuria.

General George Marshall is reported to have stated that the Nationalist Kuomintang had an opportunity to have peace in Manchuria but have failed to capitalize on their opportunity. The Communists are gaining strength every day. The Nationalists are dangerously oxerextended and have rejected American military advice.

The Generalissimo ignores all advice and continues to insist that he will accept nothing less than complete control of all Manchuria.

May 10. . . . A few days after the farewell dinner for the Christian General, I made a trip to inspect the ship which was to take the Embassy goods, chattels, and me through the Yangtse Gorges. It was to be the SS *Ming Pen,* which had been sunk by a single Japanese bomb last year. The missile had penetrated the ship's stern right through the bottom. The ship had, however, been patched up and floated ready for inspection. A representative of the company accompanied me in a small motor boat after introducing me to General Feng Yü-hsiang's adjutant, who was also to inspect the ship.

"There she is," said the company man.

"Where?" I asked.

He pointed, and I saw a ship whose bow seemed to be reaching for the sky, while her stern hung very low in the water. I asked how the cargo, if not the passengers, could be prevented from sliding down and piling up at the stern. He replied there would be no danger of that. Before the cargo and passengers were boarded, twelve locomotives would be loaded in the bow of the ship, which would then be as level as other Ming Sung ships. I remembered that twelve locomotives had been sent to Chungking a dozen or more years before for the Chungking-Chengtu Railroad, which was never started. The company man then explained that the present unseemly and unshiply pose assumed by the *Ming Pen* was due to the cement that had been used to patch the bomb hole.

The Christian General's adjutant felt that he could not let his boss take the risk, but for me there was no choice. We were building ships in Canada for the Ming Sung Company and, even as a lowly First Secretary, I could hardly show lack of confidence in the firm.

May 20. . . . "Two-gun Cohen" is in Shanghai. You may remember him as General Morris Cohen, the title he acquired in China as Dr. Sun Yat-sen's bodyguard. He is a Canadian from Montreal who was frequently involved in business deals on behalf of Chinese like the Soong brothers and foreigners like Chennault.

June 2, Nanking. . . . In preparation for the move here, General Odlum had negotiated with Mr. Lu Tso-fu, owner of the Ming Sung Industrial Corporation, for transportation through the Yangtse River Gorges to Nanking. As I said before, we are building ships for Mr. Lu in Canada, the loan to be guaranteed by the Canadian Government. Mr. Lu offered us transportation for our furniture and supplies from Chungking to Nanking at regular commercial rates.

When I come back from Nanking to Chungking in April, I began detailed negotiations for specific allocation of space, rates, and tickets for the staff of servants and myself. It was not long before I discovered the task was rapidly becoming very complicated. The Ministry of Communications took everything out of the hands of the Ming Sung Company's Manager, and I was forced to negotiate with men who planned to capitalize on the tremendous demand for transportation.

The manager was a little reluctant to admit this, and I continued to assume that the agreements we had previously reached were final. We were to have tickets for suitable accommodation at regular rates and commercial freight rates rather than the suddenly inflated baggage rates for all the goods and furniture. When I began hearing about the competitive bidding by influential individuals for passage, I found that the company was completely powerless. The "right man" in the Ministry had assumed full control.

My efforts to talk to him were fruitless. In the first place, I was unable to locate his office. When I finally did, he contrived to be absent every time I arrived, despite firm appointments. One day, accompanied by an officer of the Australian Embassy, who had also been promised transportation with us by General Odlum, I walked past the messenger boy outside the "right man's" office, saying I had an appointment with his boss, which I did. The young man opened the door and showed us in. The boss was bargaining with two Chinese gentlemen. He suddenly stopped, bowed, and spoke to us in English. He did not know me, but promised to do his best for us. Space on the ship, he said, was very limited, and it was doubtful that we could be accommodated. I protested that we had been assured by the company through our Ambassador that we would have accommodation on the *Ming Pen*. He quickly assured me that he would do his best, but that it would be very difficult.

Then he asked the messenger boy in Chinese to escort us to the outer door. While we were still in the office, he scolded the boy severely for admitting us, adding that, if the boy did not carry out his instructions, he would be fired. I stopped and said to the boy in Chinese, without looking at his boss: "Do not be afraid, young man. When I come back tomorrow, I shall explain to your honourable manager that it was my fault, because I walked past you, and he will not fire you."

The boy made no effort to stop us when we arrived the next day. We were quickly issued with all the necessary documents and paid our bills. I did not learn until later how the "right man" outwitted me. He sold all special, first-class, and second-class accommodation to the notorious war lord and ex-Governor of Yunnan, Lung Yün, and his entourage of wives, children, concubines, and servants.

We learned that the SS *Ming Pen* was too large to come alongside and that it would be necessary to engage sampans to take the goods out to shipside for loading.

Two days before departure, I had to go to the Canadian hospital, where the doctor put me to bed with "Chungking fever"—nearly everyone got it some time or other. Before going, I discussed with our chauffeur, Lao Chu, about all arrangements and asked him to take immediate action when the old ship came up to load the locomotives. Lao Chu told me a few days later that he posted a look-out to keep watch and report as soon as possible the arrival of a ship with its bow up and stern down. When our Number Two came to the Hospital to fetch me on the morning of May 21, he reported that all our staff was aboard. (Lao Chu had been one of Vinegar Joe's drivers and got things done like his hero.)

Out in the stream was the resurrected SS *Ming Pen* on an even keel, set for Shanghai and for major repairs if she got through the gorges.

I have seen steamers loaded and boarded in Hankow and Shanghai with unbelievable noise and confusion, but never, during over two decades in China, had I seen anything like this. Swarms of sampans surrounded the ship, each laden with people and piles of bundles. Passengers were using ropes to haul their baggage up themselves. On every deck, relatives were shouting instructions to relatives below. As each sampan was cleared of baggage, the people started crawling up to the overcrowded decks, assisted by ropes and the hands of their families.

I could see no way to get aboard, but just then, one of the ship's company's representatives spotted me and came to my assistance. He helped me out of my wicker hospital chair, engaged a sampan, and in it we somehow wove through the maze of small boats to the foot of a ladder.

The Australian, a Norwegian, and I had been promised, and paid for, "special class" cabins, but it was soon evident that we were not getting them. We were not even getting first, second, or even third class. The company representative escorted us to a 5′ by 9′ cabin next to the boiler room, with a narrow door to the deck and no window. Since I was still weak from the fever and was supposed to keep to my bed, I chose the lower of the two six-foot bunks. My Norwegian friend took the upper. The Australian and his Chinese assistant were left with the lower and upper five-footers. All the remaining space, except for a wash-basin, was taken up by our baggage, and we had to eat our meals sitting on the two lower bunks.

The Ming Sung representative apologetically explained that our "special class" cabins had been commandeered by Chiang Kai-shek for his captive, Lung Yün, who was to be kept under surveillance in Nanking to prevent him from returning to Yunnan.

By noon, the Lung Yün crowd had not arrived, and until it did, the ship could not leave. Food was served by experienced waiters, who skilfully manoeuvred round the crowds of deck passengers dispensing rice, steamed vegetables, and tea. The fact that no one was scalded was a small miracle.

Finally, the humiliated war lord arrived with his vast household. There was much talk about them among the passengers, but no one rushed to catch a glimpse of them—and with good reason. There simply wasn't room to move.

As we began to pull away, the hubbub gradually subsided, the engines throbbed, the ship trembled slightly, and the temperature in our cabin rose sharply. Deck passengers' baggage had been piled from deck to ceiling, cutting off any possibility of a breeze, and we wiped the sweat from our faces with towels.

After the evening meal, people settled down and dozed off. Our Australian friend sprinkled his bunk generously with DDT as a precaution against bed bugs. The closest toilets for deck passengers and us were at the very stern of the ship. To get there, one had to walk from midship through and over the deck guests, who had perhaps paid more for their passage than we had. Once there, one found a row of dozens of thin board doors which stretched right across the width of the ship. Each door opened into a tiny box stall suspended over the water, which could be seen, through a convenient hole, churning and boiling below. One was not tempted to perch too long.

The first night we stopped at Wanhsien, the last little city before the gorges and reputed to have the best pomelos on earth —more tasty than the fabled melons of Kabul. We tied up for the night, as ships can navigate the gorges only by day.

The following day, we entered the gorges, and I made my way early to the bow of the ship. Dr. James Endicott and some friends had a cabin similar to ours on the other side of the *Ming Pen* from us. It was so difficult to make the journey around either the bow or the stern that we had not visited each other more than once. He had also picked his way to the bow of the ship, but was not as excited as I. He had gone through the gorges before and recited to me the statistical average percentage of junks which do not get through. Suddenly, conversation stopped completely when we realized that our ship was being drawn into the Hsin Lung T'an, the New Dragon Rapid, the first of many treacherous rapids. The Yangtse churned and boiled, plunged and twisted. The turbulent waters shook the patched-up, overloaded *Ming Pen* as we raced headlong towards our first gorge, the Feng Hsiang Hsia, Wind Box Gorge. While it is only four miles long, it is considered the grandest and most striking of all gorges. The perpendicular sides of the Wind-Box are 3000-foot-high, solid cliffs. As we were hurtled down stream, the mighty corridor, some 300 yards wide, rapidly narrowed to a slit through which we could barely see the sky, and we seemed trapped and heading for a crash into sheer rock that closed the passage. Momentarily, I was unconscious that the ship was not completely at the mercy of the Yangtse, but was being piloted by a human being who had spent his life going up and down through every one of these gorges and over each of the more dangerous rapids. He knew every twist and turn and exactly how the waters churned and swirled at high, low, and mid-water levels. I looked up at the ship's bridge to see if he was on the job. A jangle of bells urged the engineer below to make "full steam astern," and our speed was checked. A sharp turn revealed the continuation of the narrow gorge. The river was still hemmed in by a mighty corridor which widened and narrowed several times before we cleared the gorge.

The story goes that the Wind Box Gorge was cut through the mountains by a furious blast of wind from the nostrils of the legendary wizard Wu Tzu, and it is kept open to this day by the "eternal wind." Before we entered Wind Box, Jim Endicott drew my attention to a series of square holes which had been chiselled into the limestone cliff. Each hole was four-teen inches square and two feet deep, reaching from water level 526 feet up the perpendicular cliff to the top. It was here that the famous hero General Meng Liang, whose feat I had heard of since childhood days, had his men build a ladder of beams fitted into the holes and escaped with his army when his fleet of junks was trapped in the gorge.

Jim also pointed out to me, as we came through the Iron Coffin Gorge, three huge metal boxes or coffins in a cleft 600 feet above the water level. I remembered that, near this gorge, Chu-ke Liang had buried his magic sword and mystic war books to keep them out of the reach of warmongers. We used to enjoy an annual picnic at the mountain temple across the Han, where Chu-ke Liang had studied as a young man before becoming Prime Minister of one of the Three Kingdoms after the collapse of the Han Dynasty.

After the Wind Box, we successfully negotiated the Precious Son Rapid, a deep cleft through high mountains, the exciting Dismount Horse Rapid, around which no horse could pass, and the False Gorge, so named perhaps because it was more dangerous than a gorge and almost as bad as a rapid. Then we emerged into a ravine which cut through a thirteen-mile-wide valley.

Most dramatic for me was coming down the thirty-mile-long Wu Shan Hsia, the Witches Mountain Gorge. The solid white and yellow limestone cliffs, some 2,000 feet high, shut out enough light to create a weird feeling of looking into mysterious gloomy depths. The yellow water of the crowded Yangtse turned into a moving black mirror disturbed only by a sudden whirlpool. The water, over millennia, has gradually gouged out huge caverns in which small junks can escape a heavy downpour of rain. Somewhere above is a cave called Yü Shih Tung, Jade Cave, which legend says is the opening of a narrow passage to the earth's centre.

The gorges have all been carved by the river from vertical limestone cliffs. The depth of the water varies from sixty to seventy fathoms. The rapids have all been formed by enormous landslides of soft shale and sandstone, which obstruct the stream. The rate of the current varies with the water level from one and one-half to thirteen knots at special places, and the level of the river drops by several feet in a few yards. One of the worst and most feared of the rapids was caused by a fall of rocks in 1640, but it is still called the Hsin T'an, New Rapid.

Towards the end of a tense and exciting day, we began to emerge into the extensive plains of Hupeh Province and the city of Ichang, where we anchored for the night. The turbulent stream had finally become quiet as it spread into the great plains of China, bringing water to hundreds of millions of Chinese peasants.

It took two days to get from Ichang to Hankow, where we again stopped overnight. Some passengers got off. Their places, however, were immediately taken by newcomers, and the total population of the ship increased. The bow of the ship was occupied by Chinese troops from an American-trained Army corps. At one port of call a major-general of the Chinese Army, followed by his troops, forced his way on board with a drawn revolver. The deck passengers made room for them in no time.

After Hankow, we landed at Kiukiang, the famous porcelain centre and gateway to Kuling, and at Wuhu late at night. On May 29, the last day, we reached Nanking at 10 A.M. after a rapid journey of only eight days from Chungking.

June 6. . . . The cost of living here climbs rapidly, and inflation accelerates astronomically. The cost to us in Canadian dollars, at the official exchange rate, which is only one fifth of the black-market rate, is now five times as high as corresponding prices in Canada. There seems to be no hope whatever of any improvement as long as civil war continues.

The war in Manchuria has gone into high gear. The Nationalists, according to American sources, are in a virtually irretrievable situation. The Communist forces roll on, gathering irresistible momentum.

The Generalissimo benefited from aid, which the United States poured into China for the war against Japan, amounting to $1.5 billion, Lend-Lease, the construction of airfields, the training and equipping of his troops, and over $600 million from the United Nations Relief and Rehabilitation Administration. Chiang could therefore ignore the sound advice of US military advisers. His power, he thought, was infinitely greater than the simple guerrilla forces of the Communists.

The Nationalists, however, are defeating themselves by the colossal corruption and greed which has infiltrated the whole political structure and much of their military structure. Many of Chiang's generals are accumulating fortunes which are safely banked in Singapore, Geneva, and New York. Many of his political appointees are fattened by the increasing profits of their private economic monopolies. Truly, the state of affairs in China is in a sorry mess.

One day, after we had learned that some new generals had been appointed overnight, despite the fact that not a single one of them had any military training, our Ambassador, General Odlum, asked Chiang Kai-shek how many generals there were in the Chinese Army. The Generalissimo hemmed and hawed, as he usually did when he had nothing to say. Odlum then commented: "Mr. President, in the Canadian Army, we know how many toothbrushes have been issued to every private, and you seem to have no record of how many generals there are in your whole army."

June 30. . . . The Nationalist Minister of Information announced today that the truce with the Communists has expired and expressed the hope that General Marshall would continue to mediate an agreement to get the fighting stopped.

Mr. Wang Ping-nan, who calls on us nearly every week to keep us informed about developments as analysed by the Communists, says that the Nationalists now want the resumption of a truce agreement, because they are gradually being driven out of Manchuria. He says that the Communists have three ways of getting arms and ammunition from the Nationalists. The easiest way, and the way the Communists prefer, is to buy them from the generals who operate the arsenals. In Chungking, I learned that the product of many arsenals was secretly sold to the Communists. The second way, Wang said, was to bribe the generals in command of a Nationalist garrison to leave all their military supplies behind when they evacuated, in exchange for money and a guarantee of safe conduct through Communist lines. This way, he said, cost more money than buying from the arsenals, but had the advantage of saving the lives of PLA troops. The third way—to be avoided because of the loss of men—was to storm the garrison and take all military supplies. This method did, however, frequently result in the garrison defecting to the Communist side almost as soon as the fighting started.

We learn that the United States has extended to the Nationalists another $50 million in long-term credits. Nevertheless, the Nationalist Government continues to print vast amounts of new money in ever-increasing denominations. Imports of consumer goods are stimulated, and exports depressed. Middle-class people are critical of continued US aid, which benefits only the political and military bureaucracy.

July 5. . . . The Nationalist Armies are making gains in Manchuria by the occupation of important cities, and we are receiving reports of looting by Nationalist troops. The Chinese of Manchuria are regarded by the Nationalists from south of the Great Wall as Japanese lackeys. Their property and personal possessions are therefore considered legitimate war booty.

In the occupied cities of Manchuria, everything left by the Russians was taken, including the plumbing and heating equipment of private houses, tools, and hospital equipment. The unfortunate Japanese civilians were relieved of their personal possessions and shipped back to Japan by sea. The wealth which not only the Japanese but the Chinese had accumulated disappeared completely in the looting.

The Soviets had already confiscated all the gold, and the people were forced to sell their commodities to the Russian troops for Soviet Army notes. They suffered more from the Russians than from the Japanese. Now, Chinese Nationalist generals are competing with each other for power and possessions.

Like the Chinese people of Taiwan, the Manchurian Chinese expect that when the Japanese are defeated, they will be freed from domination and exploitation. Instead of treating the Taiwanese and Manchurians as fellow Chinese, the Nationalists consider them "collaborators." In Taiwan, they are not only denied a voice in their own government, but are ruthlessly executed by the thousands. In Manchuria, they are driven by the Nationalists into the ranks of the Communists.

July 10. . . . Although the truce has expired, Chou En-lai has been persuaded to remain in Nanking. Dr. J. Leighton Stuart, appointed, at General Marshall's suggestion, United States Ambassador to China, commenced immediately to negotiate a new truce agreement. It was, however, too late. The Nationalist Armies have gone into full-scale military action in North China and are winning battles.

The Communists have renamed their military forces the People's Liberation Army.

July 18. . . . Last week I had an exciting air trip to Shanghai. At 2:30 P.M. sharp, the plane taxied out to the runway, and in another five minutes I was headed east over the city wall past the old Ming tombs and the Sun Yat-sen tomb on Purple Mountain. The whole countryside was covered with a thick carpet of various hues of luscious green in patterns of every conceivable shape. China is beautiful from the air.

We circled considerably south of the regular course. This took us over several large, beautiful lakes with numerous small islands and hundreds of junks going in every direction, all sailing in the same wind. Past the lakes, we flew over the great alluvial plain of the lower Yangtse. As far as the eye could see, the land was as flat as a pancake. Canals and irrigation ditches cut the vast plain into millions of irregularly shaped patches. Junks plied the canals. Men with straw rain cloaks stood knee-deep in the rice fields cleaning out the weed growth between the rows of rice.

Then came Shanghai with its skyline, which is more pretentious than that of many North American cities. Its 6,000,000 inhabitants are, for the most part, poorly housed. The remainder, perhaps, enjoy greater luxury than the richest dwellers of the richest cities in China. The outskirts have only hovels; the centre has palaces. In the slums, millions crowd together, sweat together in summer, and shiver together in the winter. For the landing, we came in lower than some of the pagodas on the outskirts of Shanghai.

I rode in a truck and then took a rickshaw to our office on the Bund. In the Whangpoo were as many warships as ever, but instead of belonging to many nations, as they did in former days, they now all belong to one—the United States of America. There is much anti-American feeling in Shanghai.

You have no doubt read about the great drive of the Communists across Honan and Hupeh. In a few days, they captured Hsingyang, Tungpeh, Tsaoyang, Hsinyeh, Tengchow, Hsiangyang, Ichang, Nanchang, and Paokang.

What it means is difficult to say just yet. I can tell you this, however. A few days ago, a Canadian doctor, sent out by Canadians to inspect the hospitals in Communist-liberated areas to which Canadians have given some financial assistance, gave us a long report of what he saw. He was critical of the Communists before he visited them, but came back with glowing reports on the way they are conducting affairs compared to the Nationalists. He says that going into their territory is like going into a different country. The people are well treated and give support to the People's Committees established in each community. He says that there is no graft or "squeeze," that the Communists are friendly to Protestant missionaries, that their hospitals are exceptionally well managed, that they give the people free medical attention, that they control food prices, that the people are not over-taxed, and that there is no starvation. They are not, of course, perfect, and the doctor pointed out certain weaknesses, but claimed on the whole that they were so superior to the Nationalists that one could scarcely realize they belonged to the same nation.

August 1. . . . Our diplomatic bags have been so irregular you must have the impression that there is no longer any continuity

in my series of letters. One of the reasons for the failure is that the Royal Air Force, which carries the King's messengers, has been gradually forced out of China, and it is becoming increasingly difficult for them to get permission for flights in China. The treatment of the Americans is different, as Uncle Sam is still pouring blessings—the Communists would add a question mark—into China. Anti-American feeling is nevertheless growing, and the US is going to be faced with the choice of either pulling out altogether or coming in with even greater strength. I hope they do not do the latter.

Yesterday, an important Communist spokesman, Wang Ping-nan, came to interview the Ambassador. I acted as interpreter. Wang asked the Ambassador to use his influence to get the great democratic powers to tell China that she must stop fighting and settle her problems by peaceful methods. He said that unless something were done very soon, a general civil war would break out all over China. The prospects just at present are not very bright.

Last Saturday afternoon, I went out for a very interesting hike into the hills about fifteen miles east of Nanking. Professor Lossing Buck, Pearl Buck's first husband, was my guide. We took the jeep as far as we could. Then we started out on foot over narrow paths between the rice fields towards the hills. We came at last to a valley of solid walls of black rock. Upon examination of these walls and the floor, which was flat, it was evident that it was man-made.

Almost a millennium ago, this had been a stone quarry. We were on our way to see the never-completed order of the first Ming Emperor for a colossal monument to be erected in his honour, perhaps at the site of the Ming Tombs near Nanking.

A solid rock had been cut from the mountain side. It was to have been a great stone tablet, which had been chipped out lying down, but the base had not been completely cut loose from the mountain. Only the top end and four sides of the great slab had been completed. A support for the top end and the foot of the slab were not cut out. Otherwise, the monstrous monument was nearly ready for the move to Nanking. I paced the height of the rock and found it to be 150 feet. It was fourteen feet thick and thirty-five feet wide.

An old farmer who came walking by told us about the orders of the Emperor. Each stone-cutting peasant had to chip more than a bushel of fine rock per day or lose his head. Thousands of heads were cut off, he said, before the problem of moving the rock was considered.

Not even modern machinery could even begin to move a stone that size, and how the tyrant expected to erect the rock was not explained by the old peasant, whose family passes on the story of the cruelty from generation to generation. There were two other rocks—one for the turtle that was to support the tablet and the other to support the turtle. Such grandiose designs with so little thought for the consequences!

August 22. . . . I have just returned from a week in Kuling. The Ambassador was invited by Generalissimo and Mme. Chiang Kai-shek to spend a week in a villa on Kuling, and I accompanied him. The American Ambassador and Mrs. Marshall were spending ten days in another villa as guests of the Generalissimo for a rest and for consultations. Every evening, we were all dinner guests, usually in the garden, where the food was prepared in an outdoor oven.

The Ambassador and I had left Nanking by Chinese plane for Kiukiang, whose airport is across the Yangtse River from the city. The Chinese Navy had assigned us a launch to take us across.

On the Kiukiang side we were met by the Generalissimo's private car. It was brand new, and the driver proudly explained that he had driven the President for the past eight years and that he hardly ever drove the car now unless the Generalissimo was himself a passenger.

In the city, we were entertained to tea by local officials and finally whisked off in the car at 70 m.p.h. through small villages to the foot of the mountain.

For the first time in China, I saw road signs, giving advance notice of curves and telling drivers where to sound their horns. For the latter sign, under the Chinese characters was the English word: "Alarming." Every time the driver saw one of these, he duly alarmed the villagers with tremendous blasts of the horn.

A fifteen-mile drive brought us to the end of the motor road, at which point, sedan chairs with four bearers each were provided for us. After more tea, we started off up the steep slopes of the Lu Shan Mountains, at the top of which is the Kuling, where foreigners and wealthy Chinese go to escape the intolerable heat of the plains.

We climbed 3,500 feet to the rim of the mountain before reaching the mountain pass which is Kuling.

An American officer once remarked to me that the author of *Lost Horizon* must have got his inspiration from Kuling, as no place could be more like the original Shangri-la. It is enchanting. In the evening light, it has an air of mystery. Luxurious vegetation, splendid trees, rushing mountain torrents, rocks and caves, summer cottages of stone, and Gothic churches make Kuling a wonderful resort.

The Chinese Department of Foreign Affairs sent a representative to escort us to the house assigned to us. After a sound, refreshing sleep, we woke up to a grand morning. Clouds, drifting by, touched the top of the mountain.

Early in the day, the Generalissimo's secretary called and made arrangements for an interview at tea the following day. This gave us a day of rest and an opportunity to prepare the presentation of our case.

At five the next afternoon, the President's secretary escorted us to the residence. We passed several sets of guards and were asked to be seated on the shaded porch so that our arrival could be annnounced. In a few moments, we were taken into the main reception room. The Generalissimo was in his uniform.

He stood to greet us and shake hands. He looked young and alert but seemed definitely nervous. When he listens to what is being said, he keeps up a continuous "Hm, hm, hm, ha, ha, ah." He hesitates frequently, as if searching for the right term. He has a pleasant, winning smile.

Suddenly Mme. Chiang walked in. We stood up. The Generalissimo was called away on some urgent matter, and she took his place, the conversation continuing in English. She is a very impressive woman. She speaks English with an Eastern American accent. When the Generalissimo returned, she acted as interpreter, speaking to him with a Shanghai accent, although her Mandarin is perfect. She is quite bitter about the Communists, and her eyes flashed as she denounced them.

August 26. . . . Code telegram from External received August 26: "Your telegram No. 714, regarding Ronning's family. We are taking steps with the Embassy in Washington to provide space to China for Ronning's family. As the war shipping administration allots space, we cannot promise that passage will be available before September 30 but we will do our best. External."

August 30. . . . The United States has sold $100 million worth of war surplus equipment to the Government at bargain prices. It was designated as civilian-type equipment, and General Marshall has explained to Chou En-lai that it consisted mostly of non-combat material such as machinery, motor vehicles, and medical supplies.

Nevertheless, the Communists have issued a statement bitterly attacking the American policy of supporting the Nationalists and interferring in the internal affairs of China.

Communist strength continues to grow in the Manchurian rural areas, including towns and villages.

September 26. . . . On Sunday I had lunch with General Pai Ch'ung-hsi, Minister of National Defence, who is second only to the Generalissimo as regards China's military and naval forces. The General thinks he can defeat the Communists by taking all the key cities which they now occupy and by holding the lines of communication. This he hopes to do this fall. Then he will gradually wipe out the isolated Communist troops or give them the opportunity of joining the National Army. However, he will have to induce the peasants of China to like the National Government much more than they do now before he can change the popular support which sustains the Communists in some of the areas occupied by them.

On Monday, I had dinner with the Communists. They are determined to withstand to the last man and say that, however hard the Generalissimo may try, he will never be able to wipe them out, in spite of American war equipment. They say that he has been trying for twenty years and that unless he reforms his government, the Chinese people will rise in revolt until they eventually succeed in overthrowing the corrupt government. They seem resigned to a bitter struggle.

October 30. . . . General Odlum returned to Canada earlier this month, and I am in charge of the Embassy as Chargé d'Affaires.

It turned out, after I had been in China half a year, that the Department wanted me to stay, and I wanted very much to continue my work, which I found completely absorbing. I replied that I would stay, but that the Department must live up to the agreement that my family would come for my second and subsequent years.

The Department cabled that there was simply no transportation available. I cabled that, in that case, I would return at the end of my first year. In less than twelve hours, the Department cabled that transportation would be found on the SS *Marine Lynx* and that my family would leave for San Francisco very soon to board the famous, only-passenger vessel crossing the Pacific.

December 29. . . . The National Assembly went into recess on Christmas Day, and I attended as the representative of Canada. In the evening, I was the guest of Generalissimo and Mme. Chiang Kai-shek at the Chinese opera. The famous Chinese actor, Mei Lan-fang, whom Inga and I saw many times in Peking in 1922–23, performed. He is old now, but still marvellous. He played the part of a woman and was as graceful and smooth in his movements as a seventeen-year-old girl.

I have finally concluded the land deal, and the Canadian Embassy is the owner of a fine site of high land just west of Ginling College. We are the first embassy to purchase land in China's capital since the abolition of extraterritoriality, so my advice is being sought by several other embassies with regard to the new procedure. It took nearly five months, but we are now ready to build.

7

NANKING
1947-8

January, 1947. . . . At long last, on the last day of 1946, Inga arrived with Meme, Audrey, Kjeryn, and Harmon. They are all in good health and in good spirits. I met the *Marine Lynx* at the dock in Shanghai and was the first civilian on board by special pass, although the husband of another family beat me by getting aboard at Woosung. I had quite a time finding them, as they were all out of their cabins attending to the baggage. We went ashore and had a big New Year's Eve feast in our room at the Cathay Hotel. The following day, we came by rail to Nanking and are now installed in the house in which we shall be living for the next seven or eight months.

January 4. . . . In Peiping (as Peking was called when Nanking became the capital), there have been student demonstrations today, but they were not as serious as the two demonstrations we had here. The second ended only after police had beaten scores of students, knocking them down, swinging their belts, and cracking skulls with brass buckles. The students are seething with resentment.

January 10. . . . This month the exchange rate of Chinese national currency went wild. From 7,700 yuan per US dollar, the rate climbed to 18,000. Thousands of people who know nothing about exchange rates or inflation and kept their spare yuan under a mattress have lost their life's savings. Fortunately, China is an agricultural society, and modern, Western-style rates of currency exchange, bankruptcy, and so on have little effect on planting, harvesting, and eating rice. China is not brought to her knees when governments based on Western finance collapse.

February 15. . . . Dr. and Mrs. George Patterson have arrived to take over as Chargé d'Affaires until our new Ambassador, T. C. Davis, arrives. George has had years of experience in Japan and reads Chinese characters.

We have rented the vacant Pearl Buck house as our Chancery.

Professor Lossing Buck heads the Agricultural Department of Nanking University and probably knows more about agriculture in China than any other foreigner.

February 16. . . . The financial situation in China's cities is becoming more and more disastrous to city people and more profitable for the Soong financial interests. Chinese currency is down to one third its value of only a few days ago, and prices are three times as high.

March 1. . . . The people of Taiwan are revolting against barbarous suppression and looting by Governor Ch'en Yi's troops. Thousands of Chinese who made their home on the island centuries ago are being slaughtered. The harassed Taiwanese

expected liberation from the Japanese. The Governor, appointed by Chiang Kai-shek, made promises to keep the peace until units of the mainland Nationalist Army arrived. Taiwanese are now being executed in a holocaust more terrible than anything inflicted upon them by the Japanese since China surrendered Taiwan to Japan in 1895 at the conclusion of the Sino-Japanese war.

March 24. . . . Nationalist troops have marched into Communist headquarters at Yenan. They took jolly good care to wait until the place had been completely evacuated by the People's Liberation Army. It may actually be a move to lead the Nationalists away from more important areas. For the Communists, there are no strategic positions in China, including their own capital, as long as guerrilla warfare is the order of the day. The Nationalist Armies are already over-extended in the Northeast.

May 21. . . . When we were here in the Twenties, conditions in China were bad. We were in the midst of the great political and social upheaval of 1926–27 and its cruel suppression. Today, we hear the rumblings of a similar outburst. China is again in turmoil. Canadian missionaries in North Honan, evacuated by military aircraft, describe the terrible suffering of the people in the battle zones. Thousands of soldiers die from neglect of very ordinary wounds.

May 21. . . . Communist General Lin Piao's People's Liberation Army is supported by Mongol and Korean troop units. More than 250,000 men are reported to be marching rapidly south from the Sungari River to central Manchuria. The Nationalists are abandoning all outposts to retire to the cities.

There they are surrounded, isolated, and fall easily to better equipped, indoctrinated, and organized Communist forces.

The PLA, equipped with Japanese weapons left behind by the Russians when they withdrew, have now defeated the Nationalist Seventy-First Army, equipped with American weapons.

The Nationalists are withdrawing to the defence of Mukden, while the Communists claim the capture of scores of cities and towns where the Nationalists were cut off, with no alternative but to surrender.

May 27. . . . The event of the week was the presentation of credentials by our new Ambassador, Mr. T. C. Davis.

You have read about the controversies between foreign plenipotentiaries and the old Imperial Court of the Middle Kingdom about the ceremonial kowtow and the refusal of some of the stiff-necked barbarians to conform to this age-old custom. Well, we didn't kowtow, but we did stand to attention while the military band played "God Save the King," and we bowed, stepped forward six paces, bowed again, stepped forward another six paces, bowed a third time, and stood in formation in order of rank. The Ambassador read his speech. It was interpreted. The Generalissimo read his reply. It was interpreted. Our bones waxed creaky with old age while standing rigidly through this ceremony. It would have been easier to kowtow and get it over in one bump. It took almost as long as the Chinese train on which an old gentleman presented a half-fare ticket explaining that when he got on he was a boy.

July 24. . . . The Wedemeyer fact-finding mission has arrived. Unlimited US aid for the Nationalists is expected by those who remember that Wedemeyer was sent to Chungking to pacify the Generalissimo when he was furious with General Stilwell.

August 24. . . . Wedemeyer left today after visiting every part of China still under Nationalist control.

It is rumoured that the Generalissimo was furious. The two generals apparently minced no words in exchanging opinions. The Gimo will probably calm down before Wedemeyer does —he needs US aid.

August 28. . . . Colonel Freddie Clifford arrived this month. He is to be our new military attaché, replacing Brigadier William Bostock. Bill was a tower of strength during the difficult months of getting established in Nanking.

September. . . . The Chinese people are increasingly disillusioned with the Nationalist Government. It is evident to everyone that the Nationalists are diverting US aid to their own corrupt ends. Today, even the merchants sympathize with the Chinese peasants who have risen in revolution against Chiang Kai-shek.

The scholars of China are also alienated.

October 28. . . . The Government has outlawed the Democratic League. Leaders and supporters are threatened with execution, and some professors have already been executed.

The Nationalists are reported to have secured millions of rounds of ammunition from the United States at a very low price. The Nationalists, however, are not satisfied and are asking for $3 billion dollars over a three-year period. Washington had proposed only $300,000. The Nationalists call it "a drop in the bucket."

Mme. Chiang has flown to Washington to plead for immediate assistance. The US has apparently granted 150 transport planes and 131 naval vessels at low cost to Chiang Kai-shek.

December 25. . . . The Christmas message from the armies of China is that there are now 2,700,000 Nationalist troops prepared to wipe out the Communists.

The Communists claim that 2,000,000 Peoples Liberation Army troops are poised to liberate the people of China.

January 1, 1948. . . . The Generalissimo's New Year message announces: "The Bandit Suppression Campaign (referring to the "Communist Bandits") that is now taking place can be accomplished in one year."

Mao Tse-tung said at the close of 1947: "The Chinese people's revolution has now reached a turning point, and the People's Liberation Army is on the offensive."

The famous Christian General Feng Yü-hsiang, who at one time threw in his lot with Chiang Kai-shek in the late 1920's, and Nationalist General Li Chi-shen have formed a Kuomintang Revolutionary Committee in Hong Kong to cooperate with the Communists.

January 5. . . . Mao's New Year's resolution is being carried out. The People's Liberation Army has isolated Mukden by capturing Anshan south of the city.

Chiang Kai-shek counters Lin Piao's move by naming a new chief of "Bandit Suppression."

Washington has instructed Major General Barr, senior officer of the United States Army Advisory Group here, to make military advice available to the Generalissimo.

March. General Barr has advised the Nationalists to withdraw their forces from Manchuria.

The Generalissimo is furious and states that under no circumstances will he order his troops to withdraw.

US Ambassador Stuart is of the opinion that the "demoralization and deterioration" of the situation is accelerating alarmingly. Even the Generalissimo now realizes victory is impossible.

April 20. . . . The Communists have recaptured their old headquarters at Yenan, and Manchuria continues to be the main theatre of the civil war. Chiang has rejected General Barr's advice, and the Communists have unexpectedly become active in North China south of the Great Wall.

After the capture of Yenan, they surrounded the city of Kaifeng, cutting off communications and transportation. The Generalissimo was himself directing the battle by telephone from Nanking. The Communists overwhelmed the defenders and demonstrated that in large-scale positional fighting they are as superior as they have always been in guerrilla tactics. If they can take Kaifeng, the fear is that Nanking could also fall to the PLA.

The Communists evacuated Kaifeng after capturing military supplies to retain their mobility, a strategy which has been so successful in Manchuria.

July 4. . . . Communist Armies in Manchuria are closing in on the Nationalists. Wang Ping-nan informed me that Communist Airforce bombers had dropped bombs on Nationalist troops winning an important battle for the People's Liberation Army. He was so jubilant at a Fourth of July reception at the American Embassy, I asked him why and he gave me the news which was verified later by foreign observers.

8

❁

KULING
1948

❁

General Odlum and I had, of course, been guests of Generalissimo and Mme. Chiang Kai-shek in Kuling in 1946. During
the summer of 1948, my wife and I, together with our four
children, decided to spend our holidays in the hill resort. They
might not have been so enthusiastic, had they known how
difficult the trip would be.

I made reservations on one of the older Yangtse River steamers—the only one available. My wife and I, with our two
youngest, Kjeryn and Harmon, boarded the ship early. (I knew
from experience what a terrific scramble it would be to get on
board.) Meme and Audrey were to come a little later, accompanied by their boyfriends.

In all the confusion, we in due course saw Meme with David
Westlein and Audrey with Seymour Topping battling their
way forward through a crowd of people trying to board the vessel.
For a while one of the girls seemed to disappear. We learned after
they finally got on deck that Audrey had been pushed over, but
had, with the help of Top and Dave, regained her feet—only after
experiencing what it might be like to be trampled underfoot. The
young men had only a little less trouble getting back. The people

began to disperse only after all doors were closed and our old tub steamed up the Yangtse. The only ship I have ever seen more crowded was the *Ming Pen* coming down from Chungking two years earlier.

We stayed on deck until dark, enjoying the cool breeze. Then, after dinner, came the family council as to who should sleep where. (We had one first-class and two second-class cabins.) The two second-class cabins—inside cabins with no portholes—were roomy enough, but hot. We went to inspect the first-class cabin. It had windows to the deck, but a curtain was drawn across the length of the cabin, and we could hear the gentle snoring of a person sleeping in a screened-in bed, leaving us one single bed. As we went in, we caught a glimpse of several rats jumping out of the window. My wife immediately decided she was not going to bed at all. The girls decided to try the second-class cabin, leaving Harmon and me to the single bed. Harmon was not afraid of rats, and I was an experienced rat-chaser.

Harmon and I dropped off to sleep with a lovely breeze coming through the open window, but all of a sudden, I was conscious of rats in our bed. Harmon had some chocolate bars. When I turned on the light, the rats scampered out, leaving chocolate stains all over the bed. I closed the window. It was too hot to sleep. I opened the window. The rats came in just as I was dropping off. It was broad daylight when I wakened and was shocked to find that the sheets were covered not only with chocolate but with blood-red stains. Could the rats have started to eat Harmon? I shook him awake. If he was being eaten, the rats must have used acupuncture on him. He seemed to be all splattered with blood, but perfectly sound. He said: "Look, Dad. The rats have eaten all my red paint."

Harmon loved to paint cars, trucks, and fighter aircraft. Red was his favourite colour, and the rats had apparently enjoyed it even more than their Chungking relatives enjoyed my soap. We dressed and joined the rest of the family below. The person in our other bed was still snoring gently.

Late that afternoon, we arrived at Kiukiang. The wharf was under water and we had to be taken off in row-boats. We got a bus to the foot of the mountain.

Usually, there are a great many home-made wicker sedan chairs available, but we arrived late in the day, and only two chairs were available. One of the girls was not well, and we had to get her up to Kuling and to bed, so my wife and two of the girls took the two chairs and started up the mountain.

Audrey, Harmon, and I spent the night with the luggage, as no coolies were available to carry our luggage at night. And since no house was available either, we camped out.

Early the next morning, after eggs, bananas, and tea, we started up the mountain with several coolies carrying the luggage and one chair for the youngsters.

Kuling, far above the intense heat of the plains, is ideal for rest and recreation. Near the top of the mountain, surrounded by higher hills, the business centre of Kuling provides all food and shopping requirements. Many porcelain shops displayed wares from the famous Ching Teh Chen kilns—for everyday use, for connoisseurs, or for ordinary collectors.

My wife and I occasionally visited some of the shops to purchase useful household wares. The proprietor of an attractive shop tried to get us interested in some of his special displays, but I explained to him that I could not afford to purchase his really good stuff.

One day, as the proprietor caught sight of us walking past, he came out calling: "Come in, come in. I have something very special to show you." He brought out a box from the back room and opened it to exhibit a beautiful vase about eighteen inches high in an unusual cone shape and with a typical T'ang painting. We admired it, thanked him for showing it to us, and prepared to leave. "You must have this vase," he said. "It has a coating of genuine Ch'ien Lung glaze and is available for the ridiculously low price of one hundred twenty Chinese silver dollars." We thanked him again, saying we were not in the market for his fine things, even for US $60. "Make me an offer," he begged.

"No," I replied. "I have children to feed and educate."

"Come again," he pleaded, as we left.

A few days later, when we attempted to walk past, the performance was repeated, with the same result. The third time, he called to us: "I have the owner in my guest room. He is anxious to sell and will reduce the price." He left the vase with us and walked back to his private quarters and returned to announce that the owner would sell it for 100 Chinese silver dollars. We left. The next time we were walking past his place, he again asked us to come in, saying the owner would now sell it for half that price. We were not interested. He insisted upon us making some offer, any offer. I finally said the only offer I could make would be five silver dollars. He laughed, and we made for the entrance, but he asked us to wait. He went behind the curtain and reappeared saying: "He will accept ten." I insisted I could not increase my offer. He ducked behind the curtain again very quickly and said: "The vase is yours. You have purchased the finest vase in China for only five dollars." He put it in the box and handed it to me. By this time, I was not certain that I wanted to part with five silver dollars. Since I had promised, however, I paid, and we carried off the priceless vase. When we got home, I noticed that the inscription indicated the vase had been given to Tzu-wen respectfully from "younger brother." That meant nothing to me.

Three years later, when I was getting ready to return to Canada, and my stuff was being packed, I asked our custodian, Mr. Chen, to look at the vase from Kuling. When he read the inscription, he asked me if I knew to whom the vase had been presented. I said that it was apparently a present to someone named Tzu-wen, adding that there must be a lot of people in China with that name.

"Oh, no," said Mr. Chen. "There is only one person called Tzu-wen in China—the famous brother of Mme. Chiang Kai-shek, T. V. Soong."

I realized then why I had obtained the vase for five dollars. It was one of several which had been fired at one time, all alike. Only one was to be kept, the rest destroyed. Some employee at the kiln had kept one or more to sell for his private profit. Before I left, I was offered, at a ridiculously low price, one of the most beautiful vases I had ever seen in private hands. The inscription indicated that it was a present to President Roosevelt from Generalissimo Chiang Kai-shek. I refused to offer even a red copper. Some foreigner who couldn't read the inscription probably has it, ignorant of its history. I knew that Ambassador Leighton Stuart had been entrusted with the one selected, while the duplicates were to have been destroyed. It was presented to Mrs. Roosevelt after the death of the President.

We were still in Kuling when Chiang Kai-shek changed the basis for China's national currency. On August 19, 1948, the official exchange rate had been US $1 for 12,000,000 Chinese currency yuan. The new "gold yuan" was fixed at the rate of US $1 for four gold yuan, which was guaranteed to be stable. This was to be the "great currency reform." This useless step was, it was claimed, to stop inflation, which had gone berserk. All national currency, gold and silver bullion, gold and silver coins, and American bank-notes were to be exchanged for the new currency. Campaigns were organized to compel everyone to carry out the exchange at the declared rate within a certain period. A few weeks later, the new currency started slipping, and reluctance to obey the new law increased.

Chiang Kai-shek's son, Chiang Ching-kuo, was sent to Shanghai to enforce the law. Many of Shanghai's wealthiest men failed to comply with the law, and some of them were publicly executed. The rest came across. The new currency behaved as its predecessors had, but with even greater alacrity. The Government had, in the meantime, acquired control of practically all the gold, silver, and United States dollars in China. Before the Government left Nanking, inflation, accelerating at geometric rates, was accompanied by the issuance of bank-notes of astronomical denominations. (China's new regime eventually replaced the "gold yuan" with new People's Bank notes.)

The salary and wage classes of China have been reduced to desperation. Money has lost its value so rapidly that whenever they are paid they spend it the day they lay hands on it. The following day its value would be almost nil.

The people of China wait impatiently for a change of government—it matters not by whom.

September 15. . . . The economic situation continues to deteriorate rapidly. In Shanghai, the wholesale commodity price index is now more than 3,000,000 times higher than the prewar level. This month, the prices are forty five times higher than in January, and the rate for American dollars is fifty times higher.

More and more towns still held by the Nationalists in rural areas are blockaded by the Communists, who control the food supply, with the result that, one by one, they capitulate. When I visited Peiping this year, the only way to get there was by air, as most of the rural areas between Nanking and Peiping are now known as "liberated areas."

September 24. . . . The city of Tsinan, which has been surrounded by the People's Liberation Army for some time, has fallen to the Communists. With the city went the Cheeloo University, where Dr. Menzies' famous collection of oracle bones is kept. At Tsinan, the Nationalists lost 80,000 troops and great quantities of military supplies. With losses like this in northern China, the Generalissimo is finally withdrawing his troops from Manchuria, but too late. Eleven divisions have defected to the Communists with all their equipment.

October 15. . . . The Nationalists have lost the city of Chinchow, and five regiments capitulated to the Communists.

At Changchun, the Nationalists Sixtieth Army from the Province of Yunan has defected. This was Lung Yün's army before he was outwitted by Chiang Kai-shek. (You may remember that it was Lung Yün who crowded me out of the cabins reserved for me on the *Ming Pen.*) Lung Yün's former troops will now march with the PLA, and I may see them before long in Nanking.

October 20. . . . Chiang's troops in Manchuria continue to topple like tenpins. The latest victory of the People's Liberation Army is over the Seventh Army, when they attempted to break out of besieged Mukden. These troops were trained and equipped by officers under General Stilwell. I saw them march through Nanking last year and have never seen smarter, better equipped, or more disciplined troops in China. They were the cream of the Generalissimo's armies.

October 28. . . . The Canadian Government has decided to evacuate all Canadian women and children from the Canadian Embassy in Nanking, and we are trying to obtain transportation.

9

✺

THE
LIBERATION OF
NANKING

✺

November 1948. . . . It was inevitable that Nanking would fall, but no one knew whether or not fighting would create an unsafe situation for its residents. This means that Inga, Audrey, Kjeryn, and Harmon will be leaving for Canada. Meme and her husband, David Westlein, will also be leaving soon on their next posting.

I have been in China for three years, and am long overdue for home leave. At Inga's insistence, I have informed the Department that I would return with my family. In reply, I have been asked to remain until the expected change-over has taken place—perhaps within a few weeks or less, judging by news from north of the Yangtse River. If I am prepared to stay on, the reward will be a posting to Norway. A foreign service officer is usually requested to list in order of preference the places to which he would like to be posted. I had chosen Norway, because Inga has never visited Norway.

Inga is, of course, delighted with the prospect of going to Norway and the family will obey External Affairs orders without complaint, expecting that I shall follow them to Canada in a few weeks.

November 7. . . . The Communists have taken Yingkow, so now all of Manchuria is under their control.

The United States Navy has withdrawn from Tsingtao, as the Communist advance continues southward.

Two Chinese armies are locked in battle. This time, the armies are more evenly matched—some 500,000 troops on each side.

The Communists are employing the same strategy which proved so successful in Manchuria, Kaifeng, and Tsinan. The Nationalists again seem to be unable to do anything about it, perhaps because they fail to cooperate among themselves. The Communists manoeuvre overwhelming forces against the weaker KMT units, which never seem to get help in time. After crushing the isolated unit, the PLA moves swiftly to outnumber and cut off other units, one at a time.

It can only be a matter of time before the Peoples Liberation Army occupies Nanking and Shanghai, unless the Nationalists can stop the Communists in the Huai-hai area, where 1,000,000 men are engaged in a battle which may decide which side will win the civil war.

December 2. . . . As this year draws to an end, the new "gold yuan," like its predecessors, is plummeting, and the Chinese people have been fleeced again, this time more effectively than ever before.

Now it is not only the poor peasants who have lost confidence in the Nationalist dictatorship and the Generalissimo (who, it is rumoured, will soon be deserting the sinking ship). The Government blames it all on the Communists. Reports from the Communist "liberated areas" however, are that the economic situation there is relatively better.

January 1, 1949. . . . The Generalissimo's New Year Message does not refer to the Communists as "bandits," nor does it predict how soon they can be exterminated.

This year he says: "If the Communists are sincerely desirous of peace, and clearly give such indication, the Government will be only too glad to discuss with them the means to end the war."

Too late. The people know that there will be peace only after Chiang Kai-shek abdicates.

January 20. . . . The Nationalist Government's request that the United States, Britain, the Soviet Union, and France intervene on its behalf has been rejected by all of them.

January 21. . . . The Generalissimo has gone through the ceremony of handing authority over to Vice President Li Tsung-jen. He has "retired" as President.

January 22. . . . The Battle of Huai-hai lasted sixty-five days, ending on January 2. It will probably be recorded in history as one of the greatest in modern times. It was a battle of annihilation in which Chiang Kai-shek's military power was utterly crushed. He is fleeing to Canton.

Ch'en Yi led the People's Liberation Army in this final victory against Chiang Kai-shek. The Generalissimo's second son, Chiang Wei-kuo, led the Nationalist Armoured Corps. The Generalissimo himself again directed the Nationalist military operations in this last of countless defeats which lost him the civil war and China.

At the end of the sixty-five-day battle, the Nationalists had lost five Army groups, seven full divisions, and the Armoured Corps—a total of 550,000 men and all the generals who led their troops, with the exception of General Liu Chih and Chiang's son Ching-kuo, who escaped by air. The Communists won enormous war booty.

The way to Nanking is now open.

January 30. . . . The situation in Nanking is tense with rumours, and there are new developments every few hours. It looks as if we may have a peaceful take-over by the Communists, but the civil war will probably rage on south of us. We may be cut off from communications for a while. We are well stocked up with rice and silver dollars. The Communists are just across the river. The Americans, French, British, and most smaller missions are staying on. The Russians pulled out for Canton today. Our plans may change. A Canadian destroyer is coming out here just in case.

Most of the Americans have gone to Canton, but their Ambassador, Stuart, remains here. There were scenes of wild excitement when the people from the north side of the river streamed over here before the advance of the Communists.

February 2. . . . The peace talks may have been merely an attempt by the Government to gain time for the withdrawal of its troops to the South. The terms offered by the Communists have been pretty stiff, but they seem to know that they will have the whole of China in due course, so why make terms that give them less?

There is much glee in Nanking diplomatic circles regarding the possibility of Canton being attacked before Nanking. The more timid souls went to Canton to escape! Out of the frying pan into the fire maybe.

February 11. . . . The railway has been cut off for short periods, but all is quiet here. Several recent executions have put a stop to armed robberies and looting.

April 1. . . . General Fu Tso-yi has capitulated to the Communists on their terms, and the Communists now occupy Peiping.

A Nationalist delegation led by Chang Chih-chung has arrived in Peking to negotiate a peace settlement. The Communists have imposed a deadline of April 20 for concluding negotiations.

April 20. . . . We are all afluster here today over the reported sinking of the British destroyer *Amethyst*. We still do not know the details—only that many lives were lost. Last night, there were practice manoeuvres in the streets with thousands of troops and tanks. The tanks thundered past and kept us awake half the night. A terrific battle has been going on all night just across the river.

April 21. . . . The Communists crossed the Yangtse River above Nanking last night with 60,000 troops backed by heavy artillery.

Yesterday, the time limit of the Communist ultimatum expired. Starting about five-thirty in the afternoon, we could hear the distant rumble of big guns west of the city and on the other side of the Yangtse. By eight, we could hear heavy machine gun firing, then heavy artillery north of the city. At ten in the evening, Chinese Navy destroyers opened up with brilliant flashes of gunfire which rocked the whole city. I climbed to the roof of our third storey and had a grandstand seat for spectacular fireworks accompanied by thunderous reverberations.

The shooting continued steadily all night with occasional explosions that rattled the house. Fires started everywhere across the river, and one could tell that the Communists were advancing steadily as the sound of machine gun firing moved forward. It was nine this morning before the shooting stopped.

The news today is so conflicting that all we can be sure of is that the fighting was intense. China's peasants are dead and dying today, and their homes destroyed in ever-increasing numbers.

British sailors are also dead and dying as a result of British ships passing through the war zone. Ten killed on one ship and seventeen on another, including all the officers except two, when the bridge of the *Amethyst* was blown off by Communist shore batteries. The doctor was killed, and the medical supplies destroyed. British sailors are suffering from terrible burns with no relief tonight. War is hell.

April 25. . . . After months of certainty that the Nationalists would eventually topple, Nanking was liberated on April 23. Following a thunderous night of cannonading, I finally dropped off to sleep only to be suddenly awakened by Top, who burst into my room. Off we went in his jeep to stand inside the North West Gate to see the first thousands of PLA troops walk, at ease, into the city carrying their war equipment and *pei-wo,* sleeping bags, to take possession of the capital of China with no fanfare or triumphant pomposity.

For three days prior to liberation, wild yet systematic looting by the people was widespread. Amidst shouting and laughter, the people stripped the residences of top Nationalist officials and army generals, carrying out the contents, ripping out plumbing, electric fixtures, doors, windows, floors, and all wood for kindling. Like vultures, the looters waited patiently until the Nationalists evacuated their homes in panicky flight to escape with as much as possible of their possessions.

At the height of the chaos, I accompanied my friend Philip Crowe, who had suffered a heart attack, to the airport, winding through piles of loot in the streets. Crowe was flown out in the last aircraft to leave Nanking.

At the airport, I witnessed confusion worse confounded. The families of the wealthy had climbed into scores of aircraft with their baggage—in at least one case, which I saw, with their grand piano. They never got off the ground. The pilots defected or disappeared.

In the utter confusion, our Ambassador, Judge T. C. Davis, arrived from a visit to Shanghai, in high spirits as usual. He had gone in the last aircraft to Nanking until the People's Liberation Army re-established law and order.

May 31. . . . There is only a small group of foreigners left here now, and Nanking will soon be a country village. All diplomats will go either to Peking or home.

We have been having some troubles as usual—never a dull moment. Barrels of oil have been stolen, and the bamboo fence goes every time it rains. There are fewer air raids. We had great excitement one night when an alarm went off at about eleven o'clock. Raids had always been during the day. The aircraft kept flying round the city and anti-aircraft artillery went off from all quarters, shaking our house. When shooting stopped, the plane landed. It had escaped from the Nationalists. At five thirty the next morning, we had the real thing—another visit from a strafing Mosquito.

We all hope it will soon be over. I hope our Government will recognize the new Government here as soon as it is formed and that the civil war will finally come to an end.

June 2, Shanghai. . . . I didn't think that it would take so long after the fall of Nanking and Shanghai for communications to be reestablished. Tomorrow, the first boat goes out of Shanghai with the first mail to you since before April 24, when Nanking was liberated.

The man in charge of Foreign Affairs here is Chang Han-fu, with whom I travelled from Calcutta to Chungking in 1945. He assures me that you will be allowed to return.

I was told yesterday that no foreigner in Shanghai had yet been allowed to see him and that it would be useless for me to try, but I had only a five-minute wait before I was admitted. We talked for three-quarters of an hour.

After writing the first two pages, I had to go out to call on the Public Safety Bureau. While out, I witnessed strafing by American pursuit planes and heard the explosions of bombs hitting the Standard Oil tanks, which are now burning fiercely down the river a little way from where you docked in 1946. A British Blue Funnel ship was also hit. It is going down by the stern now.

Yesterday afternoon, we saw Canadian Mosquitos flown by Chinese Nationalists bombing and strafing Shanghai. They were so close that the empty machine gun shells dropped into the compound in front of the Pattersons' residence, where we were having tea.

Over a month ago in Nanking, Mosquitos strafed a crowd at Sun Yat-sen's monument and killed and wounded thirteen. Also four-motor bombers hit a small school when they were probably aiming at a power house in the vicinity. Some forty youngsters were killed.

I shift about from office to office, so you will find this very disjointed. I have had more contacts with the Communists than any other foreigner, and I have been liaison between the Diplomatic Corps and the Communists regarding many problems. In Nanking, they call me "Ambassador at Large."

News has just come that many lives were lost on a British ship, which is now sinking.

July 15, Nanking. . . . I am taking advantage of an opportunity to get a note out to you with a special plane which will carry the American Ambassador out of China. You undoubtedly know that we are still cut off from the outside world and that no ships are coming into or out of Shanghai due to the blockade by the Nationalists. This is a situation we had not expected.

Since the liberation of Nanking, our work has been gradually decreasing, so that I have much more time for rest and exercise. I have been riding a great deal and swimming at the American Embassy Club a few times.

Acting as unofficial liaison officer beween the Diplomatic

Corps and the Foreign Nationals Department of the Military Control Commission, I did help to create some goodwill which resulted in several concessions. Our Ambassador will be leaving here as soon as he can get transportation, and I shall be in charge during the period of negotiations regarding eventual recognition.

The new regime shows every indication of effective administration with the old corruption eliminated. This is unheard of in China, but it is being achieved. They have the support of the great majority of students and intellectuals and also peasants. The city people are, to a considerable extent, opposed, as they fear that their business will not be as profitable as formerly. Money-changers and black marketeers have been driven away. This affects the livelihood of many people, and they are, of course, very bitter. The revolution is certainly gaining momentum, and there is every indication of a release of the tremendous energy of which the Chinese people are capable. There will probably be great social changes in China. In Shanghai, foreign concerns are worried. Even private Chinese corporations are suffering. With the present blockade, many companies are hit very severely, and many of the parasitic businesses will undoubtedly perish. Missionary work goes on as usual—so far at any rate.

August 1. . . . We have been dismissing surplus servant staff, which has been pretty difficult. This has continued for four days, and today I had a chap who was His Excellency's assistant cook, who rampaged around the office shouting. I finally got him quieted down and gave him some fatherly advice about not losing his temper if he wanted to make a real contribution to his chosen profession of working for Chinese workers. I added that I was glad to see that, at long last, there were people in China who wanted to help the common people of China. (He is an official of the Labour Union.) Strangely enough, he took my advice, admitted that he had a bad temper, and apologized

for flying off in my office. The others could hear it from the larger outer office and thought the man was going to attack me.

We have daily air raids. The KMT planes are after the water-works west of town, the power house down by the river, shipping in the river, and the railroad.

10

❊

PEACE
AND REFORM

❊

After a century and a half of war and violent turbulence, peace finally came to continental China when the People's Liberation Armies occupied all of China's cities in 1949. Since the beginning of the 19th Century, China had suffered a continuous series of wars and sporadic turbulence, including foreign invasions, the Opium War, war with France, military action to obtain territorial concessions in port cities and extraterritoriality for foreigners, the Taiping Rebellion and mass extermination of the rebels, war with Japan and loss of territory, the Boxer Rebellion, the Republic Revolution, extortion by war lords, the Northern Expedition and the blood bath to exterminate revolutionaries, the atrocities of Japanese occupation, and finally the ravages of civil war. The people of China had known only a continuous succession of wars, rebellions, and devastation. The end of war, the coming of peace, and the establishment of law and order was almost too good to be true.

I was in China when it happened. Seymour Topping, who later became my son-in-law, and I stood together on that memorable day just inside of the Northwest Gate of Nanking watching battle-weary troops of the People's Liberation Army coming through the city wall into the capital of China. Top had been chasing around the city all night keeping in touch with developments, while I had been watching the spectacular artillery duel north of the river from the top of the Canadian Embassy residence. Top came early to inform me that troops of the PLA were expected to come through the Northwest Gate very soon. We rushed off in his jeep, anxious to see the triumphant entry of the People's Liberation Army.

What we saw, however, was not the triumphant entry of a conquering army with fanfare and fire crackers that had characterized the entry into Nanking, almost exactly a century earlier, of an army of angry, determined, but ignorant peasants of the Taiping Rebellion, fired by visions of establishing a "kingdom of heavenly peace."

The peasant army that Top and I saw was made up of literate, well armed, well clothed, well fed, and well informed seasoned veterans, disciplined and indoctrinated to serve the people and liberate their fellow peasants and workers. They came trained in the tactics of guerrilla and conventional warfare. What made them different, however, was their training and experience working with peasants in construction and agriculture. They had come not to rule and exploit, but to liberate and cooperate, and this was most unconventional in China's armies.

China's illiterate masses had always borne the brunt of disaster and suffering. Only in an atmosphere of peace could reforms flourish which would liberate the people from China's ancient, multitudinous evils and the never-ending cruelty of man's inhumanity to man. In addition to the millions who suffered from man-made disasters, millions of Chinese had been killed or had become victims of widespread natural disasters. Floods, drought, and pestilence had caused famine, disease, death, and destruction.

Many of the so-called natural disasters were the result of man's neglect. They would not have occurred—at least not as frequently —had man not neglected the continuous work necessary to prevent them. The building of dikes, the constant dredging of silt, the construction of drainage canals to prevent floods, and the construction of irrigation canals to prevent drought received no priority when war was of the essence. The coming of the People's Liberation Army changed all that.

Misapprehensions of Foreign Observers

Westerners with no actual experience of what China was like before the People's Republic cannot possibly understand what the early reforms meant to the masses and the why the peasants, especially the younger ones, were willing not only to accept but to support changes that were begun before 1951, when I closed the Embassy to return to Canada.

It was in the villages around Nanking that I came into contact with the first reforms initiated by the new regime. I learned from some of the young men that they were participating in newly organized committees, and they enthusiastically showed me their new farm implements. They also talked about being supplied with chemical fertilizers, about the fact that students from the Agriculture Department of the University of Nanking visited them periodically, and about the soil samples the students took.

I had no knowledge of the extent to which Communist cadres had organized these peasants until one day, when driving through the streets of Nanking, I found traffic stopped at a main thoroughfare and a colourful parade passing. Our gate-keeper and I got out of the car to get a closer look. Peasants from seventy-two villages were marching through the city in a holiday style of celebration. Young people proudly carried white flags with the names of their particular villages, and there were hundreds of huge red flags. Many of the peasants, men and women, were beating side drums and paused occasionally to dance the new Yang-ko.

The gate-keeper suddenly started jumping up and down and shouting: "There goes my wife!" She was carrying a flag, and he explained that she was a member of one of their new village committees. Apparently, Red Army troops had helped bring in the harvest for no pay, not even food, so that it had not been necessary for him to go home to help, for which his wife was grateful.

I had often witnessed peasant pilgrimages, but never had I seen them given the right of way on a main thoroughfare for a celebration of any kind.

The interest that students were beginning to take in the community came as no surprise to me. Several of my Chinese friends' daughters, after a few months' training, had become completely involved in constructive activities. Whenever they visited me, they were so enthusiastic about their work that they could talk of nothing else, and their involvement was the key to the tremendous release of energy that was generated after the fall of Nanking.

In the rural areas, the end of the war meant that defeated Nationalist troops who were not incorporated into the People's Liberation Army could return home. In the past, disbanded troops became brigands who swelled the numbers of robber bands already preying on the people. A large proportion of the manpower that should have been used for producing food was diverted to building mud walls in the attempt to keep out the predators. Watch towers had to be built and manned every night. The People's Liberation Army not only relieved the peasants of all the defence work, but worked in the fields too.

An important reform started very early was freeing urban and rural people from constant harassment by organized, parasitic gangs. In cities and villages throughout China, beggar gangs had made demands upon restaurants for food, merchants for goods, and the public for donations. Children had sometimes been mutilated to appeal for help. Men with boils, sores, or contagious diseases sat in crowds to prevent customers from entering establishments whose proprietors refused payment of regular alms.

Yellow Ox

A more modern parasitic organization, the Yellow Ox gang, had operated anywhere tickets were sold for admission to theatres or for railway transportation, sometimes cooperating with ticket sellers on the inside. In some port cities, underground gangster groups had paid employees in foreign concessions to keep silent about their vicious activities.

Money-lenders

Almost as vicious as the completely parasitic organizations, were the money lenders. The Chinese peasants had been, during the Imperial days of China, the victims of unscrupulous money-lenders whose exorbitant interest rates forced many peasant tenants to become itinerant beggars.

War lord's taxes

In addition, during the war-lord period, a new scheme of taxation was enforced. After current taxes were paid, the war lord suddenly discovered that to defend the area against invading brigands (the term used for the enemy war lord's troops), an emergency had arisen which necessitated the collection of next year's taxes immediately. The peasants were given the alternative of either paying next year's taxes or accepting the looting, raping, burning, and destruction for which troops were notorious. The peasants paid. There were times when they had been forced to pay several years' taxes in advance. The following year, however, the war lord started again to collect current taxes first and then future taxes as before. Not only the war lords, but even some of Chiang Kai-shek's Army generals, with whom they were frequently allied, were not above this type of extortion.

Distribution of land

A very important reform was the distribution of land to the peasants. A great deal of misinformation was published about this reform measure as a result of the treatment of the former landlords. Many landlords were put to death in many parts of China, not because they were landlords, but in retribution for crimes committed by them, including, in some cases, brutal murders. In parts of China where landlords were relatively benevolent, they were given exactly the same treatment in land distribution as the peasants. In the area where I was born and brought up, northeastern Hupeh, the landlords suffered no atrocities. One of my boyhood friends, who lived in Nanking, was requested by his landlord father to return to his ancestral home, which he had left many years before, when land was distributed according to the number of members in the family. My friend went home, and as a result, the landlord's family received more land. Distribution of land was a prelude to collective farms and ultimately to the communes of today, which have been an important factor in the solution of the food problem.

Rice

Under Nationalist control, the price of rice fluctuated, not as the result of market demand, but entirely for the profit of the private rice corporations. During the harvest season, when the peasants had to sell to repay loans at excessively high interest rates from money-lenders, the price of rice fell. As soon as private dealers had secured the crop, up went the price. In China, there is a limit to the length of time rice can be stored, and prices remained at such extremely high prices that much of the rice rotted. When I arrived in Chungking in 1945, there was a famine in parts of Hunan, a rice-producing area. Reports came to Chungking that rice in bins controlled by Army generals was rotting and that prices were too high, but it paid to sell at the highest rate, even if a portion rotted in storage, since total profits were greater.

Following liberation, prices were stabilized.

In all areas controlled by the Communists, including newly liberated areas, prices remained at the same level in and between harvest seasons.

When the Americans pulled out of China, it was predicted that the Chinese would, within six weeks, beg for ECA (Economic Cooperation Administration) rice, which had been generously distributed by the United States. That did not happen. As a result of the stabilization of prices, all rice produced in China was distributed, and enough surplus was saved to exchange for rubber from Ceylon. This reform achievement alone won for the new regime the gratitude and support from the peasants of the rice growing areas of China, involving as it did the most basic food of central and south China.

Canals

The first task undertaken by the People's Liberation Army in Nanking was the cleaning out of all the many canals—for the first time since the Ming Dynasty probably. Where the water was deep, thousands of troops used small boats, and where it was shallow, they waded in to shovel out the purple, almost black muck. Thousands of peasants from seventy-two villages around Nanking eagerly carried away the muck to fertilize their fields and gardens. In a matter of weeks, the canals of the city and the moats outside the city walls were filled with clean water.

Public nuisance

Simultaneously with this work, a campaign was organized by young people throughout the city to end the dirty habit of men and boys urinating, publicly, in back alleys or street corners and voiding excrement in any convenient place. The back alleys of every Chinese city stank to high heaven, and when walking in out-of-the-way places or near walls, one often had to step gingerly.

Early one forenoon, on my way to the new Municipal headquarters, I noticed in the middle of a street intersection a gaily dressed group of teen-age boys and girls dancing the Yang-ko, a new, very popular dancing step, while beating side drums carried at the waist. A crowd gathered quickly. One young man got up on a box and began the recitation of a rhyme, the rhythm of which was punctuated by the clickety-clack of two flat pieces of bamboo in his hand. The subject matter was the committing of "public nuisance" in the street not being in the interests of the "people." The rhyme was delivered with all the attention-attracting technique of Chinese story-tellers. The whole performance concluded with a formal speech about the iniquity of urinating and defecating in the streets, when there were places for such conveniences in the toilets provided by farmers who collected night soil to fertilize gardens or fields. More public and more modern places were, he said, being erected to make unnecessary and inexcusable the offensive practice of "public nuisance." The speech ended with a warning that, after ten days of campaigning to give everyone a chance to learn how detrimental to public health this revolting practice was, there would be fines for one or two offences and then, if necessary, a jail sentence.

There were similar performances in each section of the city, and each team moved on to another section every half day. The campaign worked. When it was over, one could walk anywhere in Chinese cities. The air was wholesome, except, of course, in the country near night soil cisterns, where night soil was collected, processed, and stored for fertilizing gardens and field crops.

More important than canals and nuisances were the stabilization of prices, especially rice, and the end of disastrous inflation. When the new "jen min pi," people's currency, was issued and proved stable, the new regime won universal approval. These reforms were carried out in an astonishingly short period of time.

Before I left, I saw reforms which I did not expect would be introduced during my lifetime. Having seen the instigation of completely unexpected, bold, fundamental reforms capable of transforming feudal China into a more modern civilization, I was hoping to have an opportunity some day to return to see if it was really genuine or, like so many previous attempts, merely transitory. Could the Chinese bring these initial changes to fruition without foreign aid? Except for a loan from the Soviet Union, entirely too small for China's needs, no foreign aid seemed to be forthcoming.

February 28, 1950. . . . The British have gone to Peking. The Americans have gone home. Only the Dutch, French, Italians, and Egyptians are left here with the Australians and Canadians.

Just as I was writing that sentence I heard some tremendous explosions, rushed to the door, and saw great clouds of debris rising from one side of the power plant. It is a daily occurrence. We had a raid at 4 A.M. today.

Just as I came back into the office, I got a telegram from External saying that you have informed them Father is very ill and is not expected to live. Other members of family have all been called home. External adds that a further message from them will follow.

Although your letter had prepared me, it is a stunning blow—especially as I am trapped here and do not know what I can do. No transportation is available. It would take two weeks to Canton and Hong Kong, even if the local authorities granted me permission to go. And before I could leave, I would have to advertise in the Nanking papers and apply for an exit permit, which takes at least two weeks. All I can do now is to wait for External's second telegram and see what plans they have. Then I shall have to explore every possibility and press hard for permission to leave and try to find some means of getting out.

March 17. . . . My plans for the next few months all depend upon decisions reached in Ottawa. It is impossible for me to get away now before recognition. I shall have to stay to perform the task the Government has assigned to me of negotiating the estab-

lishment of diplomatic relations and supervising the move to Peking. Then I shall be free to return.

April 12. . . . . After the arrival here of MIG jet fighters from the Soviet Union, air raids have finally stopped. What a relief! We have been bombed from the air for over ten months—sometimes as many as five raids a day. This morning, we had an air-raid alarm warning, but the enemy planes didn't arrive, and it was said the MIGs got them before they got as far as Nanking.

July 29. . . . . I have just been for a tour of inspection around the compound. Our trees, shrubs, flowers, and particularly the bamboos are all doing wonderfully well. We have the finest park in Nanking.

Until a few days ago, we had been confined within the walls of Nanking for a year and a half. Now we may go to the Sun Yat-sen Park, Lotus Lake, and the railway station. It is like being let out of prison. We have looked at Purple Mountain from inside the walls, but kept at a distance for long months.

I may go to Shanghai for a few days next week to meet Dr. Pannikar, who will be visiting there for a few days. I have not seen him since he became the new Ambassador to the People's Government, and am most anxious to exchange views with him.

These are the hot days in Nanking, but with our small air-conditioners it is not too intolerable.

To keep myself busy during the past months, I collected snuff bottles and a few other things. I have about eighty snuff bottles—no two alike. I also picked up a few pieces of Han ceremonial jade and am starting to appreciate some of this stone's wonderful qualities and colours. A few days ago, I acquired a really old piece of Han—about 2,000 years or more. It is a jade mortuary pig with brownish colouring in the most unusual carving. The artist cut the hard jade as if it were green cheese. It is marvellous. It is a very rare specimen which I can leave to my children and grandchildren down through the ages. You have to see it to appreciate it.

September 7. . . . Last week, the house of the Egyptian Chargé was entered by three armed men after midnight. The Chargé refused to open his safe and fought with them. He was stabbed in the lung, but succeeded in frightening the robbers off. He has been in the hospital ever since, but is gradually improving. He was foolish in not having a night watchman in the first place and in fighting with the men in the second place.

October 13. . . . The news from Korea seemed for a while to indicate that the fighting would soon terminate, and my hopes for your trip out here by Christmas were revived. With the crossing of the 38th Parallel, however, the day of peace seems again to be postponed, and it is impossible for me to make any recommendations yet.

November 22. . . . For the first time in my life, I have had to take a driving test—our chauffeur, Lao Chiang, was too old to get a driver's licence from the new regime. I use the car very little, so I decided not to get a new chauffeur but to drive myself. It took two whole days of testing. First, I had a physical examination. My eyes were perfect. My height was so great that their measuring apparatus was not high enough. My lungs and ears passed 100 per cent, and my grip was three times that of average Chinese applicants. Then came the oral tests in road regulations and automobile mechanics. Next day came the driving test. First I had to drive a jeep (with my knees up to my chin) forward and backwards through stakes without using the clutch or brake, and the throttle was geared to a pretty fast pace. I made it, but they would not believe I had been a driver for thirty-five years. Most of the applicants failed this test. Then came a road test

through the streets of Nanking. I drove through Fu-tzu Miao, and the next day curio dealers came to ask if I had been arrested, as they saw me in an official jeep with Communist officials. Now I have a bright yellow booklet permitting me to operate a car. Only one Frenchman out of five passed.

January 24, 1951. . . . Ottawa has requested me to close the Canadian Embassy and return to Canada. I therefore made application to the local authorities eleven days ago for permission to advertise in the local press, but permission has not as yet been granted. After that, ten days must elapse before the application for a travel permit to Canton can be considered. If approved, an exit permit may be issued in Canton after arrival and customs inspection there.

This will be the fourth time I have left China, and each time has been more or less associated with the most important events in China's recent history.

The first time was just as the Boxer Rebellion was breaking out. The second was prior to the revolution that established the Republic. The third was at the climax of the "Great Revolution." The fourth is during the period when the new People's Republic is in conflict with the United Nations in Korea. The dates: 1899, 1907, 1927, and 1951. It has just occurred to me that each stay here has been six years—nearly a quarter of a century altogether.

While I am overjoyed to be coming home to you, I leave here with a heavy heart, because I have not been able to accomplish that for which I have been working and waiting all this time—recognition of the real Government of China.

11

LAST
DAYS
IN CHINA

Jim Staines, my administrative assistant, and I were the only Canadians left in Nanking.

It became necessary to reduce the size of the Embassy compound, which was composed of two areas, an upper portion and a lower one, connected by a narrower strip of land. The upper portion had been intended for a Chancery and Ambassador's Residence. We decided, using the bamboo fence around the upper part as material, to fence off the lower, larger area, consisting of three prefabricated Canadian lumber houses for officers and a number of brick buildings for other purposes.

We arranged to have a large enough crew of workers to complete the job in one day, as it was essential to have a fence surrounding the buildings to prevent anyone from infiltrating the premises at night.

Soon after the fence around the upper compound came down, the people of the district started to move in to cut the grass for fuel. We could hardly protest. Removing the fence was an invitation to the needy to help themselves. Armed with axes and hoes, hundreds of people cut down every tree and shrub and dug out the roots. Since we were abandoning the land, it was perfectly legitimate to denude it of everything which would burn when it was dried. The mountains of China, except in the roughest terrain far from human habitation, were naked due to a never-ending onslaught like the one to which our compound was being submitted.

Near riot

For lunch that day, Percy North, a British Foreign Service officer, left in charge of the former British Embassy in Nanking, was my guest in the pleasant dining room of the centre prefab. All of a sudden, the cook burst in, shouting that the mob had invaded the main compound and was cutting down all the vegetation. I rushed out, but they were too busy to pay any attention to me—until some of their assistants who were carrying the stuff away noticed me. They tapped their relatives on the back:

"The foreigner is trying to say something to us."

Gradually, it became quiet enough for me to explain that, since we had not objected to letting them have everything in the area which we were abandoning, would it not be fair for them to let us keep the grass, flowers, shrubs, and trees in the area we were keeping? They were in a good mood and said: "*Pu-ts'o, pu-ts'o,*" not wrong, not wrong. Many of them were from nearby and knew me. They persuaded the rest to walk out politely. I was not too surprised, knowing their respect for what they called *chiang-li,* speak reason.

The excitement died down, and the new rush fence was being erected before the day ended. Jim and I remained outside, however, as a deterrent. Later, as it was getting dusk, some ruffians, not from the neighbourhood, began helping themselves to the old bamboo fence. The crowd became a mob and began taking the bamboo away from the workmen, trampling a neighbour's vegetable garden in the process. The new fence was completed shortly after dark, and the mob was becoming nasty. A few men started tearing down the new fence. I would have been unable to stop them if the neighbouring gardener and other neighbouring friends had not threatened to call the police. It helped when I called out to our neighbour that I would pay for the damage to his garden. The crisis passed, except for sporadic minor attempts to break through the newly-built fence when it became too dark to identify the marauders. Jim and I stayed up all night patrolling the fence. Only at dawn was quiet finally restored.

Early in the morning, Mr. Ch'en, who was to be our custodian, prepared a written report to the Foreign National Bureau giving full details of the affair. I asked him to add a final paragraph requesting police protection, especially at night. I carried it to the Chief of the Bureau. At his office, I was escorted by an attendant to an inner waiting room. After the usual wait, a young officer with whom I had dealt many times walked in, and I handed him the report. He accepted it, but did not open it. Instead, he suddenly accused me of having started a serious riot at the Canadian Embassy.

I am not easily riled, but to be accused of doing what, with the help of our Chinese staff and neighbours, I had stopped took me off guard. I blew up.

The young chap looked surprised. He walked quietly out of the room, and I paced around the room trying to recover control of the beast within. I finally sat down, still trembling. It was more than an hour before he returned, preceded along the corridor by a very dark man. My friend came in to the waiting room and announced that the new Chief would receive me shortly—he would let me know when.

I was escorted to a room I had not been in before and was asked to sit in a chair facing a low platform on which sat four young women, two at each of two desks. They were apparently secretaries, as they started writing when the Chief stood up and talked. He charged me with having deliberately incited a riot and disturbed the peace. I immediately stood up and protested that the accusation was false. He requested me to be seated and said I would have a chance to talk as soon as he had finished.

It was obvious the man was new at his job. He read the accusation in a subdued tone of voice and hesitated over a few of the more complicated phrases. He then gave me the floor.

After saying that I could not accept the statement, I explained the whole incident in detail and pointed out how ridiculous it would be for me to start a riot. Canada had been negotiating to recognize the People's Republic of China and to establish diplomatic relations with Peking. In fact, that had been my job, and I had been in communication with Prime Minister Chou En-lai for that purpose. I had even rented a house in Peking. The war in Korea had held things up temporarily, but Canada would continue to give consideration to recognizing China in due course. I added that, if he did not send troops or police to protect the premises of the Canadian Embassy, I would report the previous night's near riot to Chou En-lai, who would certainly be disturbed if the Chief of the Foreign Nationals Bureau in Nanking failed in his duty to prevent an incident which might damage the possibility of the restoration of international relations. In conclusion, I demanded that the charges against me be dropped and repeated my demand for immediate police protection.

The Chief talked in whispers to some of his officers who knew me and announced: "You may go now."

I replied: "I shall not leave this room until you inform me that there will be police tonight to prevent a real riot."

He repeated: "You may go home."

I repeated: "Not until you say the Canadian Embassy premises will be protected."

"But," he corrected, "it is the former Canadian Embassy."

"Yes," I replied, "it is the former Canadian Embassy, but the premises are still occupied by Canada's Chargé, and Chou En-lai has not requested me to vacate the premises."

This went on for some time. Finally, after further consultations with his staff, he said: "You may return to the former Canadian Embassy now. I have sent troops to protect the grounds and your safety."

I departed with thanks.

When I got home, the place was surrounded by police and troops.

Since Canada had not recognized the Government of the People's Republic of China, it became necessary in 1951 to close the Canadian Embassy in Nanking. Our translator, Mr. Ch'en, who was a Chinese scholar, was engaged to remain in the Embassy compound to take charge of the place pending sale or removal to Peking.

Oracle bones

In preparation for our departure, I was taking inventory. I suddenly found myself most unexpectedly in possession of perhaps the finest collection of oracle bones in existence at that time.

In the store-room we noticed a very large box, and I asked the head servant what it contained. It had come from Shanghai with a shipment of groceries. Inside, we found a tall cupboard with two rows of shallow drawers, each row held in place by an iron rod and padlocked at the top. We forced a lock, removed the bar, and opened a drawer. It was divided into small squares about 4″ × 4″, each of which was carefully covered by cotton batting. I removed one and to my astonishment recognized an oracle bone.

After the invention of written ideographs and long before the invention of paper, ancient Chinese used a metal stylus to write on the flat bones of animals—skulls, shoulder blades, and turtle backs. Bones upon which ideographs had been inscribed were cracked by heat and used for divination purposes to guide monarchs and potentates.

There is archaeological evidence of their historical existence in the Shang Dynasty prior to 1122 B.C. and prior to the recorded history of China.

I had never seen an oracle bone, but I had read everything that had been written about them and had seen photos. I knew that a collection had been made by Dr. Menzies, a scholarly Canadian missionary and father of Arthur Menzies, who became our High Commissioner in Australia. I assumed that, in some unexplained way, Dr. Menzies' collection had found its way to our store-room. Much later, I found out that Dr. Menzies' daughter had asked Ambassador Davis in Shanghai, before his return to Canada, to take her father's collection of oracle bones to Nanking and eventually to the University of Toronto.

The servants crowded eagerly around Mr. Ch'en and me, asking what the box really contained. Mr. Ch'en whispered to me in English that he simply could not assume responsibility for oracle bones. I immediately covered them up carefully, got a new padlock, replaced the iron rod, locked the cupboard, and nailed up the box. Before doing so, I suggested to the servants that they were probably medicine bones (which is actually what they are). Dr. Menzies had first seen them in an apothecary shop and made his collection from the same source when he learned where they had been found by the apothecary, who ground them up for medicine.

That evening, Mr. Ch'en repeated that he could not take over as custodian of our property unless I found some other place for the oracle bones. I consulted a few foreign friends who still remained in Nanking. They had never seen or heard of oracle bones and unanimously advised that I should destroy them by burning. I could not for a moment envisage such a solution, as I knew them to be invaluable for historical research work. My friends were more concerned about me than the bones and said that if the authorities found out that I had them, I would get into serious trouble, such as had befallen some Americans who had obtained valuable national treasures. The authorities would never believe that I had simply found them in an empty store-room.

The next day, I had a brain wave. I decided to entrust them to the Nanking National Museum until they could be sent to a university, where specialists could study them. That evening I called on a friend who was a scholar associated with the Nanking Museum, and he agreed to take them to the museum. The same evening, I delivered the bones to his tender care, asking him, if possible, not to mention my name. The problem was, I thought, solved to my complete satisfaction.

A few days later, I was visited by two municipal policemen. They had called on me a number of times previously, and I assumed it was one of their occasional routine checks. They asked questions, and I answered. We talked all forenoon. At twelve o'clock, they finally suggested that I might wish to have lunch and that we could meet for further discussions at, say, one o'clock. I agreed.

We met at one. They then asked if I had not given some valuable curios to my friends. "No," I replied. "I do not have any really valuable curios." In fact, the closest thing I had to a valuable curio was a small Chinese brush-holder. I showed it to them on my desk in front of us. I turned it over to let them see the stamp, which indicated that it had been made in the first year of the Hung Hsien Dynasty. (President Yuan Shih-k'ai had ordered the old Imperial kilns at Ching Teh Chen near Kuikiang to manufacture a great quantity of porcelain to commemorate the first year of his reign as Emperor of the Chinese Empire in 1915 before he passed away.)

The police seemed neither to care about my precious, if humble, brush-holder nor to be interested in the Hung Hsien Dynasty.

The policemen continued to insist that I had given my friends curios, and the conversation went round and round in circles, always coming back again to the same topic. I finally said: "I haven't given away a single thing since Christmas."

"And what did you give away at Christmas?"

"Oh, some cheap things I picked up near the Confucius Temple."

"What kind of things?"

"Just some of those cheap trinkets—you know, the things merchants sell to unwary foreigners."

The police promptly asked me to make a list of every item I had purchased and a list of each recipient. By this time, it was again time to eat. They said they would return the next day to collect the list.

The next morning, when I arrived at the office, Tessie Wang, our receptionist, said: "Do you know what the police were after yesterday?"

"No," I replied. "I certainly do not."

"They must have been after the oracle bones," she said.

I protested and said: "But they asked about '*ku-tung*,' ancient things. If they were after the oracle bones, why did they not say '*chia-ku*,' oracle bones?"

"They have never even heard of that name," she said. "Only scholars like Mr. Ch'en know it."

I decided she had put her finger on it. I had completely blocked out the possibility that the police were enquiring about oracle bones. For me, that problem had been solved. Realizing my mistake, I immediately went to my learned friend's home. He was not there. His wife was frightened and informed me that he was at the police station. I rushed to the station to find he was being interrogated, and I asked to join him. When asked what I knew about the oracle bones, I related the story exactly as it happened, explaining that when the police called, I had no idea what they were really enquiring about.

I was then cross-questioned as to how many oracle bones there were. I did not know. I had opened only one drawer. They asked me how much they weighed. I did not know. How many had I kept? None. This continued until my friend finally said: "Why don't you let him go? He has told you exactly what happened as I did. Let him go home. Friends told him to destroy them, but knowing their value, he asked me to give them to the National Museum for the use of Chinese scholars."

The investigation finally came to an end.

On the morning of the day we were leaving by rail for Shanghai and Canton to return to Canada, Jim Staines and I went to the railway station at 6 A.M. to clear our trunks and suitcases for on-ward transportation. We had made an appointment with the police for inspection. One of them received us politely and started to go through our baggage. He first inspected every article in my trunks and took out a few. He held up one and asked: "What is this?"

"That is a snuff bottle."

"What actually is a snuff bottle?"

I explained that no snuff bottles in China were over 300 years old and could not therefore be considered ancient curios. He nevertheless put my snuff bottles aside, together with a few other articles. He also went through Jim's stuff and set aside a few old *chops* used to imprint private or firm names in ink on documents. Since it was now almost noon and I was getting hungry, I said: "What is troubling you? Can't you see they are just things curio dealers sell to unwary foreigners?"

He paid no attention and requested us to accompany him. He took our junk along in two small baskets. We were then escorted to a private room in the police station and asked to sit down and wait for the Curator of the National Museum. We waited until 3:30 P.M.

The Curator was dressed in an old-fashioned gown, wore old style glasses with very thick lenses, and had a cute, scraggy little Fu Manchu moustache. He bent over to within six inches of my snuff bottles, gave them a quick, passing glance, and exclaimed rather severely to the policeman. "There is nothing here over three hundred years old. These are not national treasures."

The policeman asked: "But what are these things?"

"Snuff bottles."

"Actually what are snuff bottles?"

The Curator impatiently explained what they were. He bent lower to inspect Jim's *chops* and ash trays, then scolded the police-man: "Can't you see that these are only the kind of things curio dealers job off on foreigners?"

I decided not to give in to my instinct.

In Shanghai, station police again went through our baggage, but they were better informed about snuff bottles and stuff for foreigners.

After travelling another night, we arrived in Canton, where our baggage was again meticulously inspected, this time by two eager young men who had very recently been appointed and were eager to prove themselves. They confiscated everything they thought looked at all suspicious, including all the transparencies I had taken on a long journey through Africa and India, all of the ones taken in China over a period of six years, and . . . Jim's collection of *chops*. I had obtained permission from the Nanking police to take my shot-gun out of the country. When the two young police officers found it, we were escorted to the police station. Jim was ordered to sit down near the exit door guarded by a soldier with a tommy-gun. I was conducted to a counter, behind which sat a young policeman, who seemed to be in charge. He began: "Have you a licence to take out these things?"

"Only for the shot-gun," I replied.

"What about these things and the gold glasses you are wearing and the ring on your finger?"

"I was not required by the Nanking police to have a licence for anything but the gun."

"Are you accusing the Nanking police of failing to carry out their duties?"

"I am not. I am merely saying that I was not required to have a licence for anything but the shot-gun."

"Then you do accuse the Nanking police of failing to require the necessary licence from you to take these things out of the country."

"No, I am making no formal accusations against anyone. The only thing I had to obtain to take my things out of China was a statement by a guarantor that all the things which I am taking out of China are my own possessions. This is the bank's guarantee." I handed it to him.

"Why did you not give me this when I asked you for it?"

"You asked for a licence to take out my glasses, watch, and ring. You said nothing about a guarantee of possession of goods."

He made no comment, but said authoritatively: "I order you to go to the Licence Bureau to get one to take gold out of China and return here this afternoon promptly." I consented and said: "My friend and I will carry out your orders. What is the address of the Bureau, please?"

"You speak Chinese. Find out."

I protested: "Unfortunately, I do not speak Cantonese, and the rickshaw men do not understand mandarin."

"That is your bad fortune. You are both dismissed."

Jim did not know what it was all about and was pale as a sheet. No wonder. The guard let the tommy-gun slope towards him.

I then said: "You are putting us in an extremely difficult position. We have permission to stay in Canton only until six o'clock tomorrow morning, when our train leaves for Shen Chuan on the border. I cannot leave without a licence for my watch, ring, and glasses. I do not know where the Licence Bureau is." He made no comment, but added, "Your gun will have to be wrapped in strong paper and sealed before you are allowed to have it."

We went out. I found two rickshaws and asked Jim to stay with them. I ran to the nearest open shop and asked if anyone spoke mandarin. Fortunately, one man understood a little. I asked him to tell our rickshaw men we wanted to go to the Licence Bureau. He did, and off we went.

When we arrived, I made signs to the rickshaw men to wait. The Bureau, however, was closed. An armed guard of the People's Liberation Army stood by the locked door. I asked if he would let me in. He smiled and said in a strong Shantung accent: "You are from the North."

"Yes," I said, "and I have just arrived. These people do not understand me very well."

He immediately conducted us to the back door.

Inside, he called out in a loud voice: "Here are two men from the North in trouble. They have to have a licence for something and get back to the police station. You must, with the speed of a horse, help them."

A clerk asked me what the problem was. When I explained, he told the guard that licences had to be stamped to be valid and that the boss had gone home. The necessary *chops* were in a locked cupboard. The guard said: "Send someone on a bicycle to get the keys." The clerk sent a young chap to fetch the key. The licence blanks were properly filled in describing our things. While we were waiting, I persuaded the guard to take me to a shop where I could purchase a large piece of tough paper and some twine. Everyone worked at top speed. In fact, one of the young men thought it was "lots of fun."

The rickshaw men were told by the guard to take us to the police station with the speed of horses. They didn't understand a word he said, but they did read his hand signs.

The police station was still open. Maybe police stations always are. The man in charge was still there and must have been most disagreeably surprised to see that we had secured duly stamped licences. He had probably deliberately kept us until he knew it was too late for us to get to the bureau on time.

At 6 A.M. the next day, we were headed for the border.

We arrived at Shen Chuan, the rail terminal, across the international border from British "New Territories," and found ourselves nearly at the end of a long line-up of hundreds of Chinese who had been wise enough to get out in a hurry as soon as the train stopped. We were carrying all our baggage except the trunks. The line moved very slowly, but we eventually got to the counter, identified our trunks quickly, and caught the attention of an officer who spoke mandarin. He cleared our baggage after opening only one suitcase, and off we went to the bridge across the stream separating China from Chinese territory leased to Great Britain. I got our exit permits stamped. Jim followed me as fast as we could carry our luggage to the little three-foot-wide gate in the barrier across the end of the bridge. The guard examined my exit permit. He was still doing so when I heard heavy footsteps behind me. All of a sudden, someone held me firmly by both shoulders. I turned around and saw several troops. They escorted us back, after I had retrieved my exit permit, to an almost empty house, in which there was a long narrow table and one light bulb suspended from the ceiling. For the third time, Jim Staines was seated under the surveillance of a tommy-gun guard.

I asked why we were brought back. There was no reply. Two men started searching me carefully from head to toe, and I realized they were looking for oracle bones.

When I had been thoroughly searched, I commented to the two searchers: "I know you cannot answer, because you may not be too certain what you are looking for, but it may be that someone thinks I am carrying 'oracle bones.' You have done your duty, and I understand you must carry out your orders. I want to assure you, nevertheless, that I have no oracle bones, and I am glad that they are all safe and are in the National Museum in Nanking. I wish the scholars who will study them every success. Visit the museum in Nanking some time, and you will see what you have been looking for."

To my surprise, one of them said: "We hope you are not offended. We had to carry out our instructions. Someone accused the Customs man who passed your baggage of being too lax. We wish you favourable winds on your journey and hope you will return to China."

When we got to the bridge gate the second time, escorted by the two gentlemen who had searched me, the guard was instructed to open the gate. I learned that I had been searched by two of the higher Customs officials.

On the other side of the bridge, the British guards were still waiting for us. They had been notified by our Trade Commissioner in Hong Kong that we were coming. They had already held up the train for half an hour when they saw us being taken back. Nearly another hour had passed before we returned. The train was still waiting. The British guards insisted on taking us into a small guardroom to serve us hot coffee. They saw we needed it and told us not to hurry. They said the train had waited so long it could wait a little longer.

In Hong Kong, at the Gloucester Hotel, I stayed in bed for five days to recuperate from a cold and also to think things over. I did not want my personal inconveniences to prejudice my analysis of the tremendous changes that had begun to take place in China.

At midnight on May 24, after a visit to Hanoi and to Saigon to see my daughter Audrey, Seymour Topping, and my grand-daughter Susan, I left Hong Kong.

12

RECOGNITION
OF THE PEOPLE'S
REPUBLIC OF CHINA
THE CANADIAN EXPERIENCE

In January 1949, Chiang Kai-shek invited the foreign diplomatic corps in Nanking to accompany his fleeing Government to Canton. Aircraft for the move were offered to the personnel of all foreign embassies and legations.

Canada decided, without hesitation, not to accept the invitation. I took Ottawa's reply to the Foreign Office. As I walked up the steps of the main entrance of the old Waichiaopu building, whom should I meet coming out but General Roshchin, the Soviet Ambassador. When I remarked that he had been even more eager than I to reject the invitation, he said dejectedly that he had been ordered to accept and planned to leave for Canton immediately. General Roshin knew there was not the slightest possibility of the Nationalist Armies regrouping to resist the advance of the Red Army troops and that it was inevitable that a new Government would be established before long.

It was significant that the only ambassador of an important power in Nanking to decamp with the Nationalists was the Ambassador of the Soviet Union. Even the United States Ambassador, the Reverend Leighton Stuart, remained.

The Soviet Union had virtually given up the Communist Party

of China in 1927 and had not raised a finger to help the Communists during the Civil War, except for some Japanese small arms and ammunition which the Soviet Army left behind in Manchuria when it marched home. The Russians denuded Manchuria of everything really valuable in industrial and military equipment before their evacuation.

The Soviet Union had not even helped the Chinese Communists in their fight against the Japanese. Assistance was given only to Chiang Kai-shek, who used it against the Communists. In return, the Nationalists made important concessions to the Soviet Union in Manchuria.

This information was first given to me by Mr. Tung Pi-wu and Mr. Chang Han-fu when I flew with them over the "hump" in 1945. Mr. Tung said at the time that if and when the Communists established a Government in China, they would nullify the concessions made to the Soviet Union by the Nationalists. The Chinese Communists had accepted no important advice from Moscow after 1927.

When General Roshchin left for Canton with the Nationalists, it was probably because the Soviet Union was anxious to see a Nationalist Government set up in the South to challenge the Communist Government which they expected would be established in the North. The Russians must have reasoned that, to win the Civil War, the North would have to become dependent on the Soviet Union.

In 1949, the People's Liberation Army defied Soviet advice and crossed the Yangtse to take Nanking and Shanghai.

The US State Department's analysis, nonetheless, when the Government of the People's Republic of China was established in October 1949, was that the new Government *was* a puppet of the Soviet Union and that it should not be recognized because it could not last. The Soviet Union, on the other hand, was quick to reverse its position and recognize the new Government.

Nanking was liberated in April 1949 and Shanghai a month later, but the new Government was not organized until October, when the whole of continental China was under its control. Foreign representatives in Shanghai did not wait for the announcement of a new government, but tried immediately to get *de facto* recognition for their consulates, thereby hoping to postpone as long as possible the necessity for *de jure* recognition while reaping the benefits of the continuation of their consulates. The Chinese, however, would accept nothing short of *de jure* recognition.

Policy differences between the United Kingdom and the United States occurred early and continued to grow, especially in Shanghai, where conditions had deteriorated as a result of a Nationalist blockade of Shanghai's harbour. The United States tended towards withdrawal from, and isolation of, China, while the British, with heavy vested interests there, were anxious to work out a *modus vivendi*.

On the question of the Shanghai blockade, the State Department feared that American and British private enterprise in the city would, if left alone, cooperate with the Communists and deprive the US government of bargaining power. The State Department, for example, pressed Northwest Airlines to stop negotiations for international service in any areas controlled by the Communists on the grounds of not assisting a hostile regime.

The United States had no intention of breaking the blockade to please the British, while the UK emphasized the importance of the shipment of supplies rather than evacuation. The British, in fact, hoped that the Chinese Communists would capture the offshore islands to break the blockade, but the Nationalists thwarted every attempt at circumvention and insisted on searching every ship for forbidden cargo.

In August, Mr. Davis and I interviewed Mr. Huang Hua, Director of the Foreign Nationals Bureau in Nanking. He anticipated the creation of a government in the near future that would welcome recognition on the basis of friendship, equality, and withdrawal of recognition from the Nationalists. Mr. Huang charged that the blockade of Shanghai was supported by the United States as a way of weakening China and endangering the new movement, but he said that China could get along despite the blockade. He then added that China had plans to industrialize and therefore needed foreign trade to make China a strong, independent, and prosperous nation.

On October 1, 1949, the Director of the Foreign Nationals Bureau summoned the members of the diplomatic corps in Nanking. He announced the organization of the Central Government of the People's Republic of China in Peking and requested the representatives of all foreign powers in China to invite their respective Governments to recognize the Government in Peking and to establish diplomatic relations with the People's Republic of China. The speech was in Chinese, and no interpretation was given.

Chinese Foreign Service Officers had always conducted business with foreign diplomats in English or French—the two diplomatic languages, but Huang was making it clear that the Chinese finally had enough confidence in themselves to use their own language in their own country. However, I did expect Huang to interpret what he had said into English. (After all, he was a graduate of Yenching University, and all graduates of Yenching spoke English.) But the Director of the Foreign Nationals Bureau waited in silence after his announcement.

The ice was finally broken by Mr. Keith Officer, the Australian Ambassador. He stood up and said in English that, except for the Canadian representative, the members of the diplomatic corps had not understood what the Director had said and asked if the Canadian representative might be allowed to act as interpreter. I translated Mr. Officer's request. The Director replied in Chinese that I could act as the interpreter, and I did. Huang and I have frequently exchanged reminiscences about that occasion.

The organ which brought the People's Central Government of the People's Republic of China into being was the People's

Political Consultative Council, "comprised of delegates of all the democratic parties of China, all People's Bodies, the People's Liberation Armies, various Regions, various Tribes, overseas Chinese, and other Patriots and Democratic elements" which met and elected Mao Tse-tung Chairman of the Government. The People's Political Council announced the establishment of the People's Republic of China, and selected Peking as the capital of China.

In China, it was frequently said that Peking, meaning "Northern Capital," was the capital when China had a strong government and that Nanking, meaning "Southern Capital," was the capital when China's government was weak. For example, after the death of the first Ming Emperor, who was buried in Nanking, the Ming Dynasty moved to Peking to indicate the power of the new Dynasty. The subsequent thirteen Ming Emperors were all buried near Peking.

The Manchu Dynasty retained Peking as their capital. When Chiang Kai-shek seized power in 1927, he chose Nanking as his capital. The name of Peking was then changed to Peiping, Northern Peace, to indicate that there was only one capital in China—Nanking. Countries opposed to the recognition of the People's Republic of China continued to call the capital of China Peiping, although the new regime changed China's capital back to Peking. The deliberate refusal to accept the name of the capital as decided by the Government in power was no doubt due to the hope that Chiang Kai-shek would return to Nanking and that China would be brought back into the fold of the "Free World."

With the establishment of the new Central Government, the right of communication with our governments by code and cypher, which had been withdrawn, was now restored, and my recommendation to Ottawa was that the new Government should be recognized. The Government of the People's Republic of China was in control of all mainland China, thus fulfilling the accepted international criterion for recognition.

When I received a reply that the Canadian Government was consulting other Commonwealth governments, I urged an early decision, because I felt that the benefits of recognition and the establishment of diplomatic relations would diminish inversely as the square of the length of the time taken to reach a decision.

In November, India announced her decision to recognize Peking as soon as all Commonwealth representatives in India had been consulted. India was not allowing any fear of curtailment of United States aid to decide her foreign policy. She would naturally consult with other countries, but the decision would be hers and the time would be determined by her. There was no doubt in the minds of Indians that the new regime in China was well established, stable, and likely to endure. (India decided that the proper time for recognition should be soon after the conclusion of the United Nations General Assembly—between December 15 and 25, 1949.)

Canada had hoped that India would have deferred the decision to recognize China until after Commonwealth members had discussed the matter during their meeting in Colombo to consider a plan to aid developing countries. Canada, however, fully understood India's reason for not waiting until January 1950.

India recognized the Government of the People's Republic of China on December 26, 1949, Pakistan on January 4, 1950, the United Kingdom on January 6, 1950. Canada deferred a decision until after the Colombo Conference. Nevertheless, I received authority from Ottawa in January to rent a house in Peking for the Canadian Embassy, and I promptly carried out my instructions. It was necessary for us to rent a house because, unlike the United Kingdom, Canada had never had a diplomatic mission in Peking. Canada's first Embassy in China was in the wartime capital, Chungking.

After the Colombo Plan Conference, when Mr. Lester Pearson returned to Canada via Hong Kong, he tried to contact me by telephone in Nanking, as previously planned, to give me instructions regarding recognition. He did not get through, and the question was temporarily postponed. In any case, the earliest date suggested as possible was the end of January.

On January 16, 1950, the Danish Government announced that it had accorded *de jure* recognition to the Government of the People's Republic of China. I was becoming convinced that the continued recognition by the United States of a regime that had been thrown out of China was exhausting the fund of friendship that had existed in China for Western nations, especially the United States, which had been the most popular foreign power. Because Chiang Kai-shek was still recognized, he could with impunity blockade China's coast and use American bombers to raid her cities.

In a letter to my father from Nanking on February 23, 1950, I wrote: "When you stand for months at the receiving end of bombs falling from aircraft sent by a corrupt and discredited regime and see the wanton destruction of life and property long after the civil war has ended on the mainland, you pray daily that the support which continued recognition gives to that regime will be withdrawn."

Such activity was having little effect on ultimate developments, but it did create ill-will for nations like Canada which continued to recognize Chiang's government. It also made it imperative for the Chinese to seek naval and air strength from the Soviet Union.

When Mao Tse-tung went to the Soviet Union for assistance, he returned from Moscow bringing back most inadequate aid for rehabilitation and industrialization. He received mostly promises for the future relinquishment of Soviet-controlled Manchurian railways and ports in Manchuria. The failure was a subject of much discussion and discontent in Nanking.

For the United States, the fear of Communism nonetheless became the determining factor in dealings with China, despite the latter's profound differences with the Soviet Union.

Public and Congressional opinion, which might have been

able to accept recognition during an earlier time—for example, when Leighton Stuart thought recognition might be the only practical policy, became crystallized against Peking through the myth of an international Communist hierarchy, headed by the Soviet Union, which supposedly won China for the Soviet Union and lost it for the United States.

By the publicity given to the Chinese seizure of United States Consular property in Peking, the United States elected to make it a major incident, and withdrawal of American representatives from China when the representatives of nearly all other Western powers remained in Nanking substantially increased the difficulty of preparing the way for eventual recognition.

The problem of Taiwan also influenced the United States position. Before the Nationalists moved to Taiwan, the island was considered by the United States not to be strategic. All of a sudden, however, Taiwan became strategic for the security of the United States in the Pacific. Taiwan was, of course, not vital to the United States, but it was thought to have the physical resources to hold out indefinitely if attacked by China. The doubtful factors were morale and political stability. Recognition of Peking would have had an adverse effect and was a reason for reluctance to recognize Peking.

When Mr. Pearson returned to Canada from Colombo in February 1950, the Canadian Government gave further consideration to the question of recognition of the Peking Government. No decision was reached, but there was general agreement that, unless there was a change of conditions, recognition should be accorded. It was thought possible that Canada would recognize Peking during the latter half of March.

By March 1950, America's China policy was having a considerable influence on Canada. Our decision was postponed from time to time, waiting for Peking to reciprocate the recognition that had been extended by the United Kingdom.

Peking had kept India waiting for almost exactly the same length of time it had taken India to recognize China—nearly three months. India's "negotiator" was then accepted as a

Chargé d'Affaires. The United Kingdom, however, was kept waiting for nearly four and a half years before Anthony Eden and Chou En-lai reached an agreement at the conclusion of the Korean Conference in Geneva in June 1954 to exchange Chargés d'Affaires.

In reply to the UK's note of January 6, 1950, recognizing Peking and expressing the desire to establish diplomatic relations, the Foreign Office in Peking stated that the Government of the People's Republic of China was willing to establish such relations with the UK on the basis of equality, mutual benefit, and mutual respect for territory and would accept Mr. J. C. Hutchinson as Chargé d'Affaires *ad interim* as representative of the United Kingdom, sent to Peking to "carry on negotiations on the question of the establishment of diplomatic relations between the two countries."

The United Kingdom's recognition had not resulted in full diplomatic relations for several reasons. One was that the UK had abstained, instead of voting for Peking, on motions in the General Assembly to change China's representation from Taipei to Peking. Another was that London overruled the Governor of Hong Kong's decision to turn over to Peking Chinese Nationalist aircraft in Hong Kong. The most important reason was that the United Kingdom was not considered to have fully broken off relations with the Nationalists in Taiwan, since the British maintained in Tamsui a *de facto* Consulate. In general, although the United Kingdom recognized China, it continued on many important issues to support the policy of the United States.

In June 1950, Anthony Eden was of the opinion that the United Kingdom's decision to recognize Peking was unfortunate, both in timing and method. It was thought by many in London that the United Kingdom should have kept more in step with partners in the Commonwealth and with the United States. Keeping in step with the United States was the very reason why full diplomatic relations with Peking had not been achieved by the United Kingdom. Without such relations, it was not possible to capitalize on the benefits that could have been derived from recognition. It is also true that diplomatic relations do not count for very much if the functioning policies are not mutually beneficial to both countries concerned.

The United Kingdom did keep step with two of its Commonwealth partners in recognizing Peking, India, and Pakistan, but Eden's reference was, of course, to the necessity of keeping in step with the other "white partners" of the old Commonwealth, none of which had recognized Peking, and with the United States, with whom the "white members" were in turn keeping step.

It was my opinion at the time that the United Kingdom could expect no "advantages" as long as it extended its right hand to Peking in recognition, while voting against Peking in the United Nations with the left.

In March, the Australian Embassy staff in Nanking was ordered by Canberra to come home. They planned to leave as soon as the last members of the British Embassy went to Peking. That would vacate a building in which the Australian furniture could be stored in the event of a return to China, if and when Canberra reversed its position not to recognize Peking. (Sometimes, even furniture is important in diplomatic movements.) The real reason was that Australia followed the United States rather than the British lead in China policy. There was a great deal of talk about a Pacific Pact, including Japan, the Philippines, South Korea, and Taiwan, but excluding India.

In the meantime, more and more effective counter-measures were being taken by Peking against the blockade of China, including anti-aircraft artillery and MIG fighters from the Soviet Union.

Before the end of March, due to the continuing difficulties of the United Kingdom's relations with Peking, Canada decided on a further delay of recognition.

On March 27, 1950, the Netherlands announced their proposal, to recognize, thus raising to six the number of Western governments to have recognized Peking.

Canada did not have the impediments of Great Britain to the

establishment of diplomatic relations. We had been a British colony, and our dealings with China had no dark past. We had not participated in the Opium War; we had not taken concessions in China's port cities; we had no Canadian troops there, and no police and law courts exercising jurisdiction over Chinese citizens. All we had, as British colonials, was extraterritoriality, which gave us immunity from Chinese law. Prior to World War II, we had not even had diplomatic relations with China.

The Canadian Government was nonetheless reluctant to have its representative in Nanking go to Peking and perhaps wait indefinitely for the establishment of diplomatic relations after the Canadian Government had recognized Peking. The Department of External Affairs wanted to find a way of avoiding the difficulties encountered by the British. Canada hoped that, by working out some suitable procedural arrangement before recognition was made public, Ottawa and Peking could make simultaneous announcements of Canada's recognition and the establishment of diplomatic relations.

Canada was therefore considering having me communicate orally with the Foreign National Bureau in Nanking, stating that I had been instructed by my Government to inform the Chinese authorities that consideration was being given to the recognition of the People's Republic of China and an agreement to exchange diplomatic missions. Before doing so, my Government would wish to know whether such a procedure would be agreeable to the Chinese authorities to authorize me to proceed to Peking to discuss in advance any questions which Chinese authorities might wish to raise in this connection.

The understanding would be that if the discussions resulted in agreement, I would hand the Peking authorities a note informing them of recognition. Canada and China would then exchange notes recording the understandings reached on other points, regarding such matters as withdrawal of recognition from the Nationalist Government in Taiwan, support for the seating of Peking's representatives in the United Nations, and so on.

As soon as I mentioned to an officer of the Foreign Nationals Bureau that I wished to discuss Canadian recognition of Peking and diplomatic relations, I was invited to have informal talks with the Director of the Bureau, who immediately communicated with Peking.

A week later, the Acting Head of the Foreign Nationals Bureau handed me an unofficial written statement stating that the Ministry of Foreign Affairs would welcome the Canadian Government's representative to Peking to discuss preliminary and procedural matters with a view of establishing diplomatic relations if the Canadian Government would "formally indicate" its desire to recognize the Government of the People's Republic of China.

My recommendation was that, since Canada had taken this informal initiative, it was urgent that a decision be reached at the earliest possible moment to take formal action. I was convinced that the sooner Canada followed the informal proposal with the acceptance of the Chinese invitation, the greater would be the chances of achieving success. I was gradually coming to the conclusion that the time had arrived to decide whether to keep step with the United Kingdom, India, and Pakistan or with the United States. Continued indefinite postponement of the decision meant, in effect, keeping step with the United States.

Ottawa's interpretation of Peking's reply was that it did not constitute full acceptance of Canada's suggestions. Peking had made counter-proposals which limited the scope of the proposed negotiations. It became necessary, therefore, to give further consideration to these counter-proposals. As time went on, Canada's hesitation was due more to American influence than any other single factor.

In my opinion, the Chinese reply had been an acceptance of the Canadian proposal, not a counter-proposal. The Chinese Ministry of Foreign Affairs had said the Canadian representative would be welcomed to Peking if Canada would "formally indicate its *desire* to recognize." The reply did not require prior recognition, but an indication of such a desire. If there was no desire or intention to recognize, why send a representative to Peking at all?

On June 25, 1950, I was informed that Canada had decided to proceed with negotiations. I was instructed to deliver a confidential oral message to the Director of the Foreign Nationals Bureau stating that the Canadian Government was prepared to announce recognition of the Government of China, if and when a satisfactory agreement had been reached on the establishment of diplomatic relations. I was then to ask that the message be transmitted to Peking as confidential.

But Canada had waited too long. June 25 was the day war broke out in Korea, and a few days later, I received a message stating that the unprovoked attack on the Republic of Korea by North Korean Communists and the firm action by the United Nations, which the Canadian Government had supported, had introduced new and important elements into the problem of relations with Peking.

It was felt that in the prevailing circumstances, it would not be appropriate to open negotiations with Peking. Rather than make a decision against recognition, however, Canada decided to defer the question of proceeding with negotiations until the immediate crisis in Korea was over, until China's attitude toward the Korean action had become clearer, and until Peking's reaction to the message delivered on June 17 by the United Kingdom's Chargé, recognized only as a "negotiator," was known.

I cancelled the house in Peking and, a year later, in 1951, after closing the Canadian Embassy compound, left Nanking.

The Korean War ended in an armistice on July 27, 1953, and a conference of the former belligerents and the Soviet Union met in Geneva to negotiate a political settlement of the conflict.

On March 12, 1954, the Canadian Prime Minister, Mr. St. Laurent, was asked about Canada's attitude to the recognition of China. He replied that, while recognition merely acknowledged the fact of a new government, it nevertheless implied a certain respect. As long as the war had continued in Korea, therefore, Canada had not been able to recognize China. However, now that hostilities were over—by mutual consent—and that a solution was being sought through negotiation, Canada could once again consider recognition of Peking.

The *New York Times* published a report on March 22, 1954, which predicted that Canada would seriously consider recognizing Communist China and supporting Mao Tse-tung's regime for membership of the United Nations. Canada's shift in attitude was believed to be the result of St. Laurent's talks with Prime Minister Jawaharlal Nehru.

Mr. Nehru had indeed made a profound impression on our Prime Minister, as Mr. St. Laurent made clear during our talk before I left for India as Canadian High Commissioner in 1957. And when I arrived in India, Mr. Nehru told me that he regarded St. Laurent as one of the wisest Western statesmen of his day.

But even so, there was no real shift in Canada's attitude over Peking, and it took another two years and the establishment of full diplomatic recognition between London and Peking before Canada reaffirmed the decision to recognize.

On April 2, 1954, Lester Pearson said in the Canadian House of Commons: "Insofar as the recognition of China is concerned . . . , the Government's policy is at present non-recognition."

The United States never lost an opportunity to keep other Western powers in line with its inflexible policy on recognition. For example, in September 1954, Paul-Henri Spaak of Belgium voiced something about the importance of considering recognition of Peking. A note was quickly delivered to him stating that recognition by Belgium would embarrass the United States Government and would not serve the interests of the Western powers.

On the issue of seating China in the United Nations, Canada advised the State Department in September 1954 that the Canadian Delegation to the United Nations would be instructed to support the moratorium arrangement. (That arrangement postponed for another year any attempt to seat China in the

United Nations.) The United States campaigned faithfully each year to keep as many nations as possible lock-stepped to keep Peking out.

Canada continued to hope that United States international policy on this point would become more flexible.

At the Geneva Conference on Korea, Mr. Wang Ping-nan of the Chinese Delegation, whom I had known since 1945, broached to me the subject of Canada's relations with China. He said there were no outstanding differences between Canada and China and no insoluble problems. I raised with him the question of three Canadian missionaries, Roman Catholic priests, in prison and another denied an exit permit to return to his home in Canada. There was grave concern for them, and relations with Canada could not become normal as long as such a situation existed. Wang knew nothing about these missionaries, so I gave him their names and addresses, and he promised he would attend to the matter immediately.

Exactly nine days later, Wang Ping-nan informed me that the Canadian missionaries would be released and permitted to return to Canada if they wished. They arrived home safely. Canada, however, took no steps towards recognition.

Shortly after the Korean Conference, however, Mr. Pearson said in a speech on China:

> From information my officers gathered and which I gathered—and I pause for a moment to pay tribute to the capable officers who assisted me at Geneva—I am satisfied the view is widely held that non-recognition and non-admission of China is certainly not only standing in the way of the lessening of international tension—it is tending to keep up international tension, thus endangering world peace.

I heard about Canada's decision to recognize China in 1956, when I was Canada's Ambassador to Norway. By chance one day, in the Foreign Office building in Oslo, I ran into Halvard Lange, Norway's Foreign Minister. He said he was sorry to hear I was leaving Norway, but realized my new post would be more important and that Norway would understand why I had to leave before completing the usual term. I had not the slightest idea of what Mr. Lange was talking about. He told me that he had met my "boss" in New York the day before and had learned from Mr. Pearson that Canada had decided to recognize China and was sending me to Peking as Canada's first Ambassador to the People's Republic of China. He added that I would no doubt be fully informed very soon. I was. Halvard Lange had learned of our good intentions, but not how our good intentions merely paved the way to greater American inflexibility.

The story was that Canada had decided to recognize Peking. Prime Minister St. Laurent and the Secretary of State for External Affairs, Lester B. Pearson, went to the United States to inform President Eisenhower at a meeting in White Sulphur Springs, West Virginia, of Canada's decision to recognize China before making a formal announcement. Without saying so, they had decided to talk to the President rather than to the Secretary of State, expecting that Eisenhower would be less emotional about the subject than John Foster Dulles. To their surprise, the Canadians very quickly learned that Eisenhower was, if possible, even more emotional against recognizing China than Dulles.

The President blew up and asked how Canada could think of recognizing "Communist China, whose hands were dripping with the blood of Americans killed in Korea." And if Canada recognized China, he said, France, Belgium, Italy, and other nations would certainly follow. Canada's recognition would undoubtedly result in China being seated in the Security Council and the General Assembly of the United Nations. Public opinion was against "Communist China," Eisenhower said, and nothing could stop the United States from withdrawing from the United Nations and kicking the United Nations headquarters out of the United States if Communist China was seated.

Since Canada did not want the responsibility of sending the United Nations after the League of Nations into oblivion, our

Prime Minister and Secretary of State for External Affairs dropped the whole idea. The United Nations was already suffering the handicap of having no representation from one quarter of the world's population in China.

It was not until the next Government of Canada, headed by the Right Honourable John Diefenbaker, came into power that I heard another word about Canada probing the attitude of the United States to the recognition of the People's Republic of China.

It happened in 1959, while I was High Commissioner (the Commonwealth title for ambassadors to member countries) in India. Mr. Diefenbaker had been Canadian Prime Minister for two years, and he and Mrs. Diefenbaker had been visiting India during a tour of the Far East. On the day before their departure, I called on the Prime Minister to deliver a very important ("For PM's eyes only") telegram. I had to get him out of bed in the early hours of Sunday morning, and after he had read the telegram, he said: "Talk to me about China, Ronning."

I had been told by my friends in the Department of External Affairs in Ottawa: "For goodness sake don't talk to the Prime Minister about China when he visits India, or he'll fire you." I therefore stalled, said that it would take a good two hours, and suggested the Prime Minister could not spare that much time. Mr. Diefenbaker was not to be put off.

I explained that I considered the United States' China policy very dangerous for peace in the Far East and the world—dangerous because it was based on a fallacious analysis of what happened before and especially since the People's Republic of China came into power. For the Prime Minister, I promised to cover the ground in two hours.

The Prime Minister listened attentively and when I had completed my criticism of United States policy, I told Mr. Diefenbaker the story of his predecessors' experience with President Eisenhower at Sulphur Springs. Mr. Diefenbaker surprised me by saying that he could not believe this story. I explained that I had been invited to join the Department of External Affairs after VJ Day, because of my experience in China. How could I be wrong about an event so closely associated with the subject on which my whole diplomatic career was based? The Prime Minister then asked if I had any document to corroborate my story. I did not know if the High Commissioner's Office in New Delhi had been kept informed about recognition of China, but I said I would try to find something.

One of my officers did find a report of a meeting of External Affairs officers in Ottawa, at which Mr. Pearson was asked about a story in the *New York Times* of March 31, 1956, in which James Reston reported that President Eisenhower had told Prime Minister Louis St. Laurent and the Secretary of State for External Affairs, Lester B. Pearson, at a private Canadian-American meeting in White Sulphur Springs, West Virginia, that United States public opinion would not tolerate recognizing the Chinese Communists or bringing them into the United Nations.

I showed the report to Mr. Diefenbaker, who explained why he had at first found it impossible to believe my story. He had thought I was confusing the incident with a similar one, in which he and Sidney Smith, his first Secretary of State for External Affairs, had also gone to talk to President Eisenhower about China. Apparently, the President's reaction had excelled in emotional outrage even what I had heard of the White Sulphur Springs meeting.

The most prescient appraisal of American sentiment regarding the recognition of China was probably made by the *Denver Post* on April 7, 1956. It expressed the opinion that the President's estimate of public opinion was no doubt correct, but only so long as the President and other leaders reacted so emotionally to the China question and so long as no leader of either party undertook to give the American people facts upon which to base a rational judgment as to what constituted their best interest.

It must be said to President Eisenhower's credit, when he was convinced, after the prolonged stalemate in Korea, that many of the allies of the United States in the United Nations action in Korea were opposed to a military solution and convinced that Canada, in particular, would not actively participate in a military solution, if one was undertaken to satisfy Syngman Rhee, he gave instructions to the United Nations Command to sign the agreement to end hostilities.

Mr. Diefenbaker did not tell me whether he and Sidney Smith had reached a decision to recognize China before they consulted President Eisenhower, I assume therefore that it was merely a probe to sound out the United States.

While recognition of China was given "serious consideration" year after year, no further attempt was made to negotiate with Peking until 1971, when Prime Minister Pierre Elliott Trudeau indicated his intention of recognizing the Government of the People's Republic of China as the sole Government of China.

Negotiations to recognize and to establish diplomatic relations took place between Canadian and Chinese representatives in Stockholm. On the question of Taiwan, some Canadians had been hoping that the problem could be solved on the basis of a two-China policy—some solution involving recognition of Peking without breaking with Taiwan, but both sides eventually agreed to an acceptable formula in which Canada "took note" of the situation. Canada recognized the People's Republic and withdrew recognition of the Nationalist Government in Taiwan.

After twenty-one years and thirteen days, on October 13, 1971, Ottawa and Peking announced that the Government of Canada had recognized the Government of the People's Republic of China and that diplomatic relations had been established involving the early exchange of ambassadors.

Mr. Ralph Collins, whom I had known as a boy in knee pants in Peking when I was a student there in 1922, was appointed Canada's first Ambassador to the People's Republic of China.

Mr. Huang Hua, for whom I had acted as interpreter in 1949, when he announced to the Diplomatic Corps in Nanking the establishment of the Government of the People's Republic of China, was appointed as the first Ambassador of the People's Republic of China to Canada.

Shortly after Canada was first invited to recognize Peking and establish diplomatic relations, I expressed the opinion, in urging an early decision, that the benefits to be derived from recognition would be inversely proportional to the square of the length of time it took to recognize China. After twenty-one years and thirteen days, that should have brought the benefits very close to zero.

I was mistaken. The benefits have already been considerable.

Canada once expressed the hope that Canada's recognition would pave the way for the United States "to follow suit." That has not yet taken place, but at least Canada's recognition made it decent for Americans to talk about recognizing Peking—maybe even made it easier for President Nixon to visit Peking.

I am convinced that there is nothing more important for peace in the Pacific and the world than good relations between the United States and the People's Republic of China.

13

CANADA'S ROLE
IN THE KOREAN WAR
AND ARMISTICE

This account of Canada's role in the Korean War, and in the prolonged and difficult negotiations before the armistice was finally signed, deals to some extent with what went on behind the scenes from the Canadian point of view and, perhaps to a greater extent, my own point of view.

The war began on June 25, 1950, and continued for a whole year and two weeks before negotiations were begun to end hostilities. Then, two long years and two weeks passed before an armistice agreement was signed on July 27, 1953. When negotiations had continued at Panmunjom for nearly a year and a half without success, the United Nations General Assembly formulated armistice terms which would be acceptable to the United Nations' side. The terms were outlined in an Indian Resolution which was endorsed by an overwhelming majority including the United States, though perhaps with reluctance and only after it became evident that only the Soviet bloc would vote No. Differences had developed during the seemingly interminable negotiations on a number of issues between the United States and some of the other member nations of the United Nations. The most serious difference, especially with

Canada, involved the authority of the United Nations General Assembly in the American-controlled United Nations Command in the Panmunjom negotiations.

From the beginning, the United States made by far the most important contribution to the United Nations military effort in Korea. The United States, with the unanimous approval of the nations participating in the United Nations military action, had accepted the responsibilities of leadership for the United Nations effort. The United States also represented all the participating nations in the armistice negotiations at Panmunjom. The United Nations Command was composed of four American military personnel and one South Korean. In the final analysis, it accepted direction from the President of the United States. The Communist side was represented by two Chinese and two North Koreans.

If hostilities in Korea had not ended when the Communist side made proposals which came very close to those which had been outlined by the United Nations General Assembly, the war would have continued indefinitely.

Canada was therefore determined to force the issue by insisting that the terms of the United Nations' Indian Resolution constituted the United Nations' instructions to the United Nations Command. President Eisenhower finally agreed and instructed the American military personnel who represented the United Nations' side to accept the other side's proposals.

What were the causes of the war in Korea?

Before the end of the last century, Japan had unexpectedly emerged as an important naval and military power in the Pacific. China was the first victim of Japanese aggression. The great giant of Asia, reduced by internal corruption and foreign exploitation to abject impotence, was defeated in a short, sharp military and naval engagement, and the Province of Taiwan was annexed by Japan.

At the beginning of this century, having tested her new power, Japan attacked the Russians, and the world was startled by the sudden destruction of Russian naval power in Asia. Important concessions, which the Russians had taken from China, were turned over to Japan. Japan annexed Korea and gained a firm base on the Asian continent for future aggression and expansion.

The people of Korea worked and waited for decades for liberation from the ruthless domination of Japan. In their moment of triumph and hope for the future, the Korean people were completely unaware of the forces which would soon engulf them as pawns in, and victims of, the power-struggle between the Soviet Union and the United States.

Both the Soviet Union and the United States had been attracted by the strategic importance of the Korean peninsula jutting out into the northwest Pacific. Korea, contiguous to China on the West and Siberia on the North, also bordered offshore Japanese and Russian islands. Neither the United States nor the Soviet Union thought it could afford the other supremacy of influence or control over Korea.

Korea, which had been a unified, independent nation before its annexation by Japan, was cut in two at the 38th Parallel. The United States accepted the surrender of the Japanese to the south of it and the Soviet Union to the north. The United States thus assumed control of two-thirds of the population, the Soviet Union of one third.

In the fall of 1947, Canada was invited to participate in the UN Temporary Commission on Korea. The Secretary of State for External Affairs, Mr. St. Laurent, decided, despite some reservations, to accept the responsibility. (In many ways, Canada had special qualifications for this kind of international endeavour. The Dominion of Canada had been part of the British Empire, and only in 1939, when Ottawa declared war on Germany, did Canada for the first time become involved in war as an independent member of the Commonwealth.) And Canada had no axe to grind in that part of the world and could make impartial judgements. (The only previous contact with Korea was through the activities of more than 1,000 Canadian missionaries.)

At the time this decision was made to participate in UNTCK, Canada's Prime Minister, Mr. William Lyon Mackenzie King, was on a visit to the United Kingdom. He was there convinced that the situation in Korea was leading to a third world war and so adopted a "hands off" policy regarding any proposal which could in any way involve Canada.

Upon returning to Canada, he was informed by Mr. St. Laurent that Canada had agreed to participate in the United Nations Temporary Commission on Korea. The Prime Minister insisted that Canada could not accept. St. Laurent, however, had already agreed and would therefore have to resign as Secretary of State for External Affairs rather than fail to keep his word. The Under-Secretary of State for External Affairs, Lester Pearson, upon whose recommendation the decision had been reached, was therefore summoned to explain the Commission's responsibilities. Its chief function would be to supervise elections in the whole of Korea if possible, or only in the South if there was no possibility of an all-Korean election. The Prime Minister then suggested that if these assurances were confirmed by President Truman, he would reluctantly accept Canadian participation in the UNTCK. Mr. Pearson immediately flew to Washington.

President Truman sent assurances to Mackenzie King that the United States would not insist upon the Commission operating in North Korea, if the Soviet Union did not agree.

Dr. George Patterson, Counsellor of our Embassy in Nanking and Interim Head of the Canadian Liaison Mission in Tokyo, was appointed as our member of UNTCK.

Canada nevertheless continued to have grave doubts about the usefulness of the Commission, since the Soviet Union had already indicated that it would not cooperate. Also, Canada did not approve of American use of the Commission as an aggressive gesture towards the Soviet Union. Canada thought, therefore, that the Commission should be disbanded as soon as it had reached the limit of its usefulness in South Korea.

After the May 1948 elections in South Korea, the Government of the Republic of Korea was organized. Canada voted for United Nations membership, which constituted recognition by Canada of the new government as the Government of South

Korea only. Canada did not recognize it as the government of the whole of Korea, nor has Canada ever done so.

When the United Nations Temporary Commission on Korea was phased out, it was succeeded by the United Nations Commission on Korea (1948–50), in which Canada refused membership.

Then, on June 25, 1950, 75,000 North Korean troops crossed the 38th Parallel, and the cold war suddenly flared into open hostility.

At the time, the People's Republic of China was barely nine months old, but the Government was capable of effective action. I had remained in China to establish diplomatic relations with the new regime and so had first-hand knowledge of the Chinese attitude to the Korean War. China justified the action of the North Koreans as a response to numerous attempts by the South to invade the North.

When the Korean War started, there was no doubt whatever in the minds of the leaders of all the great and lesser powers of the West that it was a clear-cut case of an "unwarranted, aggressive invasion of South Korea by the North." The division of our globe into two worlds—Communist and Free—fore-ordained the conclusion.

That was not, however, the way the Chinese saw it. The Chinese version was that South Korean troops, armed and equipped by the United States, had repeatedly crossed the 38th Parallel in "unprovoked" border raids. The Chinese and North Koreans believed that these violent border crossings were intended to test North Korean military strength and to perfect plans for the ambitious Rhee to conquer all Korea.

Later, when Syngman Rhee resorted to every possible device, fair or foul, during the armistice negotiations to prevent an armistice in order to continue the war to unite Korea under a Rhee government, it seemed at least feasible that South Korea might not have been as innocent as the West had assumed in June 1950. The truth of what happened along the 38th Parallel before and on Sunday, June 25, 1950, has not been established.

The official report that it was a clear-cut case of unprovoked attack all along the 38th Parallel came from President Syngman Rhee's Foreign Minister to the United Nations Commission on Korea.

That version was accepted after hurried on-the-spot investigations by UNCK, and after consultations with President Rhee and the United States Ambassador. The charge of aggression was cabled immediately to the attention of the Secretary-General of the United Nations in New York. UNCK then broadcast an appeal to North Korea for a cease-fire. Consultations continued between UNCK and Syngman Rhee's Foreign Minister before the United Nations Secretary-General was requested to bring the matter of a "well-planned concerted and full-scale invasion" by North Korea to the attention of the Security Council. Again, President Rhee's version of what happened was accepted. The Security Council, in the absence of the Soviet Ambassador, declared the North Korean aggression a clear breach of the peace and called for the assistance of every member of the United Nations to repel the aggression.

On June 26, Mr. Pearson read to the Canadian House of Commons the resolution, which noted "with grave concern the armed attack upon the Republic of Korea by forces from North Korea" and called upon "all members to render every assistance to the United Nations in the execution of the United Nations Security Council Resolution and to refrain from giving assistance to the North Korean authorities."

On June 27, President Truman announced that he had ordered the United States air and sea forces to assist the Republic of Korea. He also announced on the same date that, as a result of the Korean crisis, he had made the defence of Taiwan a responsibility of the United States Fleet. The Seventh Fleet was to patrol the straits separating Taiwan from the continent, which implied some link between the civil war in China and the war in Korea.

That announcement created a problem which Canada considered could have serious repercussions. US intervention in

China's civil war carried the risk of Chinese and even of Soviet involvement in conflict against the United States and its allies in Korea. Canadian fears that the US action could involve China in the Korean War were the beginning of differences in Canadian and American policies.

Prime Minister Attlee was also worried about the United States action in Taiwan. He was reported by Clifton Daniel of *The New York Times* to have said that "dangerous possibilities" were caused by the United States defence of Taiwan against possible Chinese assault.

The situation was further complicated by General MacArthur's unauthorized visit to Chiang Kai-shek, which undoubtedly raised Chiang's hopes of being restored to power. Chiang offered to send troops to Korea to participate in the UN defence of South Korea, but neither the United States nor its allies thought it wise to accept. Canada, in particular, thought it could result only in a spreading of the war beyond Korea's borders.

General MacArthur spoke boldly of the ease with which he could destroy China's military potential. Many American observers in China were aware of the great difference between the efficiency and capability of the Chinese Communist forces and those of the Nationalists, but the fact that the latter had already sustained a total defeat did not impress MacArthur. He was certain that primitive Chinese guerrilla troops were no match for a modern army with sophisticated weapons, and China was convinced that he would try to prove his point.

China's fear of outright invasion of Manchuria from Korea was what finally decided Peking, in the interests of China's security, to send troops over the Yalu in October 1950. General MacArthur's triumphant march threatened the power houses on the Korean side of the Yalu, which would have crippled China's industry in Manchuria. That, of course, was China's immediate concern but, more important, China suspected that MacArthur had deeper plans when the General followed the route of earlier Japanese invaders into Manchuria. If he was not stopped, the Chinese feared that he would continue as the

Japanese had over a decade earlier into Manchuria and then into China proper.

A minor, but nevertheless relevant, factor in reaching the decision to cross into North Korea was undoubtedly to counter Russian influence there. In discussions with Chinese Communists, as early as 1945, in Chungking, I had learned that they resented Nationalist China's concessions to the Russians in Manchuria. The Chinese Communist Party, which came into power in 1949, was not the Party which the Soviet Union had helped to organize in China. Since the Long March, Mao Tsetung had become the supreme leader of the Party, with no obligations to Stalin whatever. The Chinese Communists, led by Mao, had ignored and defied Moscow's orthodox line. Stalin nevertheless reversed his twenty-two-year-old China policy, which insisted that the Chinese Communists should cooperate with the Nationalists, and recognized the People's Republic of China on the day it came into existence.

The Russians were better informed about the military capability of the Chinese Communists than any other foreigners, as I knew from my talks with General Roshchin, the Soviet Military Attaché in Chungking and Nanking and later the Soviet Ambassador in Nanking. Stalin knew that the Chinese would not permit the North Korean military potential to be destroyed, because their own security would thereby be threatened, just as he knew that the Chinese would appreciate assistance from the Soviet Union to save China from Chiang Kai-shek or General MacArthur, if either should be reckless enough to invade China.

It was by no means a foregone conclusion that the Soviet Union would not become involved in a general war on behalf of China, especially since it could result in China being brought into the Soviet orbit, which had been, and still was, Stalin's ambition. Later, when the Russians failed to participate actively in support of the North Koreans, the Chinese seized the opportunity to move into a vacuum left by the Soviet Union to continue their predominant interest in Korea.

In China, I had seen extensive preparations to complete the

occupation of the only remaining Province of China, Taiwan, which had not yet come under the control of Peking, but in Nanking, I realized that the Chinese were taking no chances of becoming involved in a war with the United States over an issue which involved no serious, immediate threat to China's security. All the extensive military preparations to occupy Taiwan were therefore stopped, the constant flow of supplies to South China, opposite Taiwan, was suddenly reversed, and Peking's attention was diverted to the North.

Canada was seriously concerned about three aspects of American policy in Taiwan—the speech of the Secretary of the Navy in which he made reference to the possibility of a "preventive war," General MacArthur's policy of linking Taiwan and Korea, and the dropping of United Nations' flags in China by Chinese Nationalist pilots from Taiwan.

Canada was also worried about General MacArthur's double role as United Nations Commander in Korea and Commander of United States forces in Taiwan. In fact, MacArthur had a triple role—he was also Supreme Commander of the Allied Forces in Japan. His dangerous military policies and the risks he was prepared to take regardless of international consequences became abundantly clear only after his brilliant and daring Inchon landing. That military manoeuvre stopped the North Koreans and drove them out of South Korea over the 38th Parallel.

It was then that the coast was cleared for General MacArthur's next and not-so-brilliant move. He waited for instructions neither from the Secretary-General of the United Nations nor from the President of the United States. He was certain they would never reverse a *fait accompli* and confident that he could quickly and completely destroy North Korea's military potential.

MacArthur paid no attention to Chou En-lai's statement that China "would not stand idly by" if her security was threatened. He considered Chou's threat to be a mere bluff. He boasted to my son-in-law, Seymour Topping, who reported it through the Associated Press, that with a few hundred American bombers and American fighters, flown by American pilots and serviced by American ground crews, he could wipe out the whole Chinese Communist Army.

India's warning that, if the 38th Parallel were crossed by United Nations forces, China would join the conflict on the side of the North Koreans went unheeded.

I had known of Chou En-lai since the Northern Expedition of 1926, long before I met him. I knew he never bluffed. I was certain that he meant business and advised Ottawa that if the United Nations flag was carried into North Korea, MacArthur would face the best trained and most experienced guerrilla fighters in Asia.

After crossing the Yalu and having their first encounter with UN troops, the Chinese paused for several days. Chou En-lai had demonstrated that he was not bluffing, but that he still preferred a peaceful settlement. If General MacArthur had negotiated or withdrawn from North Korea after that first encounter, the war in Korea could have ended in a few months instead of being dragged out for years. When the UN forces attacked a second time, the Chinese decided that MacArthur was determined to drive through Korea and beyond the Yalu into Manchuria.

General MacArthur was so confident of victory that he promised his troops they would be "home for Christmas." Even though the United States had said there was no intention to do so, American military authorities nevertheless did pursue North Korean forces to the Manchurian border.

The Chinese "volunteers," in overwhelming numbers, swept across the Yalu, carrying their supplies in baskets slung from shoulder yokes. These guerrilla troops in light rubber-soled shoes crossed over mountains at night to drive one of the best conventional armies of the Western world out of North Korea. The well-laid plans of General MacArthur, who had defied the American principle of never getting an American army involved in war on the continent of Asia, failed completely.

By November 1950, Canada's Lester Pearson was distressed that no effort was being made to approach the Chinese directly. He suggested a cease-fire. The Americans, however, were unalterably opposed, claiming that the technical difficulties of administering a cease-fire would outweigh its advantages and would be of benefit only to the Communists. The Military Command, which was in charge of military operations (not the United Nations Command in charge of the Panmunjom negotiations), had, it seemed, completed plans for a final campaign in northern areas. Completion of this operation was necessary before any effort would be made towards negotiations with China.

When the Chinese secured control of "MIG alley," and the United Nations General Assembly objected to the pursuit of MIG fighters into Manchuria, the Military Command protested that a war cannot be won with one arm tied behind the back. Many of the Western powers, however, were determined to have hostilities in Korea come to an end as quickly as possible. It was felt that an all-out war in China would commit to the Asian theatre a dangerously large proportion of the limited armed resources of the Western powers at the expense of other fronts such as Western Europe, where the Soviet Union might intend to conduct its major campaign if a third world war should break out.

Early in December, Mr. Pearson recommended that efforts be made to obtain a cease-fire followed by negotiations, in which the Chinese would participate. Very soon thereafter, the United Nations General Assembly approved a resolution setting up a Committee of Three (Entezam-Rau-Pearson) to determine bases on which a satisfactory cease-fire could be arranged.

The United Kingdom and other Commonwealth nations were unanimous in their opposition to an unlimited war. In Washington, however, President Truman continued to stress the importance of strengthening military defences to meet the threat of aggression. In discussing the subject, the President made some ambiguous remarks about the atom bomb, and the world press made much ado about his reference. Fearing the worst, Prime Minister Attlee rushed to Washington to urge moderation in American policy.

President Truman and Prime Minister Attlee then issued a communiqué which dealt with the Korean War in the framework of the world crisis. After a preliminary affirmation of a previous stand, they emphasized that they were ready "to seek an end to the hostilities by means of negotiations." With reference to Taiwan, President Truman and Prime Minister Attlee said: "We agree that the issues should be settled by peaceful means and in such a way as to safeguard the interests of the people of Taiwan and the maintenance of peace and security in the Pacific. Consideration of this question by the United Nations will contribute to these ends." The communiqué also stated that "the United Kingdom had recognized the Central People's Government and considered that Peking's representatives should occupy China's seat in the United Nations." The United States had opposed, and would continue to oppose, the seating of the Chinese Communist representatives in the United Nations. Their statement concluded by stating that "it would be for the peoples of the world acting through the United Nations to decide how the principles of the charter can best be maintained."

After the Truman-Attlee communiqué, it came as a complete surprise when the United States delegation to the General Assembly felt that the main issue should be naming China an aggressor in Korea.

Mr. Pearson was very unhappy about this development, and several other Commonwealth Prime Ministers viewed this hasty action with apprehension. In the hopes of finding an intermediary step before the United States proposal on Chinese aggression was considered, Mr. Pearson submitted a proposal by the Entezan-Rau-Pearson Cease-Fire Group. The objective was the achievement by stages of a programme for the establishment of a free and united Korea and for a peaceful settlement of Far Eastern problems. The first step of the proposal would be a cease-fire. The final step would be that an appropriate body of representatives of the Governments of the United Kingdom, the United States, the Soviet Union, and the People's Republic of

China would be appointed to achieve a settlement of Far Eastern problems, including Taiwan and the representation of Peking in the United Nations.

To bring the war to an end, Chou En-lai concurrently proposed to the United Nations that:

(a) negotiations be held among the countries concerned on the basis of an agreement to withdraw all foreign troops from Korea and the settlement of Korean domestic affairs by the Korean people themselves to put an end to the hostilities at an early date;

(b) negotiations should include subject matter of United States armed forces withdrawal from Taiwan, the Taiwan straits, and related Far Eastern problems;

(c) a Seven-Nation Conference (China, the Soviet Union, the United Kingdom, the United States, France, India, and Egypt) be convened. The representation of the People's Republic of China in the United Nations should be affirmed from the beginning of the Conference;

(d) the Conference should be held in China.

The United Kingdom felt that the Chinese proposal was a possible opening which the Western powers could not afford to ignore. The United Kingdom was, however, worried about the American attitude of imposing on friendly governments a policy which was the direct result of past American failures in the Far East and did not spring from the need of the United Nations and its members.

The United States, in response to Chou En-lai's proposals, recommended that no countries should recognize the Government of the People's Republic of China and that it should not be seated in any United Nations organization.

Aspects of Mr. Pearson's proposals had been so close to those of Mr. Chou that there seemed to be a real possibility of at least a breakthrough to start negotiations. The United States, however, secured the passage of its resolution condemning China as an aggressor in Korea on February 1, 1951. Canada, under pressure to maintain a united front, very reluctantly voted for the American resolution. Mr. Pearson hoped that the United States would respond by support for some sort of a cease-fire. But after passage of the condemnatory resolution, negotiations between the United Nations and the People's Republic of China broke down completely.

There was an undercurrent of deep frustration in the United Nations. Critics of the condemnatory resolution had been particularly frustrated by the tactics employed by the Americans, but when opponents of the resolution expressed critical views, the Americans would make a few unimportant changes in an effort to be conciliatory. The essence of their objections, however—to drop or at least delay the resolution for later consideration—had by no means been met.

With the Government of the People's Republic of China formally condemned in February 1951 as an aggressor in Korea, despite Mr. Pearson's near success in getting negotiations started with China, Canadians reserved the right to determine Canada's attitude, when the time came, to whatever action might be proposed in the United Nations. (That time came in May 1953, when Canada held out for the acceptance of the Sino-North Korean eight-point proposals which, in substance, were similar to the terms of the Indian Resolution endorsed by the United Nations General Assembly in December 1952.)

Under the leadership of the United States, the United Nations' main effort was, for a considerable period thereafter, devoted to bringing the war to an end by a military victory.

The US Government, however, apparently had second thoughts about the wisdom and possibility of success if a second attempt were made for a military solution. This may have been partially due to the lack of enthusiasm among so many of the friends of the United States to condemn China when prospects were bright for a negotiated settlement.

Be that as it may, it soon became evident that the United States had no immediate intention of authorizing General MacArthur to repeat the attempt made in November 1950 to occupy the whole of Korea. The forces of the United Nations were simply not strong enough and would have had to be greatly increased. Such reinforcements were not available. The Chinese and North Koreans had both the apparent intention and sufficient force available to prevent the United Nations from succeeding in another attempt to occupy North Korea.

Prior to General MacArthur's dismissal by President Truman, the military sights of the United Nations Command in Korea were lowered. In March 1951, General Ridgway, then Commander of the ground forces in Korea, said that a military stalemate appeared probable. He added that "it would be a tremendous victory for the United Nations if the war ended with United Nations forces in control up to the 38th Parallel."

That victory had, of course, already been achieved by General MacArthur in October 1950, when the United Nations General Assembly accepted the Eight-Power Resolution which gave tacit approval to terminate the military campaign just north of the 38th Parallel.

In June 1951, General Ridgway succeeded General Mac-Arthur and he was authorized to negotiate a cease-fire. After nearly four months, an agreement was reached on the principles that should govern the definition of a cease-fire line, and a tentative cease-fire line was defined. Military activity on the ground decreased greatly, but the air raids increased. Parts of North Korea were devastated.

Upon my return to Canada in June 1951, I was assigned to take charge of the American and Far Eastern Division of the Department of External Affairs in Ottawa. This gave me an opportunity to keep in close touch with day-to-day developments in Korea from the Canadian and Western point of view and to participate in discussions held in Ottawa during the development of Canadian policy, which, as I have said before, frequently differed from that of the United States. Canada was in constant contact with many of the other nations taking part in the United Nations' action in Korea, and especially with the three leading powers of that association—the United States, the United Kingdom, and France.

During the negotiations at Panmunjom, a very unsatisfactory state of affairs was developing in South Korea. Martial law was proclaimed in Pusan. Twenty-seven Assembly men were placed under arrest. President Rhee alleged he, not the Korean Assembly, represented the will of the Korean people. The United States, nevertheless, saw no alternative to Rhee—with the one exception, the Home Minister, Lee Bum Suk, who would have established an even more thorough-going dictatorship. Syngman Rhee was violently opposed to a cease-fire and continued to press for resumption of a military take-over of the whole of Korea and reunification under one government—his.

In the summer of 1952, I remember Gladwin Jebb's gloomy forecast of what was happening in Korea. Mr. Jebb, the Ambassador of the United Kingdom's Permanent Mission to the United Nations in New York, addressed a meeting in the East Block of all the senior Foreign Service officers of the Department of External Affairs in Ottawa. Mr. Jebb said there was not the slightest chance of the United Nations surviving the war in Korea if steps were not taken very soon to end the war before World War III became a reality. The next session of the Assembly, Jebb said, would most likely be its last. Mr. Pearson had been chosen by the United Nations General Assembly as its next President. When he commented on Jebb's predictions, I wondered if he were not consciously or unconsciously saying to himself: "I have no intention of presiding over the disintegration of the United Nations." Mr. Pearson worked assiduously during that session to prevent the collapse of the United Nations. Canada shared the fears of the United Kingdom as expressed by Mr. Jebb.

Americans were becoming more and more restive about the failure to get terms acceptable to the United States for a peace settlement. Serious consideration was, therefore, given to the idea of calling the General Assembly in special session. To increase pressure on China, a resolution would then be introduced calling on all members to sever commercial and diplomatic relations with China and to cut off all communication facilities with China. To induce the Chinese to accept the armistice terms which they had been offered in Panmunjom, the United States wanted a formal United Nations expression of confidence in the United Nations Command in Panmunjom and in their conduct of armistice negotiations. The United States also wanted the United Nations to condemn "the aggressors" in Korea for refusal to accept honourable armistice terms and to express a determination to continue military action in Korea, urging all United Nations members to increase their assistance and to send additional troops.

Canada insisted that the implications of such action could be very serious. Canadians had for some time been concerned about increased aerial bombing near the Manchurian border, including the Yalu power stations. Sometimes, notice was given to us by the Americans only a few hours before the bombing took place without previous consultation. This action again raised the question of the lack of consultations between the United States and the other fifteen powers participating in the United Nations' action in Korea.

Mr. Jawaharlal Nehru expressed his concern that the United States might, in an effort to secure Syngman Rhee's cooperation in the armistice, make commitments to Rhee which would make the task of the post-armistice political conference more difficult.

The United Kingdom was opposed to the United States proposal and held the view that, if the United Nations General Assembly took any action, it should be based on a less severe resolution than that proposed by the United States. The United Kingdom would definitely oppose new political and economic measures against China.

Canada also opposed the suggestion of the United States, insisting that United Nations intervention in Korea was to resist aggression in that peninsula, not to overthrow the Government of the People's Republic of China. Canada was not persuaded that additional political and economic sanctions against China would weaken either China's capacity or her will to continue fighting in Korea. Moreover, sanctions would be ineffective unless they were supported by every important country concerned, including, in particular, China's Asian neighbours, such as India. That would apply especially to proposals for a total economic embargo against China.

Adverse comments from a number of friendly governments on the American proposal that the General Assembly should endorse additional political and economic sanctions on North Korea and China seemed finally to have some effect upon the United States, and the initiative was at least temporarily postponed.

The sixth session of the United Nations General Assembly, which ended in February 1952, decided to defer consideration of the Korean question in view of the continuation of the armistice negotiations in Panmunjom. General agreement had been reached on all terms except the disposition of prisoners of war.

The United Nations Command insisted that force must not be used to compel prisoners of war to return to their homelands if they did not so wish. The Communist representatives asserted that, in accordance with the Geneva Convention of 1949, all prisoners of war must be repatriated and that the stand taken by the United Nations Command amounted to the "forcible retention" of prisoners.

As a result of Indian conversations in Peking, the Foreign Minister of China suggested several alternative proposals which offered some basis for a solution of the prisoner-of-war issue in Korea. Several variants were suggested that would save face for both sides. The stalemate nonetheless continued, and the situation was not improved when the United Nations Command informed the Chinese that they would not accept an Asian nation as a "neutral" on any commission dealing with the prisoner of war problem.

Canada wanted to know why an Asian nation could not be accepted as a "neutral." Had Mr. Nehru and Mr. Pearson not cooperated closely in the negotiations which succeeded in obtaining the support of the great majority of the members of the

General Assembly for the Indian Resolution setting out acceptable terms to solve the prisoner-of-war issue?

The Australian Government had attached great importance to the "preservation of the moral backing of the United Nations that had been so evident when the Indian Resolution was adopted by the General Assembly." Australia felt that the United Nations Command might be frittering away the "moral support" of the United Nations—particularly when it was reported that no Asian nation would be acceptable to the United Nations Command as a "desirable neutral."

Canada felt that the United Nations Command should take greater pains to convince world opinion of a genuine desire to reach an armistice agreement. Since the prisoner-of-war problem was being narrowed down almost to the point of agreement, Canada was disturbed to learn from Mr. John Foster Dulles that the United States was on the verge of breaking off negotiations at Panmunjom. Canada was reassured that this was a misunderstanding of Mr. Dulles' real intent.

Mr. Pearson finally stressed that all countries concerned should be consulted before any decision by the United Nations Command was reached to break off armistice negotiations. When the Chinese and North Koreans had made their eight-point proposal on May 8, 1953, however, the United States had given only a few hours' notice before rejecting the proposal, submitting counter-proposals without consultations. The only redeeming feature of that unilateral decision was that negotiations were not broken off.

Canada, the United Kingdom, and several other nations involved immediately requested withdrawal by the United Nations Command of their counter-proposals. The Secretary of State for External Affairs of Canada said that the eight-point proposal advanced by the other side went a long way to meet the objections to their earlier proposals. There was only one difference of substance between the new proposal and the Indian Resolution that had been so overwhelmingly adopted by the General Assembly.

Both the United Nations proposal and the eight-point proposal provided for a reference of the problem of the prisoners, who did not wish to return home, to the political conference to be called after an armistice. The other side's proposal, however, did not provide for reference to the United Nations if the political conference failed to settle the problem, and the Communists could not accept any reference of the problem to a body in which they were not represented. (Canada felt that the UN should not compromise on this point.)

Despite United States objections, Canada was not disturbed by Czechoslovakia and Poland being included in the list of countries suggested to provide guard troops for prisoners of war in Korea. Mr. Pearson believed that the way was finally open for the conclusion of an armistice, if the United States was seriously determined to obtain one.

Another favourable indication was a report from Washington that a majority of Congressional leaders desired an armistice and that there was no one with responsibility in the Administration who was not convinced of the necessity of obtaining an armistice if possible.

Nevertheless, General Harrison submitted a United Nations Command counter-proposal, which included a suggestion requiring unanimous agreement by all members of the Custodial Commission before decisions could be reached, thus giving any member of the Commission a veto to block any move to which it was opposed. The Chinese and North Koreans, on the other hand, made an additional modification of their proposal to conform more closely to the terms of the Indian Resolution.

Canada stated very frankly that, in the case of a breakdown, there would be no disposition on the part of the Canadian Government to defend the recent United States initiative in the armistice negotiations when important changes were introduced without consultation.

Incidentally, the *New York Times* reported that the American counter-proposals had been "cleared with the Allies." This was not the case. The allies had been notified only a few hours before the counter-proposals had become a *fait accompli*—scarcely sufficient clearing time on important issues. The *New York Times* had even received the text of the American counter-proposals before Canada did.

The United Kingdom was pleased that Canada put forward their point of view—British influence in Washington was at a low ebb at the time.

The United Kingdom also feared that Syngman Rhee might be able to wreck the arrangements for dealing with the prisoner-of-war problem, and Mr. Nehru shared this opinion. He felt that the Chinese, on the other hand, in their desire to reach a settlement, had declined to put forward acceptable proposals. Mr. Nehru thought these proposals followed, to a large extent, those embodied in the Indian Resolution of December 3, 1952, and he agreed with K. M. Panikkar that the eight-point proposal was acceptable.

When India was nominated to be a member of the Neutral Commission, China hoped India would accept that responsibility. This was a surprise in view of the earlier Chinese rejection of the Indian Resolution. The Indian Resolution had been turned down by the Chinese and North Koreans when the Communist bloc in the United Nations voted against it. After the death of Stalin on March 5, 1953, Malenkov, fearing the possibility of having to defend the Soviet Union on two fronts, was no longer prepared to provide military supplies to maintain the stalemate in Korea. China and North Korea eventually made the eight-point proposal, which was a virtual acceptance of the Indian Resolution.

Among a number of the nations which participated in the United Nation's action there was a general undercurrent of disquiet and criticism of the manner in which the negotiators of the United Nations Command had been handling themselves in Korea. The United Nations Secretary-General suggested to General Harrison that the tone of his dealings with the other side might be less harsh. The Asian delegates to the United Nations were particularly upset by the United Nations Command's counter-proposals.

Mr. Pearson considered that the United Nations Command had completely ignored what should have been considered terms of reference for an acceptable armistice.

Americans frequently emphasized to Canadians how "very rugged" Congressional leaders were. They were said to have not been happy about the views expressed by Commonwealth governments in opposition to the United Nations Command's counter-proposals. They were reported to have felt that Canada was even more intransigent than other Commonwealth governments.

Canada hoped that, if and when the negotiators at Panmunjom reached an agreement with the Chinese and North Koreans, the serious differences between the United States and Canada would not be made public. Some publicity, however, had already been leaked to the *New York Times*. A report by Thomas J. Hamilton stated that the United Nations Command had "decided to modify its counter-proposals at Panmunjom to make provision concerning the ultimate fate of prisoners of war more in conformity with the resolution adopted by the General Assembly in December." In Canada, it then became necessary for the Minister to make a statement to the House of Commons.

Considerable publicity was given to the differences between India and the United States regarding negotiations in Korea. Many hard things were said about each other in the press of both sides. India was severely criticized in the American press for having come down on the Chinese side, thereby allegedly disqualifying herself as the Chairman of the Neutral Commission.

John Foster Dulles was finally persuaded by countries friendly to the United States to modify some of the counter-proposals. An armistice was definitely in the offing. The United States, however, expected friendly countries also to make corresponding concessions to the US, knowing full well that such concessions would not render the counter-proposals acceptable to the other side.

General Bedell Smith considered that a "final" United Nations Command position should be presented, regardless of the consequences. He warned that Rhee had twenty divisions under his control. Rhee was reported to have said that if he launched an offensive, the United States would have to support him, since it would be militarily impossible for troops of the United States to extricate themselves if the South Korean army were destroyed.

Canada could not agree to being pinned down to a "final position" which risked a break-off in negotiations.

Canada threatened to withdraw from participation in renewed hostilities if the United Nations Command failed to accept United Nations terms for an armistice. *It was a virtual ultimatum in the sense that it was a final statement of terms, the rejection of which would have involved a complete rupture in Canada's relations with the other powers associated with the United Nations' action in Korea. It was this determined position on Canada's part which forced a decision either fully to comply with the General Assembly's terms and sign an armistice or to continue a military solution without Canadian participation.*

The United States made another concession. The United Nations Command was instructed to agree to the simple majority voting procedure in the Custodial Commission. President Eisenhower himself made this decision, because he felt that administrative terms of reference for the Custodial Commission were of "very great importance" and should not be a matter of "trivial controversy." The President felt that unless the Commission operated in a manner providing satisfactory safeguards for the prisoners, the essential principle of no forced repatriation could be overthrown.

These important modifications, made on Canada's insistence, made possible an agreement for an armistice.

To prevent an armistice, Syngman Rhee launched a violent verbal attack on the United Nations Command. Threats were made by the South Korean Government that it would withdraw its troops from the United Nations Command and order them to prevent the guards of the Custodial Commission from entering Korea. South Korea, as a "minimum prerequisite for an armistice," would demand the outright release of the North Korean prisoners who were at that time in the hands of the United Nations Command.

Rhee was in a highly emotional state—reasonable one day, and not the next, frequently reverting to impossible demands. Early on the morning of May 18, 1953, 25,500 prisoners of war broke out of seven camps when prison guards opened all doors and gates. The breakout was carefully planned and coordinated by Mr. Rhee, his Government officials, and General Won, Chief Provost Marshal. Secret orders were given to security guards to release the prisoners, and the plot was not discovered by the United Nations Command Intelligence.

Mr. Pearson cabled the following letter to Syngman Rhee on June 23, 1953:

DEAR MR. PRESIDENT:

As President of the General Assembly of the United Nations, I have been shocked to hear of the unilateral action which you have sanctioned in bringing about the release of non-repatriable North Korean prisoners from the United Nations' prisoner-of-war camps in Korea. . . .

It is most regrettable that you have taken action which threatens the results already achieved and the prospects of a peaceful solution of the remaining problems.

The action is particularly shocking in view of the progress made by the armistice negotiations in Panmunjom, which has resulted in the acceptance of principles laid down in the United Nations General Assembly's Resolution of December 3, 1952, already endorsed by fifty-three Member Nations.

The acceptance of the principles underlying this Resolution, especially that of no forcible repatriation of prisoners, which has been the basis of your position as well as that of the United Nations, has been obtained only after two years of patient and persistent negotiations by the United Nations Command.

The action taken with your consent in releasing the North Korean prisoners violates the agreement reached by the two sides on June 8, 1953, embodying these principles, and it occurs at a time when hostilities are about to cease, and when the question of the unification of Korea and related Korean problems can be dealt with by a political conference involving the parties concerned.

On the same day, Mr. Pearson said in a speech he made in Ontario: "We must keep striving in Korea to convert a setback into progress . . . Within ninety days of a truce signing, a political conference must be held. At that time, the recognition of China, a highly controversial issue, must be considered. The fact is that once we have decided to deal with China around a table, we shall have taken steps to recognize the facts of the situation."

Canada felt that the United States assurances that Rhee would observe the terms of the armistice were inadequate, and that feeling was reinforced by a statement Rhee made to the press: "We will not accept the armistice, but we have agreed not to obstruct it for a period of three months."

Rhee could still upset the armistice negotiations if those Americans who believed that the only satisfactory solution was a military one gave him the least encouragement. Had there been no Americans who preferred a military solution to peaceful negotiation, the eight-point proposal would have at least been tabled for further consideration before impossible counter-proposals were advanced.

Fortunately, the President of the United States made the decision that broke the deadlock. The last of the objectionable counter-proposals were modified, the armistice was signed by representatives of both sides on July 27, 1953, and twelve hours later hostilities ceased.

On August 2, 1953, John Foster Dulles himself left for Korea to consult with President Rhee, and the United States agreed to three basic undertakings, provided Rhee would co-operate in maintaining the armistice. They were:

1. A large amount of economic aid;
2. A security pact like the ANZUS and the Philippine Treaties, giving the US the right to station troops in Korea; and
3. A commitment to co-operate in reuniting Korea at the Conference and to meet Rhee regarding policy positions at the Conference.

Some military observers of the Korean scene have suggested that the Chinese and Koreans had signed the armistice only because the President had threatened the use of atomic bombs if they did not agree to the final terms which were offered to them.

That conclusion, as far as I know, is false. It was not Eisenhower but Harry Truman who had made an ambiguous reference to the atom bomb after the Chinese crossed the Yalu River into North Korea to stop the advance of General MacArthur.

The reason the Chinese and North Koreans signed the Armistice Agreement was exactly the same as that of the United Nations members who participated in the military action in Korea: It contained the best possible terms both sides could get.

1973. At the Summer Palace in Peking.
Front, left to right: the author, former Ambassador Li En-chu,
now Vice-President of the Friendship Association, and
author's daughter Audrey Topping; her daughter Susan
and Mrs. Li of the Friendship Association.

1973. In the Great Hall of the People, Peking.
The author chatting with Prime Minister Chou En-lai (above)
and Acting President Tung Pi-wu (below).

A visit during the peanut harvest, near Peking.

Exchanging pleasantries with a neighbour from Szechuan at the Liu Pei-chuke Liang Temple in Ch'engtu.

SHASHIYÜ

ABOVE: *Sitting on an unterraced hillside, being briefed by a leading member of the Shashiyü commune.*

RIGHT: *A terraced hillside. Soil was transported from a neighbouring valley.*

BELOW: *Cutting barley with a scythe and net attachment to catch the swathed grain on a commune near Fancheng.*

Entering the Yangtse gorges.

"East Is Red #33," sister ship of "East Is Red #32,"
in which the author and his family travelled.

The Nanking Bridge,
built after the
Russian technicians
left China.

ABOVE: *1971. A cotton tex-*
tile factory in the author's
hometown of Fancheng.

RIGHT: *1973. Grasslands*
of Inner Mongolia.

ABOVE: *Harvesting in the North.*

LEFT: *The author visiting nomads in their yurts.*

ABOVE: *1973. The historic city of Kueilin, "Cassia Forest," founded by Ch'in Shih Huang-ti* ca. *200* B.C.

RIGHT: *1971. The author's daughter Sylvia in the Hangchow Gardens.*

BELOW: *1971. The Laughing Buddha of Hangchow.*

14

TWO
PEACE CONFERENCES
GENEVA, 1954

The two most critical trouble spots in Asia after World War II and the defeat of Japan were Korea and Indo-China.

When Japan was forced out of Korea in 1945, the United States and the Soviet Union accepted Japanese surrender. With no thought for the unity of that country's oppressed people, Korea was divided between the two super-powers to fit into the plan of a world made up of Communist and anti-Communist camps. The result was a Korean civil war.

When Japan was forced out of Indo-China, the former great imperialist power, France, was restored, with no regard for the wishes of the people of Vietnam, Laos, and Cambodia. The result was a renewal of the war for independence in Vietnam against France. Representatives of the United States, the Soviet Union, the United Kingdom, and France met in Berlin in 1954 and agreed to call two conferences in Geneva to bring peace to Korea and Indo-China.

All the nations that had participated on both sides in the Korean War, plus the Soviet Union, were to be members of the Korean Conference. The Associated States of Indo-China, France, the United States, China, the United Kingdom, and the Soviet Union were to be participants in the Indo-China Conference. The two conferences were to run concurrently.

Since Canada was not a member of the Indo-China Conference, my report will be chiefly concerned with the Korean Conference. Only because there was a definite relationship between the two conferences will reference also be made to the Indo-China Conference.

The Korean Conference

The armistice of July 1953 had ended hostilities in Korea between the United Nations forces on one side and the North Korean and Chinese forces on the other.

Before the armistice was signed, differences of opinion had developed among the members of the United Nations who had participated in the Korean War about the calling of a conference to reach a permanent peace settlement. South Korea had been violently opposed to the armistice agreement and wanted no peace conference to hamper President Syngman Rhee's ambitions to unify Korea by force of arms under his control. The United States had consistently supported South Korea to prevent Rhee, it was said, from breaking away on a rampage of his own.

President Eisenhower, in deference to Canadian insistence, had ordered the United Nations Command at Panmunjom, which was composed entirely of Americans and one South Korean, to accept the United Nations General Assembly's Indian Resolution as "terms of reference" for an armistice. The State Department was not too happy about the manner in which the United States had been pressured to end hostilities in Korea. Mr. John Foster Dulles was, therefore, not enthusiastic about calling a conference to draw up a peace treaty. Also, Mr. Dulles had more or less guaranteed Syngman Rhee that if a conference was held, it would not reach an agreement unacceptable to him.

When the American Secretary of State finally agreed, at a meeting in Berlin in February 1954, to the calling of a political conference to consider "a peaceful settlement of the Korean question" and to restore "peace in other parts of Asia," nearly all of the participants in the war, including Canada, agreed to attend. The Secretary of State for External Affairs, Mr. Lester Pearson, appointed me as the acting leader of the Canadian delegation to the Korean Conference. I had just become Canada's Ambassador to Norway, and nearly did not make it. King Haakon was in mourning after the funeral of the Queen, and all official duties had been cancelled. Only by special arrangement was I enabled to present my credentials on Saturday, April 24 and, on Sunday the 25th, to fly to Geneva ready for the 26th.

On the Sunday afternoon, we were uncertain, due to a crisis in Vietnam, whether the Conference could begin on the Monday as planned. President Eisenhower had not yet decided whether to accept a recommendation by John Foster Dulles and Admiral Radford to send the American Army to relieve the French, besieged and about to capitulate to General Giap at Dien Bien Phu. Dulles was most anxious to prevent Vietnam from falling to President Ho Chi Minh. General Walter Bedell Smith used his influence to prevent American intervention in Vietnam to save the French—and said in my hearing that memorable afternoon, when France was seething with rumours and excitement: "No American boys are going to get bogged down in the jungles of Vietnam except over my dead body."

The General knew what jungle warfare was for infantry. Unlike General MacArthur, he subscribed to the traditional American military policy which was against getting involved in war on the continent of Asia. Deciding against American intervention in Vietnam, General Eisenhower made the second of his two crucial Asian decisions. The first had been to end hostilities by agreeing to an armistice in Korea. His acceptance of Bedell Smith's recommendation made it possible for the Korean Conference to open on schedule.

Considerable thought and discussion had taken place regarding the most appropriate organization of the Conference. Many United Nations members preferred a conference under the direct auspices of the United Nations which had authorized the United

Nations' action in Korea. The idea was that each of the two sides would sit on opposite sides of a round table—representatives of the United Nations on one side and representatives of China and North Korea on the other.

The United States was unalterably opposed to a conference associated with the United Nations, insisting that the nations that had participated in the Korean action could adequately represent the United Nations. The United States feared that a round-table conference under UN auspices would, in seating the representatives of Peking and Pyongyang for the duration of that conference, advance both governments' claims to United Nations membership. One of the reasons that the US had been opposed to a conference in the first place was that, should it be unable to settle the prisoner-of-war question, reference back to the United Nations would create a climate favourable to the permanent change of Chinese representation from Taiwan to Peking and the admission to the UN of the Democratic Republic of Korea. And second, the State Department did not wish to have its hands tied yet again—as they were thought to have been in Panmunjom, when the United Nations Command was coerced into accepting terms it had rejected and to which it had made counter-proposals.

Canadians began to consider whether or not Canada should accept participation in such a conference, despite her record as the third largest UN contributor to the military operations in Korea. Soon after the Armistice was signed, Canada had to weigh the advantages against the disadvantages. Participation in the conference meant sharing responsibility for its results, but if, every time there was a division between the US and Syngman Rhee on the one hand and the United Nations on the other, Canada faced demands that she accept the Washington-Seoul view or risk disrupting the Conference, Canada's difficulties would be enormous and her freedom of action seriously curtailed.

These reservations were based on the assumption that India would not be a participant. (Though she had good claims to participation, India would not press to be included. She would accept, however, if invited.) Apart from the United States and seventeen Latin American countries, only Nationalist China, Greece, and Pakistan had voted against India. The Latins had changed their tune in response to US representations, and South Korea accused India of being concerned mainly with "appeasement of Communist aggression." The problem was solved by the Berlin decision to have all the nations that participated in the Korean War, plus the Soviet Union. Australia, on the grounds of her geographical location, wished to be included, and Canada's and Australia's wishes in this respect were not mutually exclusive.

The French wanted to include Indo-China, but John Foster Dulles opposed the idea, insisting that the Conference address itself solely to the question of Korea. The United States had made certain promises to President Rhee in order to get him to accept the armistice. One was a Mutual Defence Treaty, concluded and signed in Washington in October 1953, and ratified by Rhee and Y. T. Pyun, Minister of Foreign Affairs of the Republic of Korea. Another was that the Political Conference would definitely unite Korea or there would be no agreement. Rhee assumed the assurance to mean that a united Korea would be under his Government.

If the Conference failed, there would then be no justification for another on Indo-China, and Dulles wanted to prevent such a conference until the Communists of Vietnam were defeated.

A meeting of the United States, France, the United Kingdom, and the Soviet Union, represented by their Foreign Ministers, Mr. John Foster Dulles, M. Georges Bidault, Mr. Anthony Eden, and Mr. Vyacheslav Molotov, took place in Berlin from January 25 to February 18. They reached an agreement to call a Political Conference the preamble of which read:

> Considering that the establishment by peaceful means of a united and independent Korea would be an important factor in reducing tension and restoring peace in other parts of Asia, there-

fore we propose a Political Conference for the purpose of reaching a peaceful settlement of the Korean question.

The Berlin agreement proposed that the Political Conference consist of the representatives of the Big Four (the United States, the USSR, the United Kingdom, and France), the Peking regime, the two Koreas, and all other countries desiring to attend, whose armed forces had participated in the Korean War. The conference was to meet in Geneva on April 26, 1954, "to settle through negotiation the questions of the withdrawal of all foreign forces from Korea, the peaceful settlement of the Korean questions, etc."

The South Korean Ambassador expressed concern that acceptance of the Soviet Union as a member implied recognition of China, but Cabot Lodge said there was no such implication. (On February 10, 1954, the *New York Times* reported Syngman Rhee as saying that he was determined to reopen the Korean War and that he would, if necessary, go ahead without United States support. Rhee criticized the US as "mistaken" in discussing peace with the Chinese Communists and claimed: "Unification through a Political Conference is ridiculous.")

The French Ambassador continued to maintain that an Indo-China conference should be held simultaneously and not, as proposed, after the Korean one. France was determined to negotiate a settlement of Indo-China at almost any price—even relaxation of trade restrictions against the People's Republic of China and recognition of Peking.

The State Department anticipated a propaganda battle at the Geneva Conference. The Chinese were expected to be stiff and unyielding. There would not be much ground for manoeuvring, since the Chinese wanted concessions from the West, and the only concessions the United States was willing to give were negative ones, such as refraining from increasing the pressures then being applied to mainland China.

Two weeks before the Geneva Conference was scheduled to meet, reports from Vietnam indicated that, while the battle at Dien Bien Phu had abated in intensity, a very serious political and military situation had developed in Indo-China. The implications, which the loss of Dien Bien Phu would have for the West in general and for the countries of Southeast Asia in particular, were viewed with alarm.

President Eisenhower and John Foster Dulles urged "united action" to meet the emergency through an *ad hoc* Pacific coalition along NATO lines, consisting of the ANZUS countries (France, the United Kingdom, the Associated States of Indo-China, Thailand, Indonesia, the Philippines, and Burma) to prevent further inroads by Communists in the area. A warning would be issued to China to stop aiding the Vietminh in Indo-China.

The United Kingdom proposed something approaching a "Southeast Asian NATO."

Almost on the eve of the Conference, Syngman Rhee issued another statement, published in the *Korea Times,* to explain that he had decided to send a representative to the Political Conference in Geneva. Rhee's statement read:

> The decision to attend has been made, however, because of a desire to show our spirit of co-operation with our great friend and ally, the United States. We hope sincerely that should the Conference fail, America will have come to realize—finally and conclusively—that further negotiation with the Communists would be both futile and perilous. We hope, therefore, that if and when the Geneva Conference has failed, the United States and our other friends of the Free World will join with us in employing other means to drive the enemy from our land.
>
> If a reasonable period of time has passed without Conference results, we know the United States will consult with us, as it has promised to do, on the abandonment of discussion as a way to peace with Communism and Communists.

The United States placed considerable emphasis on the importance of a "moral and propaganda victory" and the preservation of the integrity of the South Korean Government, preferably through holding elections in North Korea only.

Canada believed that any propaganda victory arising out of the Conference should be a by-product of it and not its objective.

Also Canada thought the ROK Government would have to submerge its identity in a greater Korea and that the elections should be held throughout Korea.

Mr. Nehru deplored that the Geneva Conference was being preceded by a "proclamation of what amounts to a lack of faith in it and alternatives involving threats of sanctions."

India was also deeply disturbed by the turn of events in respect to Indo-China. Development of the hydrogen bomb and Dulles' threat were interpreted as unwillingness on the part of the United States to seek a peaceful solution of the Indo-China problem. The Indians thought China was not overawed by the threat and would match increased Western assistance to Vietnam with aid to the Vietminh, thereby risking an intensification of the fighting. India feared the return of Western domination of Asia, thinly disguised as an alliance between Western countries and two or three Asian satellites.

When I arrived in Geneva from Norway to be Acting Leader of the Canadian Delegation to the Geneva Conference whenever Mr. Lester Pearson, the Canadian Secretary of State for External Affairs, was unable to be present as Leader of the Delegation, I was appalled by the great differences in position being taken by the United States and South Korea on the one hand and by most of the rest of us on the other.

I thought I had come to participate in a peace conference along the lines laid down in Berlin. Instead, the emphasis was entirely on preventing a peace settlement from being realized. I was particularly disturbed by statements—especially from the South Koreans and supported by the Americans—giving the impression that the Conference had been called merely to go through the motions of proving that there could be no political solution by negotiation. The only difference was that Rhee's statements were couched in intolerant, bombastic, aggressive language, while the cultivated Dulles discoursed persuasively on how lack of military action could lead to the horrors of a more general war.

The day before the Korean Conference was scheduled to start, the atmosphere among the Western representatives, who knew that it might be called off, was tense, but President Eisenhower took Bedell Smith's advice over Dulles and Radford's. The Conference was convened, as planned, on April 26, 1954, and the Indo-China Conference began to run concurrently a few days later.

When discussion began as to whether or not regular UN rules of procedure were advisable, Mr. Dulles interrupted to explain that no such rules were needed—he and Molotov had agreed before the start of the Conference that decisions would be reached by consensus, thus making voting unnecessary. It was not until the forenoon of the opening day that an agreement was reached on Conference chairmanship. There were to be three co-chairmen—Prince Wan, the Foreign Minister of Thailand, Mr. Molotov of the Soviet Union, and Mr. Anthony Eden of the United Kingdom. They were to rotate in that order on successive days, starting with Prince Wan.

The seating arrangement was to be alphabetic, according to the English alphabet, in two horseshoe semi-circles and part of a third, one behind the other. The Australians came first, the Belgians next to their right, the Canadians next, and so on. The Chairman sat on a platform facing the centre of the consecutive semi-circles. The inner semi-circle seated eight delegations, the second eight, and the last three. The meetings were to be closed to the press and the public. Each delegation, however, could conduct its own press relations.

Mr. Dulles preferred the agreement reached in Berlin during the organization meeting of the Conference rather than the Armistice agreement, since the former called for the "establishment of a united and independent Korea" and did not mention the withdrawal of belligerent forces. This meant that the Republic of Korea could demand Chinese withdrawal from North Korea to purge themselves of aggression without a corresponding withdrawal of United Nations forces from South Korea.

In meetings of the "Sixteen" (the delegations that had participated in the United Nations action in Korea), it was difficult to have frank discussions, because the Republic of Korea representative blew his top every time anyone made a positive suggestion in the direction of a negotiated settlement. Canada, Australia, and New Zealand were not happy about the American approach, which was based on the unhelpful assumption that we were the victors of the Korean War. We could not manoeuvre, only dictate the terms, which was exactly what South Korea wanted.

The United Kingdom expressed agreement with fundamental US aims, but suggested proposals which the world would recognize as reasonable and which the Communists would have difficulty in rejecting. France stressed the importance of everyone's not always taking the same line in our caucus meetings, even though we basically maintained a united public front.

Careful preparations were made to frustrate Molotov's "knavish tricks," but to no purpose—Molotov didn't play. His first statement was moderate in tone and substance. There was no indication, however, at the beginning of the Conference, that the other side would initiate any move towards a solution. Molotov gave the impression that he was playing second fiddle to Chou En-lai, who spoke more positively. After all, the Soviet Union had not been an active participant in the War.

Chou En-lai maintained that the United States and South Korea were seeking to block a peaceful settlement, that unification was a matter for the Korean people themselves to settle, and that foreign troops must be withdrawn. Chou attacked the United States for its "intolerable" occupation of Taiwan and for stabilizing Pacific security systems to impose colonialism again on Asia. Asian problems, he said, should be solved by Asians, just as European problems were by Europeans.

Dulles' speech was rather extreme. He developed the theme that Communists were driven by their doctrines and by their fears to seek Lenin's goal of "amalgamation of all nations." Communists, he said, believed that their system could live only by progressively destroying human freedom.

Chou En-lai named the United States as the source of tension and trouble in Asia and said that the peaceful coexistence of countries with different social systems was always possible. The Conference should, he felt, do something about American threats to the peaceful development of China, which were disturbing to Asia and the world. Chinese "volunteers" were in Korea, Chou En-lai said, because United States forces crossed the 38th Parallel and threatened the security of China. He also accused the United States of using the prisoner-of-war issue as a pretext to drag out the Armistice negotiations.

The Indo-China Conference, which was to be conducted on alternate days (since it involved many of the same delegates who were attending the Korean Conference), was already having a profound influence on the atmosphere and conduct of the Korean Conference. When the French indicated they were prepared to make more and more important concessions to obtain a settlement in Vietnam, the United States became more and more anxious to terminate the Korean Conference, lest concessions of similar importance were offered by the United Nations side, resulting in a settlement unsatisfactory to both South Korea and the United States.

When the Indo-China talks got started, it appeared that we would simply go through the motions of exchanging proposals until we saw how the Indo-China Conference was likely to go.

In a caucus of the Sixteen, General Bedell Smith insisted that our side could not agree to specific proposals on Korea. The Communists, he said, had rejected a UN basis for the unification of Korea, including proportionate free elections (i.e. based on the fact that North Korea contained one third of the total population and South Korea two thirds). Since the ROK Government had been founded on UN resolutions, any position taken by the South Koreans was, *ipso facto,* a United Nations proposal and any position taken by the North Koreans *ipso facto* anti-United Nations.

Pyun demanded that controversial issues not be raised and no concessions made at this time. Since the constitution of the Republic of Korea made no provision for all-Korea elections, his

Government could accept no such election. The important issue was that the United Nations must supervise elections only in North Korea.

Pyun was apparently not concerned about whether or not that would be in accordance with the constitution of the Democratic Republic of Korea in the North.

Mr. Pearson suggested that we rally on positive common ground. If we insisted on elections in North Korea only and only on the withdrawal of Chinese troops, world opinion would attach blame to us for a breakdown. All-Korea elections were certainly consistent with United Nation's principles.

To come to grips with the relevant issues, Mr. Pearson suggested that South Korean proposals and North Korean proposals be submitted to a smaller committee for consideration. He admitted the differences were great, but felt a decision could be reached only after the differences had been ironed out in negotiations. During the whole of the Korean Conference, not once did we come to grips with relevant issues in small committee meetings as proposed by Pearson, and in plenary session of the Conference, Pyun's proposals were offset by statements from Chou and Nam Il, and *vice versa*.

Chou said this Conference had been convened to solve Korean problems, but that it was now deadlocked because the ROK Government sought to unify Korea under its control. The Conference should, he said, create conditions for the Korean people to themselves unify the country through nation-wide elections without foreign interference. Withdrawal of all foreign troops was a necessary prerequisite, and mutual agreement between the two Korean governments was essential.

Nam Il proposed: "In order to assist an all-Korea commission in holding all-Korea elections in accordance with an all-Korea electoral law, in true conditions which preclude foreign intervention, a neutral nations supervisory commission should be formed to supervise all-Korea elections."

For several weeks, the United States had tried to persuade the ROK to modify its opposition to all-Korea elections as a first step in the unification process. In another session of the Sixteen, however, proposals by the ROK for unification were the same:

1. Elections in North Korea only and in accordance with the ROK constitution;
2. Elections under the supervision of the United Nations;
3. Chinese troop withdrawal from North Korea one month before elections in the North; and
4. United Nations forces phased withdrawal after the ROK completed effective control *over all Korea.*

If President Rhee had not made it abundantly clear before that nothing would deter him from carrying out his intentions, these ROK terms could have left no doubts about Syngman Rhee's neurotic ambitions. His persistent attitude also lent some credence to North Korean and Chinese charges about what happened on June 25, 1950, at the 38th Parallel.

At this point, Mr. Pearson suggested that if Pyun were to present proposals to the Conference, he should do so as coming from South Korea only. They certainly did not represent a consensus of the Sixteen.

By June 1, differences were considered by most of the Sixteen to be too great to make genuine negotiations worthwhile. From then on, the United States concentrated on finding a strategy for bringing the Conference to an end.

The United States delegation was instructed by the State Department to break up the Conference on the issue of United Nations authority—an issue which, to some delegations, including the Canadian, did not appear sufficiently clear-cut and defensible. To me, it was rank hypocrisy. As has been noted before, the Government and Constitution of South Korea were said to be based on United Nations principles, because the elections, which chose the members of South Korea's National Assembly, had been supervised by the United Nations Temporary Commission on Korea (on which Canada was represented).

It was argued, therefore, that it would be a defiance of the United Nations unless North Korea argeed to a similar procedure. All-Korea elections would be a violation of South Korea's United Nations Constitution.

It seemed not to matter that the United Nations General Assembly had not been consulted as to its attitude. If it had, there is no doubt that the UNGA would have endorsed a resolution providing for an all-Korea election supervised by an international commission acceptable to both sides. Most of the members of the Sixteen had expressed their attitude in favour of that solution.

Both the United Nations and the other side could have been represented in a neutral nations commission, which could not have operated without the sanction of the United Nations. The issue was trumped up to break up the Conference; "the authority of the United Nations" was phoney.

Bedell Smith further argued that the Communists, by denouncing the United Nations as belligerent, rejected the principle of collective security. Only Colombia, Turkey, Thailand, Greece, and, of course, South Korea supported him. (It is noteworthy that whenever South Korea spoke in the UN caucus, it was followed by an oppressive silence.)

As the Americans continued to insist upon the spurious "United Nations authority issue" and their responsibilities to the ROK, they hoped many other countries would, in the next plenary session of the Conference, say a good word for the South Korean proposals. Colombia and Thailand agreed to help. Anthony Eden was not anxious to speak. Australia, New Zealand, and Belgium were most unlikely to agree, but the Dutch might. The Canadians had no desire to rush into a statement.

South Korea's Pyun, talking wildly, announced to the press that the Sixteen agreed with his proposals. When asked by the press if he would accept a neutral nations commission composed of non-Communist countries like India, Burma, Switzerland, and Sweden, he launched into an unbridled attack on India, Burma, and Indonesia.

The Americans and South Koreans thought they could dismiss Chinese proposals for a neutral commission to supervise elections in Korea, but in Canada's opinion, such a commission would be absolutely essential to the unification of Korea. We thought that we should accept the fact that the United Nations, as at Panmunjom, was negotiating as one belligerent with another belligerent. We should treat the other side as an equal in strength. We could not imply that a settlement would have to be one imposed by the United Nations. In addition, the brute fact of our situation was that the United Nations was incapable of imposing a settlement on the Communists unacceptable to them, and we had all recognized that fact when we began armistice negotiations in Panmunjom. Yet the Americans and South Koreans continued to talk as if the United Nations had won the War.

If the intention was to force the Communists to profess their faith in the United Nations and its acts and thereby, as they would see it, admit their aggression, then the exercise was just silly. The Communists had come to Geneva to negotiate, as Canada certainly thought our side had.

Alexis Johnson did, however, agree with us that the Conference might be suspended *sine die*. Canada had been saying for some time that, if the Conference had to be terminated without a settlement, why not adjourn to assemble again when the time was more propitious? We thought that Chou En-lai had made proposals in Plenary Sessions which indicated much common ground. In our opinion, a fair solution to both sides was definitely possible, if the Americans wanted one. Johnson obviously thought that something could be done to meet the Canadian suggestion to refer the proposals of both North and South Korea to a committee to find common ground for a settlement. Johnson called it a "negotiating phase" and thought it might be possible that a plenary session could be held to convoke a restricted negotiating session. These positive ideas were the first, and alas the only, suggestions made by an American which promised a possibility of making real progress towards a solution.

One difficulty for the US position was that the Communist delegates had not attacked the principle of UN collective security, but had merely maintained that, in Korea, the UN acted illegally.

This raised the question of whether it was not unwise to force the Soviet Union into the extreme position of having to attack the UN Charter itself.

On June 3, Bedell Smith announced, in a meeting of the Sixteen, that out of the general debate a clear-cut issue had emerged which would command the support of public opinion.

I wondered what new "clear-cut issue" had emerged that would also be approved by the world—which seemed to be such an important determining factor.

The issue was "the position of the United Nations."

Bedell Smith was back on the same old charger. Were the Communists ready, he asked, to have Korea unified under free elections supervised by the United Nations? If not, then there was no basis for further negotiations in good faith. The United Nations representatives would then report in the plenary session that further Conference meetings on Korea were unnecessary and the Conference should close.

I maintained that the issue of free elections was important. If the other side would, as they were indicating they would, accept free elections with the requisite machinery they entailed, including supervision by an international commission acceptable to both sides, then we would be home free.

Smith, however, replied with considerable heat that the United States had not sent troops into Korea to protect free elections, but to uphold the authority of the United Nations. Free elections were important, but not that important.

With a little less heat, I reminded the General that Canadian troops had also been in Korea and that Canada attached much importance to free elections throughout Korea because they were essential to the achievement of United Nations objectives for Korea.

Bedell Smith then concluded the argument in a conciliatory mood and suggested that we were now agreed on two principles and, so long as we kept them separate, we could each give the emphasis to the one which appealed most to our public opinion.

I added only that Canada was on record in the Conference as

favouring elections throughout Korea under international supervision acceptable to the United Nations. We therefore reserved our right to advocate the continuation of negotiations to achieve this objective rather than termination of the Conference before a serious attempt to reach an agreement had been made.

In the June 6 Plenary Session of the Korean Conference, Chou En-lai said that "common ground" could be found for settling the Korean question peacefully. No delegate, he said, had come out against the consolidation of peace in Korea and the unification of the country through all-Korea elections in accordance with United Nations principles of proportional representation. Only a few delegates disagreed that foreign troops should be withdrawn within a specific time. Some, however, held that, since there was no more bloodshed, the settlement of the Korean question was no longer urgent. This was a mistake. ROK proposals should not stand in the way of an agreement being reached in view of the common ground which existed. South Korea was trying to dominate the Korean election in the name of the United Nations to impose its own constitution on the North.

At the same session, Molotov made the following helpful proposals:

1. Free elections throughout Korea;
2. An all-Korea body of North and South representatives in preparation for elections;
3. The withdrawal of all foreign forces in specified periods;
4. An international commission to supervise free all-Korea elections.

Molotov, Nam Il, and Chou helped in several important respects to advance their position very close to that of most of the delegations on our side. There was no excuse for closing the Conference without a peace agreement. Molotov's resolution, supported by Nam Il and Chou En-lai, could have been accepted as a basis for a settlement by most of the Sixteen.

Bedell Smith ignored, rather than rejected, Molotov's motion.

He said the United States would rest its case. Expressing extreme impatience, he strutted out of the Conference chamber.

The inescapable fact was that there was no possibility of seriously examining Molotov's proposals unless we were prepared to break with the ROK and the United States. The choice we faced was to break with them or to go along with them in the name of "unity" and break up the Conference.

Smith knew perfectly well that the ROK Government was determined to dominate Korean elections in the name of the United Nations if they were ever held. He told me that, although he could not say so out loud, the fact was that, so long as Rhee lived, there could be no unification of Korea. My impression was that General Bedell Smith felt obliged to accept Dulles' policies on all political issues. On military matters, however, he had emphatically opposed Dulles.

It had been no accident that in the armistice agreement, both sides had agreed to a Supervisory Commission which was not a United Nations body. Canada's position was that the same type of Commission could appropriately supervise all-Korea elections. We felt that there was no reason why the Conference could not agree on formulae for the withdrawal of foreign troops within a specified period and a guarantee of Korea's peaceful development by the nations most interested in peace in the Far East. Canada believed this would be in complete accordance with the principles of the United Nations. As a matter of fact, a study of the preamble of the Berlin statement which organized and called the Conference would reveal that these proposals were in accordance with the spirit and word of that declaration, which Dulles had himself accepted.

If only the United Nations had been represented by the Secretary-General, who could have appointed an Acting Leader of the UN Delegation, Canada could have insisted on the Conference continuing to negotiate a peace agreement, as we did in the Armistice negotiations when we insisted that the UN Command be forced to accept the UN General Assembly decisions as terms of reference.

The United Nations, however, was not represented, the Berlin meeting having taken the Conference out of United Nations hands. So we Canadians found ourselves in a totally false position, since it did not in the end matter at all what we thought was right. Canada was the last of the Sixteen to give her reluctant consent to the termination of the Conference due to United States persuasion or pressure—depending on your point of view. Yet we still clung to the possibility of a *sine die* adjournment, should the opportunity arise. It did arise, but those of us who supported it were quickly brought into line by General Bedell Smith.

Before the final session, I was instructed to state Canada's position to the Sixteen. The following is an excerpt from my statement:

> We feel bound to make clear that the declaration, as it now stands, in several respects does not represent the views we have put forward at this Conference and continue to hold. We have no intention of making any public declaration of dissent. We consider, however, that we should frankly explain that when this subject is considered again in the United Nations or in any other conference in which we might take part, we would feel free to put forward again the views which we have expressed here and which have been stated as Canadian policy by the Secretary of State for External Affairs before Parliament.

The final act was played out on June 15, 1954, in the last Plenary Session of the ill-fated Korean Conference.

Nam Il of North Korea declared that, since it was clear that the Conference could not agree on a way to unify Korea, the participants should take steps to ensure peaceful conditions there. They should agree to the withdrawal of foreign troops, in equal numbers, as soon as possible, the reduction within a year of North and South Korean troop strengths to 100,000 men each, the formation of a joint Korean commission to recommend to both governments proposals for the gradual liquidation of the state of war, and the formation of a further joint Korean body to work for improved economic and cultural relations between the two Koreas. Moreover, they should recognize that treaties between either Korea and other states which involved military obligations were incompatible with the peaceful unification of the Korean peninsula.

Molotov backed Nam Il's programme, pending the final settlement of the Korean problem. He said no action should be taken which might threaten the peace in Korea, but expressed confidence that both Koreas would act in accordance with such agreement.

It was evident from these two speeches that the other side was fully aware of what was about to happen. Nam Il and Molotov tried at least to salvage from the Conference some safeguards against a renewal of hostilities in Korea and the consequent tragic results, if hostilities could not be prevented. In contrast to the behaviour of President Rhee's representative at the Conference, Nam Il appeared to be a statesman intent on at least the preservation of the armistice agreement.

After Molotov's contribution, the Conference recessed, and the Sixteen met according to plan. General Bedell Smith termed the presentation by the other side "extremely well done."

In the circumstances, Smith felt that the joint declaration would have to be read in plenary, and Spaak agreed, even though he favoured the Molotov proposals and thought it impossible to oppose Molotov's declaration.

The General then said that he was prepared to refer to the armistice agreement as providing for the cessation of hostilities in perpetuity. This would dispose of the necessity to consider Nam Il's proposed provisions to prevent renewal of hostilities. Molotov's earlier proposal could be disposed of without further consideration as a "statement of good intent."

Anthony Eden said that he didn't see how we could avoid accepting Molotov's declaration.

It was finally agreed that Bedell Smith should make his statement on the armistice agreement and that Prince Wan would read our declaration into the record.

After the caucus, the plenary session was resumed. Bedell

Smith said that the armistice agreement would remain in effect as long as the Communists observed it. Moreover, it provided for everything in the Molotov declaration and in much more exact terms.

Casey from Australia said that the Nam Il proposals put the ROK on a par with the aggressor regime in the North and sought to deny the ROK access to its friends.

Garcia from the Philippines flooded the ground he sought to cover with rhetoric, but otherwise fulfilled his assignment.

Spaak, speaking extemporaneously, made similar points more economically. He then said, as agreed, that the time had come to separate, but nothing had been lost and that, in time, it should be possible for the parties to meet again and continue efforts to reach an agreement.

Pyun of the ROK continued his record of unfortunate interventions by saying that the Communist speeches had proved they were trying to conquer all Korea through infiltration and that the Molotov declaration was part of this sinister scheme.

Prince Wan then read the declaration of the Sixteen into the record.

The declaration roused Chou En-lai, and he made a proposal which nearly brought down the house which the Sixteen had so carefully built. As I listened to him, I noticed a tremour in his voice which I had never heard before. He appeared agitated and was trembling slightly. He had been completely shaken by our declaration and Spaak's sad farewell. Chou had come to Geneva to get a peace treaty and now rose to make a last effort to save the Conference.

Chou En-lai pointed out that the armistice agreement was binding on the two belligerent sides, but that the Conference should nevertheless reach its own agreement. He therefore made a proposal that the Conference be adjourned for the time being, but that it be reconvened by the Co-Chairmen whenever they decided that the time was propitious. He appealed to all delegations not to extinguish the possibility of arriving at a peace agreement.

Spaak, our spokesman-designate in the resumed session, turned to me after Chou had finished and whispered: "What do you think, Chester?" I said this was exactly what Canada had been working for ever since it became clear that we would never get down to negotiations in this Conference. I added that I thought we should support Chou's proposal.

While Lord Reading of the United Kingdom was saying that a break-up of the Conference did not mean the abandonment of hope for the future, it gave the delegates on our side who wanted postponement rather than termination a chance to exchange nods. Spaak whispered to the Australians on his left, and I consulted my colleague John Holmes on the Canadian Delegation. John agreed that Chou's proposal was exactly what Canada had hoped would be the decision, if the Conference was unable to agree on a peace treaty. Spaak made signs to the day's Co-Chairman, Anthony Eden, who nodded approval. (We had taken good care to choose a day when it was Eden's turn to be in the chair.)

Spaak then stood up and quickly stated that he supported Chou En-lai's amendment. The developing situation looked most promising, especially when Chairman Eden expressed the opinion that Chou En-lai's proposal deserved most serious consideration. Eden then asked if Spaak's position was generally acceptable. That was as far as Eden, as Chairman, could go. Since there was to be no voting, if no one objected to Spaak's position, Eden said that he would declare the Chou-Spaak suggestion to be the consensus of opinion of both sides.

For a moment, there was dead silence. Then we heard a rustling coming from the direction of Bedell Smith, and all eyes were turned towards him. As he rose, it was evident that there would be no consensus. His face was flushed. He said that the Chou proposal made this Conference responsible for a Korean settlement—what other purpose could it possibly have had, one wondered, except in the mind of Syngman Rhee?—whereas it was not intended to be a permanent body outside of the United Nations. It had been given a specific mission, which it had been unable to achieve. He was, therefore, not prepared to associate himself with the proposal of the Chinese delegate. Our own declaration had made it clear that the Communists could begin new negotiations any time by accepting our two principles.

Eden, as Chairman, then responded that, since there was no voting procedure, the Conference could only take note of the various points raised. No one challenged this.

Chou En-lai then said that he was pleased that the Conference would take note of the proposal made by him and Spaak. He now knew that the United States delegate had been preventing the Conference from ever arriving at a conciliatory agreement.

When rebuked by the General, realizing the enormity of the unforgivable sin of back-sliding, Spaak sought to extricate himself from this unfortunate position. He said that he supported the Chou proposal because it stressed the hope that there would be more discussion on Korea. Spaak thought such discussion should be in the United Nations.

Chou replied that this would mean that China would be excluded from further negotiations, since China was excluded from the United Nations, and would make eventual agreement on Korea impossible.

There were no more speakers, and the Conference ended in failure. Dulles had promised Rhee that the Conference would achieve nothing unacceptable to him. He had kept his promise.

Talks with Chou En-lai

I wondered what effect the action of the Western powers would have upon the Chinese who had come to Geneva with a more flexible attitude to the West, including the United States. I talked to them every day at the coffee breaks and was pleasantly surprised. When I closed the Canadian Embassy in Nanking in 1951, the attitude of Chinese towards the United States had changed from warmth to bitter resentment. They resented the American intervention in the Chinese civil war when war broke out in Korea and feared an invasion of Manchuria when General

MacArthur marched across North Korea to the Yalu. From the first day of the Korean Conference, however, I noted that Chou En-lai seemed to have high hopes of returning to China at the end of the Conference with a copy of a peace treaty on Korea signed by all the participants. The attitude of the Chinese delegation was one of willingness to co-operate in the solution of Asia's two most acute international problems—to settle wars in Korea and Indo-China.

In addition to finding out how the Chinese felt about our rejection of their proposals, I had another good reason for asking for an interview with Chou En-lai. I had received a request from Ottawa asking me to call on him regarding a Canadian pilot who was reported to have been shot down in Korea while flying an American fighter. It was not known whether Squadron-Leader McKenzie had survived and, if he had, where he was. Someone thought it would be clever to submit his name in a list of Canadians known to have been killed in Korea, asking if any of them were prisoners. I rejected this approach, knowing that the Chinese Communists appreciated a quality which they called *t'an pai,* speak truth.

I made straightforward enquiries about McKenzie through Wang Ping-nan and learned that he was alive and well and a prisoner in Manchuria. I also learned that his was a special case and that it should be dealt with through Chou En-lai.

I asked for an appointment towards the end of the Korea Conference, and it was promptly arranged at the Chinese delegation's villa in the country north of Geneva, where I was warmly welcomed by Chou En-lai and the top officers of his staff. I immediately took up the case of Squadron-Leader Mc-Kenzie. After hearing all of the details involved, Chou En-lai replied that his case was special, since he had been flying an American fighter and was classified as a prisoner of war. I explained that Canadian pilots were not participating in the air war against North Korea and that this man had only been an exchange pilot in a peace-time arrangement between the Canadian and American air forces for training purposes. Chou En-lai assured me that, after due process of law, he would be released. He pointed out that, unlike the missionaries for whom I had negotiated and who were being released, the case of Squadron-Leader McKenzie involved legal considerations and that it would take some time before he could be released. Chou En-lai assurred me, however, that he would in due course be reunited with his family.

When a much longer period of time passed than it was thought necessary, relatives of McKenzie were persuaded that the only way the Canadian pilot would get a release would be through pressure by publicity given to the case. A publicity organization was prepared to do this and offered a considerable sum for the story. Some thought I had been too naïve in accepting the Prime Minister's assurance. My reply was that, if more trust was placed in the persons who wanted to publish the story than in the word of the Prime Minister of China, I would wash my hands of the whole affair. I wanted no part in any publicity attempt to pressure Chinese authorities, or even threats of publicity. The family ruled out publicity, so I wrote to Chou En-lai from Norway about the family's concern. Squadron-Leader McKenzie was home with his wife and family by Christmas.

Speaking of the Korean Conference, Chou En-lai admitted that, while it was a great disappointment to him that a settlement had not been reached, he still felt that the eight weeks of the Conference had not been entirely wasted. Much common ground had been reached, and most of the delegates had indicated a desire to meet again to settle the problem by peaceful means. Only South Korea, Chou En-lai said, had made belligerent noises.

It appeared that the Chinese delegates had not held out much hope for a settlement even before they left Peking, because John Foster Dulles had indicated in Berlin that, while he would agree to the calling of a conference, he was not in favour of having one. Since the United States came with this attitude, it was not strange the Conference had failed. A settlement on

Indo-China, Chou thought, would have a good influence on any subsequent conference on Korea.

Chou En-lai was most anxious to stop the fighting in all of Indo-China and, especially in Vietnam, to reach a political settlement. He hoped his proposal for Laos and Cambodia would be accepted. China would urge that all foreign troops be withdrawn, including Vietnamese in Laos or Cambodia. If the majority of the people in Cambodia and Laos wanted a Royal Government, and he expected they would, China would extend recognition. The problem in Laos was more difficult, since resistance there was much greater, but solutions for the two countries need be neither the same nor simultaneous.

The Prime Minister thought that if France would take the initiative and reach a decision, free elections could be held in both North and South Vietnam to solve the problem. Partition was not a solution, he said. Bao Dai was afraid of elections, but not Ho Chi Minh.

Chou expressed the opinion that General Bedell Smith had considered Chou's proposals "moderate and reasonable." Assistant Secretary of State for Far Eastern Affairs Walter S. Robertson, however, found them unacceptable. It was difficult to decide what United States policy was, since the United States representative was not backed by his own delegation.

To Chou, Bidault was a puzzle. Bidault had seemed to me to be partially and sometimes entirely asleep during the afternoon plenary sessions of the Korean Conference. He sometimes had to be awakened by one of his officers when speakers referred to his statements. The Prime Minister said Bidault seemed to be afraid to meet him and that Bidault had insisted on complete secrecy from the Associated States, Vietnam, Laos, and Cambodia in their negotiations, while he negotiated for them behind their backs.

Although Chou En-lai was returning to Peking, he said he would come back to Geneva to carry on discussion on the "most important problem facing all of us today—the question of Indo-China," where fighting was still raging.

As I left the villa, the Prime Minister and the delegates politely escorted me out of the front door in the good old-fashioned Chinese manner. I shook hands all around and stepped into what I thought was my car. The chauffeur drove away before I noticed that he was not the chauffeur who had brought me. For a moment, I thought I was being driven only to the outer gate, where my chauffeur was no doubt waiting. We drove past the gate, however, and there was no car waiting for me. I asked the driver, whom I did not recognize, in the best French I could muster, where he was taking me. Without turning his head, he said in perfect Chinese: "I am taking you to your hotel."

It turned out that I was riding in Chou En-lai's own car. I had forgotten to ask my chauffeur to return for me, and Chou, noting that my car had not arrived, summoned his own while I was shaking hands with the staff so that I would not be embarrassed to find myself stranded. True Chinese courtesy.

The Indo-China Conference

The Indo-China Conference confined membership to the Big Four (the United States, the Soviet Union, the United Kingdom, and France), China, and the three Associated Indo-China States (Vietnam, Laos, and Cambodia).

Canada was not a member, but was interested and offered to give any help she could. Frequent discussions with Anthony Eden and occasionally with Americans gave Canada an opportunity to express views and to keep informed about developments even without direct participation.

In the early stages of the Conference, Bidault tried to initiate negotiations with Molotov, but ran into immediate difficulties over the relative positions of the Vietminh and Bao Dai. Bao Dai had been persuaded by France to send a delegation to Geneva, but he insisted on receiving invitations from the Foreign Ministers of the US, the USSR, and the UK. He also demanded for his delegation equality of status with the Vietminh.

Bidault was prepared to accept a cease-fire in Indo-China only if it was called a settlement, or armistice, and he denied a report that he planned for the partition of Vietnam, but did not rule out the possibility.

Although expected, the fall, during the Conference, of the central fortress of Dien Bien Phu came as a grave shock to the French. The Western powers assumed that the survival of Vietnam as a political entity would require protection from an international body or the support of a great power. President Eisenhower ruled against military intervention on France's behalf, but at the same time, the US, fearing that any settlement would favour the Communists, stood apart from negotiations.

The Conference was saved by Mendès-France, who came to power soon enough (and held it long enough) to work out agreements in Vietnam, Laos, and Cambodia. France was to the Indo-China Conference what the US had been to the Korean Conference—the major protagonist.

For a long time, the Conference seemed irremediably bogged down. The French insisted that military issues take precedence over the study of political ones, while the other side insisted that the "resistance governments" be recognized in Cambodia and Laos, as in Vietnam, before negotiations could continue.

Following the failure of the Korean Conference, Chou En-lai went into the Indo-China debate more determined than ever not to let it founder and especially to prevent the United States from developing in South Vietnam as firm a stronghold as it had in South Korea. (Chou's fears were, in fact, realized when the Saigon Government became completely dependent on the US, and America became engaged in a major war in Vietnam. More bombs were to fall on Vietnam, including areas close to the Chinese border, than had been dropped in all of World War II.)

It was the concessions Chou made and those he induced Ho Chi Minh to make that helped Mendès-France to reach agreements in Vietnam, Laos, and Cambodia. Despite General Giap's victory over French military forces in Vietnam, Pham Van

Dong made the most important concession when he accepted the temporary division of Vietnam for a period of two years. That concession ultimately prevented reunification.

The United States refused to sign the Indo-China agreements, the elections scheduled by the Agreement were never held, and hostilities were renewed. The United States, to save the Saigon Government, entered the war on a major scale, and President Nixon expanded it into Laos and Cambodia. The Soviet Union provided North Vietnam with sophisticated war materials, and China provided light weapons, troop training, food, and reconstruction aid.

Ironically, while the Korean Conference failed to establish peace despite the settlement, the Korean Armistice continues. And whereas hostilities have not been renewed between North and South Korea, three Indo-China Agreements were reached, but war continues.

15

THE
LAOS CONFERENCE
1961-2

Before the surrender by Japan, it had been agreed at the Potsdam Conference that after the Japanese withdrawal from Indo-China, Chinese troops were to be moved into the northern part of Vietnam. I was in Chunking, and it was there that I began to be indirectly concerned with the problems of Indo-China.

China was a partner of the Western powers, and Chinese troops were next door, but the idea of stationing Chinese troops in Vietnam was probably to make it safe for France to return in due course, which would take some time. As in the case of Korea, the feelings of the people of Vietnam seemed to be of no concern to the powers which made international decisions in the areas that came under their control after the surrender of Japan. The deciding factor in reaching such decisions was the new power struggle between the great powers which, with the downfall of Germany and Japan, had suddenly become super-powers. The question became which power should fill the newly created vacuums. Any area from which a rival great power had been driven became, *ipso facto,* a vacuum. Given this and the excuse that since nature abhors a vacuum, vacuums had to be filled for the safety and security of all people, including the people of the areas concerned, regardless of their feelings or the fact that they had more or less successfully filled those vacuums since the dawn of history.

When Vietnam was assumed to be a vacuum, China was a partner of the Western powers. China was not, however, important enough to accept the surrender of Japan in Korea. It had been conveniently forgotten that Korea had been a part of the Chinese Empire. The more important fact had also been ruthlessly forgotten that Korea was a unified viable country in which the Koreans themselves were fully capable of filling their own vacuum. Neither Korea nor China was important or strong enough even to share the territory which Japan had seized in the spectacular early, successful attempts to rise to world power. China had been acknowledged by the Western powers as a partner. Was that the reason Chinese troops were authorized to move into North Vietnam to hold the fort for France, perhaps as a sop to China for not protesting against the division of Korea between Russia and the United States?

Whatever the reason for Chinese occupation, the Vietnamese people had some very unhappy experiences during the time Chiang Kai-shek's troops were stationed in the North. When the French took over again in 1946, the only redeeming feature for the Vietnamese people was that the treatment may have been comparatively better, but the truth was that the Vietnamese did not want foreign troops of any kind in Vietnam. They desired only independence and the restoration of the freedom the French and Japanese had taken away from them.

After I closed the Canadian Embassy in Nanking in 1951 to return to Canada, I took the opportunity, before crossing the Pacific, to visit Saigon, where my daughter Audrey was living with her family, Hanoi, and Haiphong.

I have never been in any Asian country dominated by a Western power where there was as much hatred for that power as there was in Vietnam in 1951. Here and there in the main streets, I saw huge portraits of Bao Dai, the puppet of France, usually hanging at the third or fourth floor level of high buildings. This elevated position was not a mark of respect, but to keep the portraits out of range of rotten eggs and cabbage.

Anti-French feeling in Laos was never as intense or as widespread as in Vietnam. Laos was relatively isolated and far less important to the French, and both before the French were driven out by the Japanese and after their return, the French yoke lay relatively lightly there. Laos was rather a place for rest and relaxation. The Laotians, however, wanted independence and as soon as World War II was over, Prince Petsarath, the Prime Minister and leader of the Free Laos movement (Lao Issera), proclaimed Laotian independence.

The French would not tolerate this, and fighting started in 1946. The French forces occupied Vientiane and Luang Prabang, the administrative and royal capitals; the Lao Issera leaders were driven out and fled to Thailand where they set up a resistance government in exile. Prominent among the Lao Issera were the famous half-brothers, Prince Souvanna Phouma and Prince Souphanavong.

The three princes differed in their plans as to the best method of getting independence for Laos. Prince Petsarath refused to be placated and insisted on nothing less than complete independence. Prince Souvanna Phouma decided in 1949 to accept France's offer of independence within the French Union and returned to Laos to lobby for the compromise.

Prince Souphanavong was expelled from Lao Issera because he advocated co-operation with the Vietminh. He therefore organized a Laotian Communist party called Pathet Lao. The Pathet Lao forces actually fought with the Vietminh under General Giap in the battle for Dien Bien Phu near the Laotian Plain of Jars. The 1954 Geneva Agreement on Laos provided for the regrouping of the Pathet Lao forces in the two northern provinces of Laos, adjacent to North Vietnam, pending a political settlement in Laos by the Laotians.

The main thrust of the Laos Agreement was the political settlement under which there was to be unification of the country under the Royal Government and integration of the Pathet Lao forces into the national army.

The 1954 Indo-China Conference established three International Control Commissions comprising India, Canada, and Poland to supervise the three agreements in Vietnam, Laos, and Cambodia. India was asked to provide the chairman of each Commission.

The Laos Commission operated quite effectively for four years, helping to keep sporadic fighting under control and contributing materially towards the political settlement stipulated in the Agreement.

In 1956, Prime Minister Souvanna Phouma decided that neutrality was the best policy for Laos and by 1958, he had worked out a political settlement with Prince Souphanavong. The Agreement provided for the participation of the Neo Lao Haksat, the political arm of the Pathet Lao. Souvanna Phouma, as Prime Minister, then requested the International Commission to terminate its activities and retire from Laos.

I became actively involved in Indo-China affairs as soon as I arrived in India in 1957 as Canada's High Commissioner. New Delhi kept a tight reign on each Commission Chairman, and Ottawa kept in very close touch with each Canadian Commissioner. A great deal of my time was, therefore, taken up in discussions with India's Foreign Ministry regarding Commission policies in Indo-China. Our file on Vietnam was the largest single one we had in our New Delhi office. In the Indian Foreign Ministry, the veteran diplomat Mr. M. J. Desai was the expert on Indo-China, and I was a frequent visitor to his office. When Souvanna Phouma insisted that the Laos Commission had completed its work, we were both disturbed. We were not convinced that right, neutral, and left-wing elements had been sufficiently amalgamated in support of the Government to warrant a permanent adjournment of the Commission. With the US supporting and assisting the Right Wing, and the Soviet Union the Left, there were disturbing possibilities in Laos. Also, we agreed on the theory that the three International Commissions on Indo-China functioned as an interdependent group. We felt that if the Cambodian Commission was still necessary, the Laos Commission was even more so.

Both the Canadian Commissioner and the Indian Commissioner in Laos, however, seemed anxious to pull out. In one sense, this was natural, since the Commissioners would be considered *personae non gratae* if they failed to leave the country when requested to do so by the Prime Minister.

Neither M. J. Desai nor I was convinced that Souvanna Phouma may not have responded to some persuasion by certain semi-independent Americans who could function more freely with the Commission out of Laos. The new coalition also had a faction which was supported by the Soviet Union, and they would also be freer if the Commission were not present with military observers on the look-out for trouble.

Since it seemed inevitable that the International Control Mission Commission would be adjourned, M. J. Desai and I decided to persuade our respective Governments to make possible the return of the Commission to Laos, if trouble should occur. Mr. Nehru favoured this solution, and Ottawa was also in favour of the precautionary measure. If it should become necessary to revive the Commission, it could be recalled by the Chairman. Its activities were, therefore, suspended, not terminated.

As feared, the political settlement broke down. The Left Wing fared surprisingly well in the first elections, and there was a sharp reaction from the Right. Souvanna Phouma tried to hold the balance by forming a centre coalition, but he had no clear-cut political base of his own. At that time he did not have the confidence of the Americans, so he was forced out, a right-wing Government was formed, the Pathet Lao again went underground, the Government came under the domination of the army, and hostilities were resumed. As a result, a small neutralist army and the nucleus of a neutralist political party sprang up in support of Souvanna Phouma. It returned him to power. Rightwing forces, however, drove him out again. He retired to Cambodia in exile for a period before finally aligning himself with his half-brother, Souphanavong, against Prince Boun Oum. The latter headed the right-wing Government, which was really controlled by General Phoumi Nosavan, who received substantial military and financial aid from the Americans. Much of the military support for the Boun Oum Government was based in neighbouring Thailand, where the Americans were firmly entrenched.

The Soviet Union was supplying airlifted military supplies to the armies of the other two princes, whose base was in the Plain of Jars, and China assisted with small arms and ammunition.

By the end of 1960, hostilities in Laos had reached unprecedented proportions for such a traditionally peaceful country. More ominously, from the point of view of international peace and security, the two super-powers, the Soviet Union and the United States, were becoming increasingly implicated. As the civil war in Laos continued, it began to look more and more as though the Communists and their neutralist friends might take the whole country. On the American side, there was a strong feeling that direct intervention by SEATO countries should be undertaken, and some of the American military were even thinking of a drive through Laos into North Vietnam as a means of settling the Indo-China problem once and for all. The risk of a world war developing through a confrontation between the two super-powers in Laos became increasingly real.

Mr. Nehru therefore proposed that the Laos Commission be reconvened to end the civil war and prevent a confrontation between the two super-powers. This proposal was broadened by Prince Sihanouk of Cambodia into a call for a fourteen-nation conference "for the settlement of the Laotian problem"— a proposal to which the Soviet Union soon acceded.

The United States had been determined that Laos should not fall into Communist or neutralist hands. For a considerable time, the sole means of prosecuting this objective was through economic and financial support for the Royal Government in Vientiane and military support and assistance to the Royal

Laotian Army in the field. The United States was, therefore, opposed to the return of the International Control Commission and the convening of a new Geneva conference on Laos.

When John F. Kennedy became President of the United States, he was as determined as his predecessor to give no ground to Communism. He began very soon, however, to look for ways of establishing a *modus vivendi* with the Soviet Union over a wide range of problems. He did not, therefore, relish the prospect of a critical confrontation with the Russians in Southeast Asia.

Another positive factor was undoubtedly the emergence of Averell Harriman and John Kenneth Galbraith as individuals of influence in the Kennedy Administration. These men believed in neutrality as the only viable political posture for the nations of South and Southeast Asia and were probably advising the President along these lines.

The International Commission reconvened in New Delhi in April 1961 and proceeded to Vientiane in Laos. As a result of the *de facto* cease-fire, fourteen nations were invited to a conference to be held in Geneva. It was hoped that the cease-fire would be maintained throughout the Conference and that it would complete its work in a few weeks. In fact, the cease-fire was intermittently broken, and the Conference itself lasted for fourteen months, with one three-month recess. Nevertheless, the fact that the Conference was meeting took the heat out of the situation and wrote *finis* to the crisis.

The United Kingdom and India had been instrumental in persuading the United States and the Soviet Union to agree to attend the Conference. China had also agreed to participate, despite the rebuff received in the Korean Conference of 1954. She had two good reasons. In the first place, China desired participation with other world powers in the peaceful settlement of international problems in Asia, especially those which were aggravated by the international power struggle. The other reason, related to the first, was that China wanted neutrality for the whole of Indo-China. A neutral Indo-China would provide the most satisfactory land-buffer between China and the SEATO, controlled by Western powers. There was no doubt in my mind that the Chinese were genuinely in favour of complete neutrality and independence for Laos and the whole of Indo-China. I had almost daily conversations with Foreign Minister Ch'en Yi, Ch'iao Kuan-hua, Chang Han-fu, and Wang Ping-nan during the Conference, and they spoke frankly about the importance to China of good relations with Laos and Vietnam. In Laos, the Chinese were prepared to grant recognition to a Royal Laotian Government—if that was what the people of Laos wanted.

North Vietnam also had to be persuaded to attend the 1961 Geneva Conference on Laos. For them, the 1954 Agreement on Vietnam had proved a great disappointment. The South Vietnamese, backed by the United States, had prevented the elections provided by the 1954 Agreement, and which were to precede reunification. The Government of the Democratic Republic of Vietnam nevertheless accepted the invitation to attend.

The pro-Western governments in South Vietnam and Thailand were reluctant to attend any sort of peace conference. They favoured an outright military solution and saw no profit in dallying with neutralism or in holding conferences with the enemy.

Averell Harriman was Acting Head of the American Delegation to the Laos Conference and I of the Canadian. His understanding and vision as a negotiator were major factors in that Conference's success, and he brought to it a fresh breeze of determination to negotiate an acceptable settlement through peace, not an uncompromising take-it-or-leave-it attitude.

I vividly recall two incidents during the Laos Conference that illustrate the change brought about by Harriman. At a reception given by Norodom Sihanouk of Cambodia, Averell asked me if I would introduce him to Marshal Ch'en Yi, China's Foreign Minister and head of her delegation. This was a pleasant surprise, as I remembered how John Foster Dulles had refused to shake hands with Chou En-lai at the Korean Conference, even when Prime Minister Chou held out his hand when the two met accidentally.

The other incident was at the Geneva airport, when Mr. Nehru's plane stopped for an hour to refuel before taking him on to the United Kingdom and the United States. During the conversation they had, Governor Harriman stated unequivocally that he favoured neutrality as the only solution not only for Laos, but also for Vietnam. Mr. Nehru was surprised and immediately asked: "May I quote you to your President, when I see him in Washington?" Harriman replied, with considerable emphasis: "You certainly may."

A few days later, I asked Averell if there had been any repercussions. With a wry smile, he said: "Oh, I was slapped gently on the wrist and reminded that policy recommendations to the President are not usually made through the head of a foreign country."

In contrast, I recall an evening meeting in May 1961, prior to the opening of the new Laos Conference, with Dean Rusk. Most of the evening was spent in explaining to Mr. Rusk Canada's attitude as a member of the Vietnam Commission. He expressed the opinion that Canada had "leaned to the other side" in the positions she had taken in Commission decisions on policies affecting the United States. I had to cite a number of incidents to show that Canada had always attempted to take balanced, unprejudiced positions. I reminded him, for example, of the Commission's decision by a majority vote (with India and Canada voting against Poland) to accept as satisfactory evidence the manifest of each ship carrying French military equipment from Vietnam to North Africa. The United States was entitled, by the 1954 Geneva Agreement, to replace the amount and kind of French supplies. Without evidence, however, there could be no replacement. In this case, I suggested, the other side must undoubtedly have concluded that India and Canada had "leaned to the American-South Vietnamese side."

The Laotions themselves inevitably created the most difficult problems. The neutralists and the Pathet Lao were in favour of the Conference, but the Right Wing, being in power, insisted that they alone should represent Laos at the Conference. Differences over this issue forced postponement of the Conference beyond the scheduled date.

The problem of Laotian representation at the Conference was part of the larger problem of the formation in Laos of a government of national union which could speak for the whole country and which could enter into the sort of agreement which ultimately began to take shape.

The Conference opened on May 16 under the co-chairmanship of Sir Alec Douglas-Home and Mr. Andrei Gromyko, the Foreign Ministers of the United Kingdom and the Soviet Union respectively—an arrangement that derived from the Indo-China Conference. After the initial plenary sessions, acting co-chairmen were Malcolm MacDonald and Pushkin, a descendant of the Russian poet. They played a major part in the work of the Conference and deserve the highest praise for keeping the Conference going and for working out a method of negotiation that ultimately enabled the Conference to reach agreement.

In its initial stages, the Conference met in plenary sessions with the usual rounds of speeches, most of which were statements of positions and principles. The propaganda count was high. On matters of substance, the Western and Communist sides were miles apart, and neither they nor the more neutral participants could see much prospect of bridging the gap. The Soviet Union was chiefly interested only in a declaration of neutrality in general terms. When it came to terms of reference for the International Commission, the Russians wanted an iron-clad troika arrangement. There was to be complete unanimity between the three parts of the proposed coalition government before the International Control Commission could be authorized to take action or its military teams authorized to make investigations. That would simply have hamstrung every move of the Commission. The Soviet proposal was based on the troika type of government the Laotian Princes had agreed upon in their meeting in Zurich during the early days of the Conference. The meeting had actually been suggested by Sihanouk of Cambodia to get some agreement between the right, neutral, and left-wing rival Laotian groups on representation in the Conference.

Western delegates also attached importance to a declaration of neutrality, both by Laos and by other countries represented at the Conference. They also attributed equal, if not greater, significance to the terms of reference which would allow the International Control Commission to do an effective job. The Americans had a plan which would have created a highly elaborate Commission, manned, equipped, and empowered to cope with every possible contingency over a very wide geographical area.

Ottawa, concerned about the mobility of the Commission's military teams during the rainy season in areas where there were no paved roads, when even jeeps equipped with four-wheel drives were hopelessly bogged down, proposed helicopters as the only practical solution. Considerable time was taken up in discussions about helicopters, and I ended up being called "Mr. Helicopter."

In June, President Kennedy and Mr. Khrushchev met in Vienna and affirmed their support for a neutral independent Laos under appropriate international agreements. From among the problem areas involving the United States in confrontation with the Soviet Union, the two leaders had selected Laos as a sort of pilot project in *détente*. Before long, this had a beneficial effect on the Conference. Some of the Foreign Ministers returned to Geneva to confer on procedure as well as on substance, with the result that it was decided the Conference should meet in a series of restricted sessions to deal separately with each of the many issues involved and to provide a proper forum for the necessary hard bargaining and close negotiation. A list of the topics was prepared, and proposals submitted by various delegations were tabulated. The Conference then ploughed methodically through these controversial problems and reached temporary agreement on many of them. These were sent to a drafting committee to be phrased in terms acceptable to all for inclusion in the ultimate agreement. The issues that could not be resolved were temporarily set aside in what was called the "rock pile."

A new method was then worked out to deal with the "rock pile." A working committee consisting of the United States, the USSR, the United Kingdom, India, China, and France was set up to deal with them as they accumulated. The committee, however, was unable to crush all the "rocks." The rockiest rocks were turned over to the co-chairmen, and in a long series of meetings, MacDonald and Pushkin carried on negotiations on these issues in continuous consultation with all members of the Conference.

Using these various techniques, the Conference was able, by December, to draw up a nearly complete agreement. In the latter part of January 1962, the committee met and, in early March, drew up the agreement in its more or less final form.

The Conference could not, however, be brought to a close. The Laotians had not yet formed the new government, and the Conference had decided that the internal affairs of Laos were to be left strictly to the Laotians.

In June, a new coalition Government, under Souvanna Phouma, was formed, and the Conference was reconvened. By the end of July, the Agreement was signed by the governments of all Conference participants. It did not give any one of either the great or super-powers what it wanted. It did, however, represent a subordination of unilateral—and essentially military—effort to the wider endeavour of finding a negotiated and peaceful solution which would allow the local people to work out their own destiny in their own way.

The International Control Commission was finally authorized to commence its work.

The Commission's terms of reference represented a closely negotiated compromise between the demands of the two sides and were, in some respects, open to more than one interpretation. As the decisions of the Conference had to be unanimous, and as the interests of the participating countries were, to say the least, disparate, it was not surprising that there were serious differences in interpreting the terms of reference. In practice, the terms of reference may not have proved as important as we thought they were during our endless negotiating ones. Paul Bridle, Canadian Ambassador to Turkey, put it very well when, as our first Commissioner on the Laos Commission after the 1961–2 Conference, he said:

> In my opinion, the moral of the story of the revived Laos Commission, like that of all Indo-China commissions since 1954, is that it is not so much terms of reference as the attitudes of the authorities on the ground which count. [. . .] In the last analysis, the Commission can supervise and investigate only to the extent that local authorities permit it to do.
>
> Sometimes, especially if it is well equipped with helicopters and similar aids, as the Laos Commission was, it can do some effective regulatory work. But basically, the Commission's value is its presence as a symbol of the concern of the international community and as a catalytic agent which can sometimes defuse dangerous situations or facilitate negotiations between the sides. The Laos Commission did a lot of valuable work of this kind. Of course, if the parties are determined to fight, there is little the Commission can do. In that case, its value is reduced to the symbolic, it being a link with the international community which, when the time is ripe, may again be able to assist the warring sides to disengage and, hopefully, to keep the peace.

16

WASHINGTON AND HANOI, 1966

CANADA'S OFFER OF "GOOD OFFICES"

In March 1966, the Canadian Government decided to send me as a "Special Representative" to Saigon and Hanoi to offer Canada's "good offices" in getting peace talks started, especially between Washington and Hanoi. I had been retired from the Canadian diplomatic service for several months, but was, of course, willing to assist in any way possible in ending the undeclared but devastating war.

Prime Minister Pearson and Secretary of State for External Affairs Paul Martin were not proposing that Canada undertake the role of mediator. The purpose was merely to explore common ground for a settlement in the hope that Washington and Hanoi would agree to start direct talks leading to negotiations. I was also to carry a letter from our Prime Minister to President Ho Chi Minh in reply to a letter from the President regarding the situation in Vietnam.

The increasingly destructive bombing of North Vietnam was getting dangerously close to the border of China. Canada feared that the People's Republic of China might decide that China's security was threatened, as they had when General Douglas MacArthur led the United Nations armies to the Yalu River in 1950.

Canada therefore decided to do whatever she could to prevent a recurrence of what happened in Korea when General MacArthur marched to the Yalu. The first step was to revive the International Control Commission in Vietnam. On the instructions from Ottawa, the Canadian representative on the Commission proposed that the Commission ask the Geneva Conference Co-Chairmen, the UK and the USSR, to draw up new terms of reference to enable the Commission to take the initiative in peace talks to end hostilities. Simultaneously, Canada approached the United Kingdom, the Soviet Union, India, which chaired the Commission, and Poland, the other Commission Member. The United Kingdom favoured the idea. India, the Soviet Union, and Poland, while not opposed to the idea, did not think the time was propitious.

Since United States approval was important for my mission, I suggested the matter be discussed with Averell Harriman, who had led the American Delegation to the Geneva Conference on Laos in 1961-2, when I was Acting Head of the Canadian Delegation.

Governor Harriman and I met in the residence of the Canadian Ambassador to the United States, Charles Ritchie, in Washington and discussed the Canadian proposal for several hours. Harriman was heartily in favour of the attempt to get peace talks started, undertook to get President Johnson's approval, and succeeded. The next morning, Charles Ritchie and I were invited by Mr. William Bundy to discuss the details of our proposal. As a result, we received the sanction of the State Department.

I left immediately for Hong Kong and as soon as I got the all-clear from Victor Moore, our Commissioner on the Vietnam Commission, I flew on to Saigon. There I was met by all three International Control Commissioners.

Soon after my arrival, as I was relaxing in our Commissioner's drawing room, I heard a tremendous explosion. The house shook, and the windows rattled. I was reminded of the American blockbusters I had heard fall in Nanking, but said to myself that it could not be an American bomb within earshot of the US headquarters in Saigon and the seat of the Government of the Republic of Vietnam. Then a second one went off. Again the building shook and the windows rattled. When the Commissioner returned, I asked him what was going on.

"Oh, just some American bombs," he replied.

"But why so close to Saigon?" I asked.

"The Vietcong are all around us," he said.

It was sixteen years since I had seen the same type of bombing befall the people of Nanking—after the civil war was over, and the bombing served only to terrorize the population. But this was bombing the very people the bombs were supposed to protect.

That evening, the Indian Chairman of the Commission gave a dinner, to which all members, their wives, and military personnel were invited. The bombs continued to fall, and the usual small talk of necessity grew louder with every bang. I could not get my mind off the thought of more mutilated bodies, more homes blown sky high.

After dinner, the members of the Commission met and discussed the Canadian proposal. All agreed it was a good idea, but the majority thought there was no point in asking for new terms of reference under present conditions.

The next day, I had conversations with the Foreign Minister of the Saigon Government. I had known him since the 1954 and 1961–2 Conferences in Geneva. He favoured ending the war by a return to the Geneva Agreements and personally hoped that the whole dispute could be referred back to a new Conference. In fact, he seemed to be eager to return to the 1954 Agreements.

I also had a long talk with President Thieu, who also favoured a return to the Geneva Agreements, especially the provision separating the two sides by a demilitarized zone. During our conversation, he compared his own position in Saigon with that of his opposite number in Hanoi, President Ho Chi Minh, and said: "It is unfair. We do not interfere with his movements in Hanoi. He walks around anywhere on foot, and no one tries to assassinate him. I cannot go from here to my house except in a bullet-proof car, preceded and followed by an armed guard." I chose not to mention how many people of Vietnam, both North and South, had told me about their respect and support for Uncle Ho, whom they considered to be the father of the country. If Thieu had been loved by the Vietnamese, perhaps he too could have walked home without an armed guard.

I next called on the American Ambassador, Cabot Lodge, who showed me a map marking all the landing places along the east coast of Vietnam which were being supplied directly by sea from the United States. Use of these new ports would avoid the Saigon bottleneck, which prevented military supplies from getting to the battle fronts quickly enough for effective action. Now there would be parallel expeditions striking simultaneously across the country from each of the new stations. "Nothing," he said, "can stop us. We are chewing them up."

From Saigon, accompanied by the Canadian Commissioner, I flew via Phnom Penh and Vientiane to Hanoi. Parts of Vietnam looked like the surface of the moon—a scene of utter devastation. Large patches of jungle were burned out by napalm bombs, and whole villages and fields had disappeared. At Hanoi airport, I was met by the Vice Foreign Minister, whom I had known in New Delhi, the Chief of the Protocol Division, and Canadian members of the Commission's military team stationed in Hanoi.

On our way to the city, we were held up for some time by several huge trailer trucks hauling camouflaged ground-to-air missiles.

At seven the next morning, I had my first interview with Colonel Ha Van Lau, whom I had known in Geneva in 1954 and again in 1961-2. He was the Liaison Officer of the Hanoi Government to the Military Control Commission. He stated that Hanoi would be willing to return to the Geneva Agreement of 1954. There could be no peace talks, however, except upon acceptance of the Four Conditions outlined by the Government:

(1) all American troops must be withdrawn;

(2) the Provisional Government of the National Liberation Front must be accepted as the Government of Southern Vietnam;

(3) the sovereignty and territorial integrity of Vietnam must be guaranteed;

(4) Vietnam's neutrality must be guaranteed and all internal problems settled by the Vietnamese without foreign interference.

My comment was that, while there would probably be little difficulty with the last two, the first two conditions would be completely unacceptable to the Americans. I therefore suggested it might be wise to compromise on the first two conditions and negotiate the Americans out of Vietnam, since the Vietnamese could not hope to win the war against the most powerful of all nations. The talk did not end until Ha Van Lau had given me a full report of the damage done to North Vietnam by the American bombing, including the killing of school children and hospital patients. My reply was: "Why not try peace talks to end once and for all war in Vietnam?"

For the next few days, there were both formal and informal interviews, as I climbed the hierarchy, up to and including Vice Foreign Minister Nguyen Co Tach and Foreign Minister Nguyen Duy Trinh. I have never worked harder or used more arguments to put the American intervention in Vietnam's civil war in the best possible light to persuade the officials with whom I talked to try negotiations to end the war.

One afternoon, after a long interview, the Vice Foreign Minister invited me to accompany him to the Museum of the Revolution, where we saw a film of American bombing taken from below—bombs falling into the midst of houses, strafing by low-flying fighters, smoke, dust, destruction, the dead and dying. The Minister reminded me that he had accepted several invitations from me in New Delhi. He said: "I have seen so many Canadian films and propaganda, I wanted you to see at least one of our films."

Another afternoon, I walked to the lake in the middle of the "Paris of the North." (I remembered the lake from a visit in 1951, when the French were still there.) I was accompanied by the representative from Protocol, who had been with me since the airport meeting. He had been accompanied by an interpreter until I learned that he had been Third Secretary in Hanoi's Embassy in Peking and spoke Chinese.

We came to the lake. It was very attractive, especially at one end, where there was an island surrounded by lotus plants. On the island were banyan trees draped gracefully over an old Buddhist temple, and a picturesque, Chinese-style arched bridge connected the island to the mainland.

"What is the name of this lake?" I asked my companion.

"Return Sword Lake."

"Why is it called Return Sword Lake?"

He told me this story:

"Long ago, Vietnam was invaded by a great army under a great Chinese general from the North. Everywhere the Vietnamese forces fell before the invaders. Our king was sad and dejected. He knew Vietnam would soon be completely taken. He came to this lake, downhearted and depressed. He took a small boat and rowed out into the waters of the lake, his head hanging low in great despondency. Deep in the water, he suddenly saw something rushing up towards him. He stared into the depths and saw it was a great sword. When it came to the surface, he reached down and grasped it by the handle to lift."

I interrupted him and said: "If that had been in England, he would have shouted: 'Brand Excalibur!' "

My friend paid no attention and went on:

"Armed with the powerful sword, he led the armies of Vietnam in a great, victorious battle. The general and his armed hordes from the North retreated. Vietnam was saved. Vietnam cannot be subdued.

"In gratitude, our king rowed out again to the spot where the sword appeared. His Royal Majesty prayerfully returned the sword to the depths of the lake.

"If Vietnam ever again needs it to repel any invader from anywhere—North, South, East, or even West—the sword will arise again to repel the invader."

The next morning, I met the Prime Minister, Pham Van Dong, whom I already knew from the Geneva Conferences. Accompanied by a Deputy-Director, he received me and Victor Moore on the steps outside the Independence Palace. Tea was served in the Prime Minister's reception chamber, and I proceeded to explain the purpose of my visit.

The Canadian Government was concerned about the dangerous situation prevailing in Vietnam. As a neighbour and friend of the United States, and because our welfare was intricately bound up with the United States, we had some understanding of that country. Canadian foreign policy was not identical with American foreign policy, even though we were frequently regarded as blindly following American policy. On important occasions, we had had serious differences with the Americans. On the other hand, there were occasions when we agreed. I reminded the Prime Minister that Canada's Prime Minister was the first Western, foreign Head of Government to propose a halt to the bombing of the Democratic Republic of Vietnam.

Although Canada had some understanding of the United States' point of view, it was nevertheless possible for us to have some understanding of the situation faced by the DRVN. We knew something of the history of the revolution led by President Ho Chi Minh. We sympathized with, and supported, some of the objectives of that revolution. It was not insignificant that the Canadian Government had selected me for the task of offering Canada's "good offices." Our Prime Minister and our Secretary of State for External Affairs, Mr. Paul Martin, were fully aware of my personal attitude to the necessity and importance of fundamental revolutionary changes in Asia. They knew that I shared the aspirations of the people of countries like Vietnam and China for complete independence from, and domination by, strong foreign powers.

I explained that I was not sent to Hanoi to persuade anyone to change or modify his policies. My purpose was to try to obtain clarification on the two crucial points which had been declared must be accepted by the United States before there could be any consideration of peace: the demand for the withdrawal of all American troops and the demand for United States recognition of the Provisional Revolutionary Government of the National Liberation Front as the Government of South Vietnam before a peace settlement could be considered. We hoped there could be a possibility of direct, informal discussion regarding these two points between the Democratic Republic of Vietnam and the United States.

At this point, I stated that we welcomed the January 4 statement by the DRVN Foreign Ministry and the letter from President Ho Chi Minh. They gave Canadians some hope that there could be a peaceful settlement—hence my role in the offer of "good offices."

Prime Minister Pham Van Dong began his statement by saying: "I welcome your visit here, because I think you are a man of goodwill and because we think Prime Minister Pearson is a man of goodwill. President Ho Chi Minh asked me to convey to you his greetings, because you are a man of goodwill. It does not necessarily follow, however, that since we are men of goodwill, problems will be solved. That is the tragic aspect of the situation, because we think that the United States has not yet such goodwill. The political and military circles in the United States intensify the war. We know this, and you must know it too."

"Yes," I said, "we know the commitment is being increased. We fear that the application of great military power and the resultant increase in the momentum of war will make it more and more difficult later to reach an agreement than it is now."

"If you say that," Pham Van Dong commented, "it will be more difficult for us to talk."

"I can see the difficulty," I replied, "because, as before, both sides are determined to have a military victory."

"If so," he said, "you rightly understand the intention. In this respect, you and I agree with each other. The conclusion is that the United States does not have the goodwill to find a solution and, therefore, in today's talk, it is not easy to come to some agreement—not that we lack it, but there is lack of goodwill on the other side."

"My suggestion is," I said, "that the most effective and least destructive way is for both sides to decide to negotiate. At the present time, that may be the only way to secure the withdrawal from Vietnam of American troops."

"I beg your pardon," the Prime Minister said, "but your logic is not satisfactory. This logically would mean that the United States increases its military force in order to withdraw; that it occupies Vietnam in order not to stay on; that it intensifies the war in order to cease hostilities. The Americans have paid no heed to our January 4 statement. They have ignored Ho Chi Minh's letter. We are prepared, but, because of this attitude, what can we do?

"Let us look at the situation at the end of nineteen sixty-four," he went on. "American strength was thirty thousand troops. By the end of nineteen sixty-five, it was two hundred thousand. By the end of this year, it will be four hundred thousand, and they will use means of warfare more savage than the German fascists. This is a colonial war by the United States. You should not support them in this policy. The longer the war, the more bitter their defeat.

"You understand our aspirations: independence and freedom to live in our own territory. The United States of America lies on the other side of the ocean. To come to a settlement, they must go back."

"I realized this before coming here," I said, "from your Foreign Ministry statement and your President's letter. I am not surprised at the clear-cut terms of your position. I am glad, however, that you mentioned this. It is a complex problem. In the peace conference that should logically follow an agreement to cease hostilities, you could have guarantees from the great powers that have been involved."

The Prime Minister interrupted: "The Laos and Vietnam Conferences of nineteen sixty-two and nineteen fifty-four produced guarantees. Of what use were they? And that is because the problem is so complex, not simple at all."

"Yes," I said, "I know the problem is very complicated. You remember that the Americans did not sign any of the Indo-China Agreements reached in Geneva. They were not bound except by their promise not to upset the Agreements. Another complication arose out of the French signing the Vietnam Agreement instead of Bao Dai. In coming here, I had no illusions about the great gap that exists between Vietnamese and Americans. We are convinced that a solution is possible only if we can find some elements in the two positions where there can be some meeting of minds. I ask, despite your complete distrust of the United States, if it would not be worth-while to explore through direct talks the possibility of negotiations?"

"We are talking," the Prime Minister replied.

I said that I was referring to direct talks between representatives of Washington and Hanoi. Perhaps some agreement to start talks similar to the Panmunjom arrangement could be worked out, regardless of continuation of hostilities in the South. If an armistice were arranged, a conference could follow to negotiate the four points and other issues.

The Prime Minister's comment was: "All this depends on one thing only—that our Canadian friends should persuade their American friends to adopt the four points and the Foreign Ministry statement of January 4.

I again reminded him that Canada had no desire to become a mediator. If the Prime Minister could give us some specific proposal, we would have some reason to persuade our American friends to agree to an acceptable arrangement.

Pham Van Dong repeated that the four principles were essential, but that the January 4 statement had opened the way for a new step. He insisted that "the United States unconditionally stop all air raids against North Vietnam."

I immediately intervened to obtain clarification on this point. Was he implying that the United States need only stop the bombing for informal talks to begin?

He replied: "I shall answer you. If the United States Government declares that it will stop all military action and attacks against the Democratic Republic for good, and unconditionally, we will talk."

I could scarcely believe my ears. Was it really possible that Pham Van Dong was actually prepared to have direct talks with Washington unconditionally on the four points, including prior withdrawal of American troops and recognition of the National Liberation Fronts Provisional Government? He had said nothing about South Vietnam. This was too good to be true.

I had been about to give up the whole undertaking, when Pham Van Dong, almost suddenly, used the January 4 statement as his justification for the proposal he let me think I was gradually working out of him. I was completely startled, but tried not to show it. To make absolutely certain that I had not misunderstood him, I continued to ask questions.

"Are you asking for cessation of military action against the DRVN and if you get it, you are prepared to meet the United States to prepare the ground for ultimate negotiations?"

"To that sentence," he said, "I must add that an official statement must be made that it [the bombing of North Vietnam] is unconditionally and definitely stopped."

"Are you limiting what you say to the territory of North Vietnam?"

"Yes."

"This has nothing to do with United States action in the South?"

"I have not mentioned it. Should I?"

"Yes."

"Our ultimate objective is United States withdrawal."

"Mr. Prime Minister, are you prepared to negotiate that issue?"

"All of the four points. The body with the authority is the National Liberation Front—two belligerents."

"Is that a precondition to talks, or can it be left for negotiations? Is there some possibility of starting informal talks between you and Washington if the United States accepts your proposal, leaving all issues with respect to South Vietnam for later negotiations—perhaps at a conference, so that talks leading to a cease-fire may start?"

"Our position embraces many aspects, but in brief, we can say that informal talks and a cessation of attacks against North Vietnam go together."

"To clarify your last point, your one requirement is an American declaration which definitely and unconditionally concerns cessation of action solely against North Vietnam?"

"Correct."

"We shall be glad to carry to the United States the proposal you make and your position."

On my return to Canada, the proposal was first discussed with the Prime Minister and the Secretary of State for External Affairs in Ottawa. Both Mike Pearson and Paul Martin were intrigued and hopeful the proposal could lead to peace talks. I went to Washington. Charles Ritchie and I met William Bundy, accompanied by an officer from the State Department, in our Embassy residence to deliver and discuss the proposal. Bundy was interested, but carefully non-committal. We went over the proposal and all the details thoroughly. He said the matter would be given consideration, and we would be informed of the State Department's reaction.

I returned to Ottawa, and we waited patiently. We waited for more than a week. There was not a peep from Washington. Paul Martin telephoned and waited. It was becoming evident that the State Department was not too interested and did not consider the proposal sufficiently important to give it the priority a serious proposal usually receives. Towards the end of the month, we were notified that a decision had been reached.

I went to Washington again, this time to the residence of our Minister, Yvon Beaulne, since Charles Ritchie was not in Washington. The reply delivered to us by William Bundy was to the effect that the United States would stop bombing North Vietnam only if Hanoi would stop assisting the Vietcong in men and military supplies. I knew this would not be acceptable and wondered if, at least, some changes could not be made in the wording of the text of the reply. A few of our objections were met, and very minor changes were made, but the gist of the reply remained unchanged.

In explanation of the extended delay in replying to Hanoi's proposal, Mr. Bundy said that the State Department had been so concerned about disturbances in Saigon and the excitement caused by the self-immolation of Buddhist priests by fire in the streets to protest against the war, there had been no time to consider Pham Van Dong's proposal. My reaction to that excuse was that self-immolation by monks in protest against what was going on in South Vietnam should have been an incentive to giving priority and attention to a peace proposal—unless, of course, there was to be no change of American policy in Vietnam.

It was with a heavy heart that I returned to Hanoi. As I passed through Hong Kong, the newspapers were publishing reports from Washington declaring that the United States was prepared to stop bombing North Vietnam if Hanoi would stop assisting the Vietcong. The only purpose I could see for this publicity was to prepare the people of the United States for an escalation of the bombing of North Vietnam by depicting the North Vietnamese as unreasonable. Only the President and the State Department knew that Hanoi was willing to negotiate peace if the United States would stop the bombing.

It was against my better judgement that I was persuaded to go on to Hanoi from Hong Kong. Hanoi's reply, as I expected, was an outright refusal even to consider such an abject, impossible condition. Subsequently, I learned that the State Department had also instructed the United States Ambassador in Warsaw to inform the Ambassador of the People's Republic of China, at one of their periodic meetings, of the condition upon which it was offering Hanoi to stop the bombing of North Vietnam. It was, of course, a foregone conclusion that the Chinese Ambassador would immediately report the offer to Peking and that Peking would inform Hanoi to ensure an outright rejection.

When I learned of the Warsaw meeting, there was no doubt left in my mind that the State Department had made public the

United States "fair offer" to stop bombing North Vietnam chiefly to justify, to American and world opinion, the bombing of Haiphong and Hanoi.

Back in Ottawa, I conveyed Hanoi's rejection to Mr. Pearson and Mr. Martin.

Paul Martin decided that, this time, the Americans should come to Canada to get Hanoi's reply, and he gave a dinner for William Bundy and officers from the State Department. All Canadian External Affairs officers interested in Far Eastern affairs also attended. Mr. Bundy spoke very ably and at considerable length on American policy in Vietnam. He assured us that the United States wanted to end the war in Vietnam, but not at the expense of the Government in Saigon, and also assured us that there would be no escalation of the bombing of North Vietnam.

Not long after the Bundy visit, the bombing was escalated, with raids on the harbour of Haiphong and in the vicinity of Hanoi.

I suffered pangs of conscience after I had reported to Washington the results of my first visit to Hanoi. I began to wonder if my report had encouraged the Americans to think that Hanoi had made these concessions because the bombing was really hurting them and that Washington therefore became all the more determined that bombing should be pursued relentlessly until North Vietnam was crushed.

It was not until Dr. Daniel Ellsberg gave the *New York Times* the Pentagon's secret study of the Vietnam war that my suspicions were confirmed. The study, as reported in the *New York Times* on July 1, 1971, revealed:

> The Johnson Administration's continued expansion of the air war during 1965 and 1966 was based on a "colossal misjudgement" about the bombings' effect on Hanoi's will and capabilities.

The Pentagon must certainly have been chiefly interested at that time in unconditional surrender by the Vietcong. If the State Department had no desire to end the war by negotiation, the

Pentagon must have been even more determined to end the war by total victory.

According to the same *New York Times* account, the sequence of events (oil bombings ordered by President Johnson) was interrupted on June 7, when Washington learned that a Canadian diplomat, Chester A. Ronning, was on his way to Hanoi to test North Vietnam's attitude towards negotiations, a mission for which he had received State Department approval. When Ronning returned, it said, Assistant Secretary Bundy flew to meet him in Ottawa, but quickly reported that the Canadian had found no opening of flexibility in the North Vietnam position. With Ronning's return and Sharp's assurances, the stage was set for the oil tank strikes. (This refers, of course, only to my second visit to Hanoi. The Pentagon may not have been informed of the first visit or deliberately ignored Hanoi's offer to talk peace.)

A report from the Seventh Air Force in Saigon called the operation "the most significant, the most important strike of the war."

17

RETURN VISITS
TO CHINA

Very soon after Canada and the People's Republic of China established diplomatic relations on October 13, 1970, I was invited to visit China by Prime Minister Chou En-lai. It was in fact the fourth invitation I had received, but I could not accept until Canada recognized China.

I suppose everyone is nostalgic about his place of birth. It was twenty years since I had closed the Canadian Embassy in Nanking, forty-four years since I had been in Fancheng. There was, however, a much more important reason for wanting to revisit China. I wanted to find out for myself what truth there was in some of the reports of newspapermen and China-watchers. Had the Chinese really all been regimented and were they hopelessly brainwashed? Had they completely lost their sense of humour? Could they no longer laugh? Did they never have fun? Did they have no differences? Did they all look alike, talk alike, walk alike, dress alike, and think alike? Were they colourless and drab and uninteresting? Had they become a race of faceless robots controlled by ruthless masters?

The best way for me to find out what the Chinese people themselves thought about what was happening in their country would be to visit and talk to the people I had known all my life and who knew me and my family.

Re-entry Point: Canton

Arriving in Canton, my daughters, Sylvia and Audrey, and I were welcomed at the railway station by city officials, who accompanied us to a comfortable, spacious hotel. It was a Russian-type building which was practical but not as attractive as the Chinese-style compound with rock gardens, pools, gnarled trees, and beautiful flowers in which we were housed on our return to Canton. From our windows, Canton was attractive. The hills, many of which had been devoid of vegetation when I was there in 1951, were now clothed in the deep green of tropical trees. Glazed tile roofs added colour. Shrubs and blossoming trees lined many streets.

We went for a walk by ourselves. In a nearby park, two clever artists were busy clipping paper profiles of any passerby willing to pose for a minute and make a very small payment. We, of course, had ours done and chatted with a small crowd which had assembled. Many spoke *p'u t'ung hua,* which has become the national language of the common people. Their responses were the same as had always been characteristic of Chinese peasant folk. When I asked the profile artists what was the difference between Russian profiles and those of other foreigners, several onlookers chimed in with the artist to repeat the conventional idea: "Russians have 'great noses' and other foreigners have 'high noses.'"

The parks of Canton were well kept and, more important, were now open to the public. There are still drab, overcrowded areas in Canton, but they are orderly and clean.

The Canton Trade Fair

At the Canton Trade Fair, we had opportunities to meet many of the young people who were there explaining their exhibits. I talked to a young man who was demonstrating a complicated piece of machinery and found that questions about his name, his home, and his age were still considered to be a friendly and polite way to establish a basis for conversation. He was so enthusiastic about the machine he had helped to create under the guidance of experienced technicians and engineers that my daughters had to keep interrupting to get at least some interpretation of what was being said. The other young men and women shared his attitude and enthusiasm. As soon as we showed an interest, and I asked questions in their language, the response was immediate and friendly. They explained the difficulties which they had encountered in constructing the machines, how these had been overcome, and how they still expected to improve them. The machines were usually too sophisticated for me. I learned very little about them, but I did learn that Chinese young people are enthusiastic about their involvement in constructive work and enjoy participation in cooperative effort.

The exhibit that interested me most and in which I became absorbed was a wooden model of a device to harness tides in river deltas. The model was demonstrated by a young woman whose home village was in the delta of the Pearl River. She ran the water back and forth several times to explain the principle of the plant and how it worked. It was simple but ingenious.

I asked the young woman if I could visit her home village to see the plant in actual operation. She replied that I would be welcome, but the one in her village was the first of many that had been built in the Pearl River Delta area and it made use only of the incoming tide, whereas the others also used the ebb tide. I said I wanted to see the first one and asked her who had thought of the idea and put it into practical use. She replied that a few university engineers had been sent to their village to do manual labour and "to find out if there was any way they could help us." They had asked what was the most important problem of the village and were told it was the job of lifting water from the river for the cultivation of rice. Working together with the peasants, the engineers finally constructed a plant which not only lifted water for rice cultivation, but also developed power for small mills and electricity for the villages.

Since a visit to the Pearl River Delta, would take three days, and I was due in Peking the next day, I decided to postpone the trip until my return to Canton from North and Central China.

Journey to Tung Kuan

The first thing I requested when I came back to Canton was the trip to the delta. It was suggested that the trip would be difficult and, as it would be necessary to stay overnight at Tung Kuan, might not be as comfortable as we would expect. It was evident they had not planned a tour for us, and I had to assure our host that Sylvia and I had often stayed in old Chinese inns and were fully prepared for whatever accommodations were available.

On the way to Tung Kuan, we passed through one of the richest rice-producing areas of China and perhaps of Asia. Before getting out of Canton's outskirts, we passed thousands of Phoenix trees in their full dress of flaming reddish-orange blossoms. People who have seen only the streets of the city centre may have some excuse for saying that Canton is drab. We saw Canton's wooded hills, attractive public parks, and coloured glaze-tile buildings in the attractive old Chinese architectural style, with great banyan trees, rock gardens, and flowers of every colour.

When we got out into the open countryside, it became abundantly evident, from the vast areas of rice paddies extending to the horizon or to the distant wooded hills and low mountains, how the millions of people in Canton and Hong Kong are supplied with their rice, meat, fish, vegetables, fruit, eggs, chickens, and geese.

Driving along the highway in a Russian version of a Cadillac, we saw garden after garden of dark green peppers, cucumbers climbing on tripods of bamboo, egg plants, and tall Chinese cabbage. The highway was lined with shade trees to shield travellers from the blazing sun. There was mile upon mile of horsetail pines and orchards of bananas bearing deliciously sweet fruit in great abundance. Even more abundant were the lichee orchards, with the first of several crops per season of exotic fruit. But more impressive still were the luxuriant, heavy crops of extensive rice paddies in thousands of acres of flat, rich delta soil.

Here there are three crops a year, and the farmers I talked to were proud of their new varieties, which have doubled and tripled the yield. Usually, the farmers give the name of their own commune to the variety they have themselves developed by scientific selection. There are nearly as many varieties as there are communes, and there is healthy competition among communes in efforts to increase yield and quality.

The further we went, the rougher the highway became. We crossed countless bridges over canals and small streams and were ferried across dozens of small rivers. Everywhere, the new network of canals and connecting tributaries of the Pearl River bringing water to the rice paddies swarmed with ducks and ducklings geese and goslings. In China today, poultry and frogs grace the tables of rural families.

Lotus is cultivated in water for arrowroot. In upland fields, in the hills, yü t'ou (which resembles Irish potatoes), beans, maize, and sorgum flourish. The soil is fertilized by animal dung, night soil, and chemical fertilizer. Up in the hills there are fields of sugar cane and sugar processing factories. On reforested hills, valuable camphor trees produce wood for beautifully carved chests, and a fast-growing type of cedar is cultivated for fuel. In the hilly country, there are old-fashioned and modern kilns producing bricks and tiles for new housing projects.

Pearl River Delta

As darkness descended upon the rice paddies, the countryside was so flat that it seemed to blur into one vast limitless paddy. All of a sudden, the earth, rather than the sky above, assumed the appearance of the Milky Way. Myriads of tiny lights dotted the countryside. "What is the meaning of all these lights?" I asked the chauffeur. I had never seen anything like this in my part of China. He explained that when the rice heads are in the pollenization period, tiny insects destroy the whole rice crop. He stopped the car and showed us a tub of water directly below a light. When the insect pests arrive at dusk, they are attracted by the light, fly into it, and fall into the water below. We saw peasants coming out with tubs, pails, basins and every household article that could hold water. Above each receptacle a light was lit—a candle, an old lamp, or a burning cattail soaked in oil, direct current electric light bulbs attached to a battery circuit, and even neon lights. The villages were dark. Every available light was out to save the rice crop. As soon as the pollenization period is over, the paddies would return to darkness and the villages to light, said the chauffeur, who had been brought up in the area.

The people of Tung Kuan gave us a hearty welcome. They had been visited by very few, if any, foreigners, since their little rural city was not on the carefully prepared itineraries of foreign tourists.

We spent a comfortable night in a clean, freshly whitewashed house, probably spruced up for our benefit, and early the next morning we set off in a motorboat to visit a village tidal power plant in Tao Chiao commune. We steamed upstream from Tung Kuan past picturesque old temples and pagodas before crossing to another branch of the Pearl River through a recently completed man-made canal which was several miles long. It was almost as wide as the river branches which it connected. It had been dug by hand—thousands of workers cooperating to bring water to restore waste land.

Arriving after a few hours at the Tao Chiao commune, we were welcomed by the fellow villagers of the young women who had demonstrated the wooden model of the Number One Plant. Altogether there are 104 tidal power plants in the area, utilizing the power of tidal water, which reverses each day the flow downstream of the many branch outlets of the Pearl River.

The villagers had hung up on a long line large ideographs done in gold paper on a red background, welcoming friends from Canada (Chia Na Ta, pronounced Jaw Nah Dah).

The men who operated it took pride in showing us the workings on the plant, which has been so beneficial to their community, lifting water for rice, providing light at night for the village and power for the mills that polish rice and grind pig feed from green weeds and other vegetation.

A huge dam impounded fresh water as it was pushed up the river by the distant tidal salt water of the South China Sea. When the dam is full, the water gate is closed. At the other end of the dam, water is conducted by gravity through a metal pipe to a small turbine, which lifts the water by direct turbine power up through another pipe to a level higher than the rice paddy. The water then pours out by gravity into the paddy or is conducted by troughs to other paddies, saving the back-breaking labour of lifting water by the many old methods—ropes and buckets, hand-operated fulcrums, or foot paddles.

At night, when water is not being lifted, the turbine drives an electric generator which lights the village. No one who has not spent nights in a dark Chinese village in the days when only a few houses were dimly lit by vegetable oil lamps—a tiny flame at the end of a wick hanging over the edge of a small bowl of oil—can fully appreciate what it means to have electric lights.

Westerners have criticized Chairman Mao's support of the great proletarian cultural revolution. They say China cannot make progress without an elite class of scientific researchers. Mao Tse-tung says that, at the present time, China cannot afford to have too many university people devoted to pure research. There is a greater need for scientists to go out into the factories and communes to apply the principles of science to the problems which the workers and peasants cannot solve alone. The universities were, therefore, temporarily closed, and university people sent out at least for a period of time to become acquainted with the problems to which highest priority should be given.

What has happened in the Tao Chiao Commune is an example of the wisdom, in China at any rate, of getting scientists, technicians, and practical mechanics out of the universities, research institutions, and industrial centres and into the rural communes.

Wen Ch'uan Hot Springs

Upon our return to Canton, we went off in the opposite direction to visit a brigade village of a commune in the mountains of Kwangtung.

We arrived in a scenic valley to stay in a luxurious rest house on the bank of a river. I retired early to enjoy a bath in the warm, healing mineral water from the Wen Ch'uan. (The hot springs were on the other side of the river and piped over to our side under the river.)

Prime Minister Chou En-lai had sent word that I should stay at the Wen Ch'uan for at least a week. He had suggested that, at my age, one needed relaxation after a strenuous tour. I expressed deep gratitude, but explained that I really did not need to rest. In fact, I could not stay because I wanted to see the mountain commune where most of the peasants were K'e Chia, "guest people," known in Cantonese as Hakka.

When I was enjoying the private pool of water from the Wen Ch'uan, I had wondered if the special water was available only to guests in the palatial rest house. Surely, it should be reserved for people suffering from rheumatic ailments. The next morning as we set out for our trip to the mountain commune, I asked if there was a sanitorium near the hot springs. We were taken over the river where we saw several sanitoriums which had top priority over the water. Only after the patients were supplied was the water piped to the rest house. That made me feel better, especially when I learned that among the patients there also were "guest people."

Lifeblood from the Rock

The guest people arrived centuries ago, but earlier migrants had already occupied most of the land and considered it their home. The new arrivals were therefore known as guest people. Most K'e Chia became landless peasants working for landlords who exploited them ruthlessly. I wanted to see what the People's Republic of China had done for them and had chosen to visit Lo Tung Ta Tui village in a mountain commune.

After two hours driving, we started up a narrow, winding gorge. Here and there, I caught glimpses of tiny rice paddies which must have been most laboriously hacked out of the steep hillsides. As we gained altitude, the valley widened. We caught up to groups of chatting and laughing boys and girls hurrying to the village for lunch. At the village, we were introduced to the leader of the Lo Tung Ta Tui and his assistant, a woman. Before long, we sat down to a peasant meal of meat balls, fish, greens, delicious monk-hood mushrooms, and steamed rice.

The people of Lo Tung Village were very proud of their success in terracing the slopes of a hill right up to the summit—as proud as the people in the village of Shashiyü in Hopei Province, whom I visited in the autumn of 1973. Shashiyü means "sand-rock valley," and that is exactly what it was. In former days, since the peasants were unable to eke a living out of rock, they were forced to seek work elsewhere, beg, or starve. After the peasants of this isolated valley were organized into a commune working brigade, they decided to raise grain for themselves and fodder for their animals. We saw the narrow terraces they had carved out of sheer rock and the huge, deep basin carved out of solid rock to store water for the dry season.

Some of the young people suggested that time and labour could be saved by digging a tunnel through the mountain to the valley from which they were labouriously carrying soil by the basket over the mountain. Their elders agreed.

Directed by an expert, a group of young men and women, using dynamite, determination, and hard work, completed the tunnel. Then, using horse-, donkey-, cow-, and human-drawn carts on discarded car tires, like the old Canadian Bennet Buggies, they transported more soil in one month than they could have carried in a year.

The reward could be seen in vegetables, sorghum, barley, millet, maize, and fruit trees. They served us delicious food and fruit produced in their Sand Rock Valley. Each family had a private little plot for vegetables, poultry, a pig, or flowers. We visited several homes—houses built of stone with tile roofs. No wonder those people are enthusiastic about the changes which enabled them to accomplish the impossible.

In Lo Tung Village we were taken out to see the terraces from top to bottom. Several hundred people had to work many days from sunrise to sunset to complete the project. A recent downpour of rain had caused a serious washout of a large section of the new terraces, and squads of men and women were busy repairing the damage. The terraces would eventually be used as rice paddies, but it would take a year or more for the earth to settle. In the meantime, the terraces were planted with sorghum or vegetables; the sides of the retaining walls were planted with fast-growing vines to prevent washouts until stone walls could be built.

A most important feature of this mountain commune was the development of several hydroelectric projects. A large penstock fed water from falls into a compact power house, where a turbine and generator produced electricity to light the village, lift water to the top of a newly terraced hill, and run a power saw.

Each family in the village had a small plot for vegetables, and many families had chickens and a pig or two. A new housing project provided brick houses with tile roofs and cement floors—a significant improvement on the old mud and straw huts and mud floors. Many families had five rooms. They could not be called suites—all the rooms were in a row without connecting doors, with a door in front and a window in the opposite wall. To get from one room to another, one had to go out onto a narrow cement porch under the eaves to enter the next room. Such housing might not be acceptable in most Western countries, but here it represented a tremendous step forward.

The people of the village were well clothed and appeared well fed. The children attended schools, and medical aid was available to everyone.

We were invited to visit a long room full of statues illustrating how poor K'e Chia peasants were treated by landlords in pre-liberation days. One group of statues showed the landlord's servants tearing a peasant mother from her breast-fed baby to be carried off to feed the landlord's child, so that the landlord's wife would not be disturbed in a marathon mahjong session. I noticed that the two young women who were in charge of the room of horrors spoke p'u t'ung hua better than most of the villagers. When I asked them if they were also K'e Chia, they replied that they were Cantonese and had volunteered to come to this commune to teach, but had decided to stay permanently. Each had a boy friend, and they would get married, but not before they were at least twenty-four years of age. They would continue teaching after marriage.

There were a day-care centre, kindergarten, and primary school in the village. There was also a dispensary and a doctor who used chiefly herbal medicines. The doctor's p'u t'ung hua was not up to scratch; his assistant had been trained in Canton and used modern methods. Before leaving, Sylvia insisted on visiting the village store, where we saw a greater variety of textiles and other necessities than I had expected to find in a mountain country store, and there were many customers.

I did not regret having given up another day at the hot springs to see the village. While it is true that the revolution which established the People's Republic of China initiated the policies, the achievements, and the revolutionary changes we saw in the mountain commune, those achievements and changes would never have been realized if it had not been for the revolution which took place in the minds of the "guest people" themselves. It was that revolution which generated the energy and willing hands to terrace the hill.

Reunion with Chou

My chief reason for visiting Peking before seeing my childhood home was that I was most anxious to talk with my old friend Prime Minister Chou En-lai.

The Prime Minister received my daughters and me in the Great Hall of the People on May Day afternoon, prior to the evening celebrations.

We also already knew when we came to Peking that Huang Hua was to be the Ambassador to Canada. He and his wife, Ho Li-liang, who is a Foreign Service Officer in her own right, were most kind to us during our stay.

A Chinese Hero from Canada

After May Day in Peking, we went south by rail. Our only stop on the way to Wuhan was at Shihchiachuang, to visit Dr. Norman Bethune's Memorial Hospital. Bethune has become a legendary hero in China. This Canadian doctor, who had served in Spain in 1936, where he pioneered a wartime blood transfusion service, went to China in 1938 to bring medical assistance to Chinese troops fighting the Japanese in northern China. The only troops at that time seriously and successfully reclaiming vast rural areas from the Imperial Japanese armies were the People's Liberation armies. Bethune organized and trained young men to deal with emergencies at the front lines. The equipment and medical supplies necessary for emergency operations and treatment were brought in quickly and neatly in the Bethune packsaddle on the backs of sturdy mules. The ingenious saddle was only one of many contraptions which this determined and resourceful man invented. Dr. Bethune lost his life due to an operation performed without gloves in extremely difficult circumstances. He contracted blood poisoning through a cut in a finger.

The Chinese were impressed with the Bethune's volunteer services to Chinese soldiers. Mao Tse-tung had urged all Chinese to make any sacrifice necessary for China and the people of China, but here was a foreigner, who owed no special debt to the Chinese people, sacrificing his life for them. What better example could there be? Bethune's body was placed in a dignified, plain white tomb in the beautiful and spacious Martyr's Park in Shihchiachuang.

Dr. Bethune, known throughout China, was almost unknown to Canadians before reports about him were published by Canadian visitors to China.

There are some Canadians who express resentment that Mao Tse-tung chose this Canadian as a hero. They suggest that it is an affront to the many missionaries who sacrified much more for many more years than Dr. Bethune, a communist, did in his eighteen months in China. They forget that the Good Samaritan was chosen as an example to be followed, despite his having been a nonconformist. They also forget that Bethune was the son of an Ontario pastor. In fact, they miss the point entirely. Dr. Bethune was honoured because he risked his life for Chinese people and certainly not to make him a hero for Canadians. Honouring the memory of Dr. Norman Bethune is a tribute to the many foreigners who gave their lives for the Chinese people. Chinese young people who visit the Martyrs' Park daily by the thousands are inspired by the sacrifice this foreigner made.

The Grasslands of Inner Mongolia

The highlight of my trip in 1973 was without doubt a visit to Inner Mongolia, perhaps because the grasslands, where Mongolians ride and round up cattle and horses just like Western cowboys, were so much like the rolling hills of Grande Prairie in Alberta before they became fields of wheat and fescue.

The Han people (people from "China proper" in the Autonomous Region of Inner Mongolia are referred to as "Han people" to differentiate them from those of Mongolian origins) are sometimes reported to be gradually pushing out the Mongolians by ploughing up extensive areas for agriculture. The Han people have converted treeless sandy areas into farmland by planting shelter belts to stop drifting. By the conservation of water and the digging of deep wells, former desert areas are now producing crops, vegetables, and some fruit. The grasslands, however, are today still the preserve of Mongolian herdsmen who raise sheep for wool and meat, cows for milk and beef, saddle and light draft horses, and camels for making the moves to summer pastures and for sale as draft animals. In the city of Paot'ou we saw teams, sometimes in tandem, of camels hauling heavy loads of steel pipe.

The authorities of the Autonomous Region of Inner Mongolia, who include a good percentage of Mongolian personnel and functionaries, have taken important steps to improve the herdsmen's way of life. We visited an experimental station managed by a military brigade of the People's Liberation Army. The organization is run by army officers. The research, animal husbandry, development of new strains of sheep, cattle, horses, and pigs, experiments with feed and pasture grasses, and water conservation are all supervised by university experts.

Australian thoroughbreds, horses from Hokkaido, Russian breeds, and others have been crossbred with the sturdy Mongolian horse to produce a popular new strain which is in great demand as saddle and light draft horses.

Since land is worthless to semi-nomadic people, each family is entitled to own as many as five sheep per person a year for food, five milk cows per family, and two horses for each rider, in addition to horses owned by the brigade or commune. All of these animals run with the animals belonging to the brigade. Most of the younger Mongolian people speak Chinese.

Mongolians today are perhaps even more grateful for liberation than are the Chinese. They were liberated not only from corrupt officials, cheating merchants, moneylenders, and landlords but also from the tyranny of the lamas. When I was a student in Peking I learned how young Mongolians and Tibetans who were acolytes in the Lama Temple in the northeastern part of the old Tartar city hated the lamas. They had been taken from their parents when they were boys to be made slaves in the name of the Living Lama. A family with two sons had to give one as a slave to the lamas, a family with three gave two, and one with five gave three. The increase in the Mongolian population in the grasslands was said to be due to Mongolian parents, no longer having to sacrifice their sons to the lamas.

Sentimental Journey to Fancheng

The most exciting part of my stay in China in 1971 was, of course, our visit to the inland walled city where I was born. When we arrived, there had been no foreigners in the twin cities for twenty years. I had left Fancheng exactly forty-four years before.

Rolling along in a comfortable railway coach from Wuhan, we stood up to catch the first glimpses of the Pien Shan mountains on the distant horizon long before we were due to arrive in Fancheng. In the old days, the villages on both sides of the Honan-Hupeh border were clusters of mud huts with straw roofs. Each village was protected against brigands by high mud walls with watchtowers and round-the-clock sentries.

There was now no sign of the obsolete walls and towers. In their place, in the first light of dawn, women were peacefully washing their clothes, pounding them clean on the smooth rocks at the water's edge. Most of the houses were of brick with tile roofs baked in old-fashioned kilns.

As we came nearer to Fancheng and the flat valley of the Han, great rice paddies extended into the distance as far as one could see. Despite considerable industrial expansion almost everywhere in China, agriculture is still by far the most important industry. While the mechanization of agriculture is still only in its infancy in relation to the tremendous demand created by China's rural communes, the application of scientific principles has enabled the peasants to double and triple the yields of rice and grain; reclamation of flooded, eroded, and barren land has increased areas under cultivation; deep wells and wind breaks have changed former arid areas into productive farming land; chemical fertilizers have increased the productivity of lands formerly too far from population centers to enable night soil to be carried there in buckets at each end of the *pien-tan,* the flat porter's pole. In the old days, one could always tell by the better crops and vegetable gardens that one was approaching a large village or city.

Cooperatives, Communes, and the Great Leap Forward

I had seen something of the first two essential steps in agricultural reform before I left China in 1951. The first was the distribution of land to the tillers, including landlords who were willing to remain on their land to work. The second was the organization of groups of peasants, traditionally accustomed to certain aspects of community village farming, into model Agricultural Production Cooperatives, which eventually prepared the way for communes.

Despite the small amount of local capital available, it became evident that even small cooperatives substantially increased production. The larger the scale on which labour could be organized, the more capital became available and the more planning was possible, which resulted in greater productivity. Another aspect of the programme was the restoration or development of cooperative auxiliary village industry, which had been crippled in many parts of China.

Agricultural Production Cooperatives had especially captivated the imagination and support of the lower-middle peasants. They had risen from the ranks of poor peasants as a result of land distribution, the availability of fertilizer, better seed and, most important, their share in the production of the cooperatives.

By 1956, peasants throughout China had benefited from membership in the Higher Stage Cooperatives, which eliminated the boundaries that had prevented large-scale farming and provided capital for tractors, trucks, and new machinery. The new communes, however, were less successful than expected and were therefore reorganized consonant with the lessons learned from the earlier Agricultural Production Cooperatives.

The cooperatives had been built on small units of mutual aid teams composed of groups of neighbours. Teams of about twenty neighbouring families, often consisting of an entire village, were formed into production teams. Groups of teams became the brigades within the communes and assumed responsibility for farming operations, while the former Production Cooperatives became the units of production management and distribution. The communes came to deal with planning and the investment of funds, the organization of small factories, water conservation, and social needs. The communes restored traditional face-to-face relationships among relatives and neighbours in the village and the extension of similar relationships between villages of the commune and neighbouring communes.

The Great Leap Forward was started in 1958 to increase agricultural production and to revitalize and diversify industry in the rural areas as well as interior towns and cities. The Great Leap Forward had made necessary the introduction of communes before the programme to restructure them had been completed. The communes did, nevertheless, withstand the effects of the great natural disaster of 1959, 1960, and 1961, and food production was sufficient to prevent famine.

A major aspect of the Great Leap Forward was the campaign to set up small workshops and simple traditional iron and steel blast furnaces in the villages. (Blast furnaces were chosen because of the peasant's rudimentary knowledge of the process.) Foreign observers have insisted that diverting manpower to construct and operate 600,000 of these backyard furnaces was "sheer madness" and a waste of labour and resources. However, they have not really understood the overall results of this experiment to introduce industrialization by trial and error to Chinese peasants. When I asked some of the young men and women who were demonstrating machines at the Canton Trade Fair how they had become interested in industrial jobs, their reply often was that their interest began when small workshops were introduced in their home communes during the back-yard furnace campaign.

The Great Leap Forward narrowed the gap between the

illiterate, feudal, rural peasant and the relatively sophisticated, trained, modern urban factory worker. Chinese leaders practiced the principle of advancing from familiar traditional skills to new skills. Large numbers of city factory workers went to the country communes to start workshops and to train peasants in the operation of new factories. Further, the face-to-face contacts and associations were important factors in breaking down characteristic class distinctions, local loyalties, and the prejudices that separated rural and urban workers.

Nearly every type of crop grown in China is seen in the rich, fertile soil of the vast plains on both sides of the Han River. From the rolling hills, we descended to the green fields of the plains north and east of Fancheng. When we lived in Fancheng, we had a stone summer house on Pien Shan. My brother Nelius and I spent many happy days in the mountains running barefoot with Chinese boys from the valleys who herded cattle, sheep, ponies, and donkeys. The valleys and terraced sides of the mountains were off limits for cattle and sheep. Like the Chinese boys, we enjoyed squishing fresh, green cow dung between our toes to flatten it out for quicker drying. If the dung heaps were left too long, they disappeared. Extremely industrious beetles called *t'ui-shih ke-lang-tse,* push-dung beetles, rolled it away in balls.

When there was a downpour, cows and donkeys were always chased into the nearest cave for shelter. In explanation for this instruction from their parents, the boys taught us this rhyme in *t'u hua,* local dialect:

> "Ma chiao fei,   (Horse soaks fat,
> Niu chiao shou,   Cow soaks thin,
> Lü-tzu chiao ti   Ass soaks soon to
> Kuang ku-t'ou."   Bones and skin.)

When we sat upon cows or water buffalos or rode the ponies or donkeys, the boys told us just where to sit by teaching us another rhyme which went:

"Ma ch'i t'ou,   (Horse ride front,
Niu ch'i yao,   Cow ride hump,
Lü-tzu ch'i ti   Ass you ride on
P'i-ku shao."   Smelly rump.)

I was suddenly jarred out of my memories as the train slowed to a halt at the Fancheng depot. I would be meeting people I had not seen for forty-four years. How different would they be?

The depot is outside the old city wall, which, except on the river front facing Hsiangyang, has been torn down. To my disappointment, we were hustled off in Shanghai-built cars to a rest house in Hsiangyang. I would have preferred to have stayed on the Fancheng side, in or near our old compound. Driving through the heart of the old city, I recognized old pawn shops, temples, and guildhalls, but then we came to the bridge over the river, and that was a complete surprise. I did not expect to find a rail, highway, and pedestrian bridge over the Han, which had never before been bridged.

On the other side, we crossed the moat encircling Hsiangyang and passed through the East Gate in the city wall, which still encircles the historic old city, now traversed by a wide avenue from the East to the West gate. We drove into a compound of spacious new buildings, which appeared to be a community centre. One building, three stories high, was equipped with suites of bedrooms and reception, dining, and conference rooms. Compared to the old-fashioned inns of inland China, it was palatial.

After breakfast, we were invited by our hosts to rest. I thanked them, but suggested, since our stay was only for a few days, that we get a bird's-eye view from the drum-and-bell tower of the old scholars' pavilion. The scholars' pavilion and the drum had disappeared, but the old bell was still there, half buried in cement. A young man began telling my daughters that the huge bell had been tolled day and night in the old days to tell people the time. He was probably referring to the *ta-ken-ti,* the gong-beating night watchman, who patrolled the streets before the young man was born, beating out the night hours on a small gong to warn off thieves and assure the inhabitants that all was well. I did not tell them that, as a child, I was terrified when the ta-ken-ti passed the *t'ien-teng,* the lamp of heaven, on a mast higher than any house or temple near us. Our amah said the sound of the gong could disturb the spirits, who were easily diverted from passing by harmlessly in straight lines by the unearthly echoes of the gong at night. That also happened to be the argument she used to stop us from making noise after we were supposed to be in bed.

From the top of the old platform, we could see how Hsiangyang had been beautified. In the old days, we could only see rooftops from the scholar pavilion; now we saw mostly trees. Beyond the city wall, I recognized three of the mountains of the Pien Shan range, the rocky ridge of Pien Shan itself, Hu T'ou Shan (Tiger Head Mountain), and Chien Shan (Sharp Mountain). The formerly naked mountains had been beautifully clothed by reforestation.

After lunch, we made our first visit to the T'an Hsi commune, west of the city. It encompassed the old Hsiangyang hospital, where our son Alton was born.

When I was a boy, the people in the area which is now the T'an Hsi Commune were steeped in the history, actual and legendary, of the "Three Kingdoms" era, which lasted from 220 to 265 A.D. The Three Kingdoms followed the Later Han Dynasty, 25 to 220 A.D., whose capital was Lo Yang in the neighboring province of Honan. (Chinese historians were not too certain as to whether anyone replaced the last Han emperor, Hsien Ti, and the period was known only as the "Three Kingdoms.")

One of the stories relates that a soldier of fortune, Liu Pei, who claimed to be a scion of the imperial Han family, attempted a coup to succeed the dethroned emperor, Hsien Ti. Liu Pei was driven out and pursued by the imperial cavalry led by the infamous Ts'ao Ts'ao. The horsemen closed in on

Liu, certain of capturing him as he galloped full speed toward the T'an Hsi, a wide tributary of the Han. As he reached the bank, Liu Pei, cried in desperation to his Arab stallion to jump: *"Ta pa ha!"* It became "the most famous leap by a horse in the history of China." The horse leaped as if it had wings and came down safely on the other side of the wide stream. Liu Pei was saved. He lived to become the King of Shu, one of the Three Kingdoms (Wei, Wu, and Shu), into which China remained divided for forty-five years.

As I looked over the area west of the village between the foothills of the mountains and the Han River, I could not believe my eyes. What had been a waste land of stagnant water, reeds, and weeds had been transformed into a green paradise. I did not realize what caused this transformation until I noticed that I could not see the river. What I saw was a high ridge with water buffaloes and cattle grazing on top.

The manager of T'an Hsi commune said: "You remember how superstitious we all were. Disaster was our fate. Nothing could be done, so we left the land waste because no matter how high we might have built dikes, dragons from the sky would descend into the Han River and angry waters flood the area!

"That was the old mentality. Our Chairman, Mao Tse-tung, has taught us that we must not allow foolish old superstitions to prevent us from coping with difficulties, even if it means moving mountains.

"Now look at our dike. We control the river! We keep it out when we harvest the rice and let it in to flood the low-lying land when we cultivate and plant. And we save the water of the mountain reservoir for the terrace paddies, which are too high for river water. We have applied the scientific principle to develop and improve new strains of rice. Our rice takes only a little more than half the time to ripen, and the heads are longer, producing twice the yield. We now have two crops annually instead of one."

An old peasant told me how very happy he was that I had

come back, so I could see for myself the great improvements. I asked him what he was doing, and he explained that he was too old to do the heavy work and so had been given the job of walking through the wheat fields to look for the best heads. He placed each head in a transparent plastic bag, which did not shut out the sun but protected them from cross-pollination with inferior heads. The best kernels from these heads were selected to seed better crops.

Women were building a forest of structures six foot high which looked like the skeletons of miniature wigwams. They were frames to support the vines of *yang ch'ieh-tzu,* foreign eggplants. (I remembered that my father had introduced tomatoes, which the peasants had called foreign eggplants.) As we watched, the women stacked the long, dry reeds together that would allow them to pick tomatoes as each layer ripened, with higher layers still green and top layers in blossom.

Young men and women were tramping down weeds in the rice paddies. The paddies are ploughed while underwater, usually by water buffaloes. Rice is planted by hand. When the seedlings are about a foot and a half high, they are carefully separated and set out in rows below the surface of the water, their roots firmly imbedded in mud. To prevent young plants from being choked, the peasants wade barefoot through the paddies tramping down the weeds between the rows. At T'an Hsi, we saw a large number of young people march abreast across the paddies leaving clean rows of rice behind them. They laughed and talked, seemingly enjoying themselves, despite the tricky balancing act, each with a light bamboo pole, that weeding requires. When I asked the young weeders about their work, they commented that their parents and grandparents, working for landlords, had to do it from early morning until late at night, while they worked only eight hours a day, could take different shifts, and could periodically change to some other type of work. One of them said, "It is not too hard to work when we ourselves are the chief beneficiaries. Also, we have meetings and make decisions about our work. All of us read and write and study and, in work like this, as we walk along we can talk, and it never becomes too much of a burden."

The countryside west of Fancheng had always been noted for its cotton, and I was not surprised to see great amounts of cotton being processed for cloth. But our visit to the new textile factory, where hundreds of power-driven, automatic looms were pouring out cloth, was the first time in my life I have been stirred by machines. They were attended by half a dozen girls dressed in white, with caps and face masks. To one side, men were packing rolls of cloth into bales to be carried off to communes, city distributing centres, and by rail to Wuhan, where some of it is dyed. The drab colours that some cynical foreign observers persist in seeing as China's only colours are not characteristic of farming areas. In rural communes like T'an H'si, millions of peasants wear white jackets for the simple reason that it costs less to buy undyed cloth for everyday wear.

Our first visit in Fancheng itself was to the old school compounds. The old Middle School, which had originally been built by Dr. J. M. J. Hotvedt as a hospital, had been replaced by a new and much larger primary school building. The playground is now used by both boys and girls, whereas in the old days education was chiefly for boys. The girls' school was in a separate compound.

We arrived just in time for the morning outdoor exercises, singing, and games. We saw several hundred children, well fed, well clothed, and healthy, playing together as wildly and uninhibitedly as children do the world over when given the chance. It would have gladdened my mother's heart to see that the girls were as graceful as the boys now that their feet and legs were normal. Today, only a few old women still suffer from the crippling deformations that the custom of binding induced in their feet and legs.

In the compound where the children played stood my mother's tombstone. The inscription, written by my father and carved deep by a Chinese stone-cutter, was still clearly visible. As soon

as I saw it, I remembered how Nelius and I had gone with
father in a *hung ch'uan,* an open sailing junk, with a small red
cabin, down the Han River to the far end of the Pien Shan
mountains, where father selected the stone in a marble quarry.

The brick church, planned by my father and built by Chinese
workers, was still standing in perfect condition. The trees
around the old pond were still reflected in the clear water.

The church is not being used, because the congregation has
dwindled to only a handful of elderly people, who meet periodically in the old guest room near the gate. It is, however,
significant that, while a former residence and the old Middle
School classroom building were taken down so that the bricks
and building materials could be used for new school buildings,
the church was not.

The Chinese constitution guarantees freedom of religion. The
young people are, nevertheless, uninterested in becoming church
members, partly because they can no longer enjoy the former
benefits of being church members. The only church members who
remained loyal were sincere Christians who were not dependent
on money from abroad. The other so-called "dollar" or "rice"
Christians dropped their membership when the missionaries left
in 1949 and their special privileges were no longer available.

The one residence that had not been needed for the construction of the new school was still in perfect condition. It was
our house, now used as residential quarters by a few People's
Liberation Army troops, and we were invited to inspect it. Upstairs, Sylvia stopped at the door of her old bedroom and confessed that one night, while her parents were sleeping, she had
secretly gone downstairs and out into the garden to see the
flowering trees in the moonlight. I suggested that it would now
be proper for her to be punished by performing the traditional
"san kuei chiu k'ou," three kneels and nine kowtows. A PLA
officer laughed at the old punishment formula and said: "That
is old mentality. In new China, one is forgiven when confession
is made. You cannot punish your daughter now. China has
changed."

The new Middle School in our old primary school compound can accommodate thousands of students. I was most impressed by the latest member to join the teaching staff. He had been a factory worker and spoke with enthusiasm about cooperation between schools and industrial institutions, though whether or not all faculty members accepted the revolutionary tendencies of the worker with good grace, I do not know. They gave the impression that they were prepared to cooperate in ridding the school of the traditional attitude to manual labour. The students, some of them grandsons and granddaughters of my old friends, were definitely enthusiastic about getting rid of the old superiority complex that characterized the attitude of the scholarly elite to peasants and workers. I remembered that students and teachers also spoke that way in the days of the Great Revolution of the Twenties, yet the traditional attitude persisted. Perhaps, after the Great Proletarian Cultural Revolution, the new attitude has gained sufficient momentum to reverse the old tradition.

Two old friends, Sung Ti-hua and Li Tsung-san, called on us in the Hsiangyang Rest House. Sung, four years my senior, brought his son and daughter-in-law. He had been my best student in an advanced course in English..

Li Tsung-san's voice and appearance were familiar, but I was unable to remember to which of the many Li families he belonged. When I asked him whether he knew Li Shih, he said: "Of course. He was my elder brother." But his brother, he said, had never returned from T'ao Hua Lun in Hunan, where he had gone in 1925. Sadly, I told him how I had unexpectedly bumped into his brother in Hankow in 1927, during the chaotic and uncertain situation following the establishment of Sun Yat-sen's Revolutionary Government. Li Shih was then trying to escape to Fancheng as quickly as possible to warn the supporters of the Revolutionary Government that Chiang's hatchet men would soon be hunting them down.

Li Shih's brother, now in tears, said: "You are the last person we know that saw him alive. He never got back. Until now, we did not know that he was in Hankow during the blood bath."

Out of the corner of my ears, while we were talking, I heard Sung Ti-hua talking to my girls in good idiomatic English, better than many a professional interpreter. The old man was still active and full of life. He asked me: "Do you know that my wife and I helped to build the bridge over the Han?" I said: "I did not know that you were a civil engineer." He laughed and answered: "Of course not, but my wife and I helped to move the earth at both ends of the bridge to build the approaches. Without them, you could not have come over in the cars which brought you here." I never thought that I would hear a Chinese scholar boast about shovelling dirt.

Shanghai Now

Shanghai has changed perhaps more than any other city in China. Some foreign observers who had known Shanghai in former days occasionally wax nostalgic over the old glamorous night life. They completely ignore or forget the criminal exploitation which made these pleasures possible. We thought we would get a look at the new Shanghai by observing the living conditions of ordinary factory workers.

We were welcomed to a residential city at a considerable distance from the centre of the city where the families of the workers of ten large factories live. The manager of this compound of three-story apartment buildings was the mother of three children. She was a charming person and evidently devoted to the several hundred families, especially the children. We saw the day-care centre, the kindergarten, and the primary school, all within the residential city. Then she invited us to visit her apartment or any other we chose to inspect. Each family had a private suite with a living-cum-dining room, two bedrooms, a kitchen with a gas stove, and a bathroom with a tub and flush toilet. It was the first time in my quarter of a century in China that I had seen a bathtub and a flush toilet in the house of a worker, or a gas stove, or for that matter a separate kitchen.

The family is still the basic unit of Chinese society. Only the old patriarchal family, with all the sons, wives, and children in one household, has vanished. It was a curse, especially to the daughters-in-law. Now, in some families, grandparents reside with a son or daughter. In such cases, they help care for their grandchildren.

I came away with the knowledge that Shanghai workers, indeed all the common people that I had seen and talked to, are so much better off now than before liberation that there is really no comparison.

INDEX

Ch'en, Mr. (translator and custodian), 127, 128, 155, 157, 158, 160
Ch'en, Eugene, 39
Ch'en Ch'eng, 46
Ch'en Kuo-fu, 42, 92, 95
Ch'en Li-fu, 42, 50, 53, 75, 92, 95
Ch'en Tu-hsiu, 37
Ch'en Yi, 40, 77, 118–19, 133, 249
Chennault, Claire L., 99
Chiang Ching-kuo, 50, 128, 133
Chiang Kai-shek, 44–5, 46, 49, 50, 51, 63, 64, 66, 69–77 *passim*, 80, 86, 93, 96, 97–8, 102, 106, 107, 112–14, 115, 119, 120, 121, 122–3, 171, 173, 243; arrest at Sian, 51–3; bandit-suppression campaign, 45–7, 49, 50, 51, 122, 132; Canton, flight to, 167; and Chou En-lai, 52, 53, 54–5; German military advisors, 46, 48; at Kuling, 112–14, 124, 128, 132–3; and Northern Expedition, 36, 37, 38, 40–2; "retirement" of, 133; and Chester Ronning, 112–14, 124, 128
Chiang Kai-shek, Mme., 53, 114, 116, 121–2, 124, 128
Chiang Wei-kuo, 133
Ch'iao Kuan-hua, 63, 249
Ch'ien Lung vase, 126–8
Ch'in Empire, 23–4
China: bureaucratic system, 22, 26, 27; corruption, 26, 68, 71; democracy, belief in, 62, 64, 70; emperors, 25–6; examination system, 22, 26, 30; foreigners in, 28–9, 36–7, 39; government, 22–4; history, 21–33; intellectuals, scholars, 61, 78, 294, 295; Japanese invasion of, 44–5, 49–54 *passim*, 141; peasants, 22–3, 26–7, 28, 43, 69, 76, 78, 142; rebellion, tradition of, 22–3; schools, 30–1, 78–80; unequal treaties, 3, 4, 25, 27; and USSR, 37, 38; village economy,

26, 28, 43; Western exploitation, 3–4, 25, 26, 27–8. *See also* People's Republic of China; Nationalist Party; Taiwan
Ch'ing Dynasty, 31
Ching Teh Chen kilns, 126, 159
Chingkangshan, 43, 44, 77
Chou Dynasty, 23, 25
Chou En-lai, 38, 39, 40, 44, 50, 52, 53, 64, 65, 66, 71, 73–80, 95, 109, 156, 195, 196, 227, 229, 233, 234, 235–9, 240, 250, 277, 280–1; and Chiang Kai-shek, 52, 53, 54–5; education, 77–80; family, 79; in France, 77, 79; on Korean Conference, 222–3, 224, 237–8; and Korean War, 195–6, 199; Long March, 46–9; vs. Mao Tse-tung, 77–8; and Gen. Odlum, 75–6; and Chester Ronning, 75–6, 95, 235–9, 280–1; on Vietnam, 238
Chou En-lai, Mme. *See* Teng Ying-ch'ao
Christians, persecution of, 27. *See also* missionaries
Chu Teh, 44, 46, 47, 48, 50, 76, 77
Chu-ke Liang, 64, 104
Ch'un, Prince, 31
Chungking, 41, 56–80, 93, 94–5, 172; exodus to Nanking, 94–5, 96–9; US Embassy in, 70–2
Civil War (Chinese), 61–2, 95, 106, 141, 168, 192–3, 235; cease-fire (1946), 74–5, 76. *See also* Nationalist Party; Communist Party of China
Clifford, Frederick, 121
Cohen, Morris, 99
Collins, Ralph, 185
Colombia, 226
Colombo Plan Conference, 172, 174
Comintern, 53–4, 76
communes, 146, 274, 275–6, 277, 278–80, 285, 286, 289

ABOUT THE AUTHOR

Born in Fancheng, China, Chester Ronning entered the Canadian Foreign Service in 1945. His first assignment was to Chungking, the war-time capital, and Nanking where he was Chargé d'Affaires until 1951, when he returned to Canada. He then served as head of the American and Far Eastern Division in the Department of External Affairs (1951–53); as Ambassador to Norway (1954–57); as High Commissioner to India (1957–64); as Acting Head of Delegation to the Geneva Conferences on Korea (1954) and Laos (1961–62); and as a Special Representative to Hanoi and Saigon in 1966. He makes his home in Camrose, Alberta.